Daniel Trotter

**Rocky Mountain Explorer,
Chronicler of The Fur Trade and . . .**

THE FIRST KNOWN MAN IN YELLOWSTONE PARK

Also, Two Additional Eye-Witness Reports:

**Beaver Dick Leigh and White Man's Sickness
1858-1876**

**The Slaughter of the Buffalo
1871-1878**

Jerry Bagley

Continental

Blackfeet Country

Yellowstone L.

Idaho

Shoshone (Stinking)

Ft. Henry

Henry's Fork

Pierre's Hole

Teton Mts.

Jackson L.

Jackson

Jackson's Hole

Lewis Fork

Grey's R.

Divide

Snake R.

Salt R.

Grey's L.

Star Valley

Soda Springs

Green R.

Bear R.

Ham's Fork

Utah

Bear L. (Sweet) L.

Wasatch Mts.

Great Salt L.

Weber R.

Utah Indians

Utah L.

Crow Tepee

FIRE

Sevier R.

(Rabbit) Sevier Lake

ROCKY MOUNTAINS, ON THE EVE OF DISCOVERY

Montana
Wyoming

Bighorn R.

rld's largest Hot spring

Wind R.

N

Oil spring

Sweetwater

South Pass

North

Platte R.

Beaver Trap

Colorado

Green R.

Daniel Trotter Potts,

Rocky Mountain Explorer, Chronicler of The Fur Trade and . . .

THE FIRST KNOWN MAN IN YELLOWSTONE PARK

Also, Two Additional Eye-Witness Reports:

Beaver Dick Leigh and White Man's Sickness 1858-1876

The Slaughter of the Buffalo 1871-1878

Jerry Bagley

For my wonderful wife and
marvelous children

Old Faithful
Eye-Witness History

4115 East 465 North
Rigby, Idaho 83442
(208) 745-9373
(208) 390-9373
E-mail: yesjerrycan@aol.com

International Standard Book Number   0-9707828-0-2

CONTENTS

Credits

A variety of experience was necessary to produce this book. For starters, I credit the early fur trappers who set off on a wild and hazardous adventure exploring the Rocky Mountains. And special credit to the ones who took time to get their story written down on paper–or elk hide or whatever. They waded through sub zero water and snow, lived like Indians, exalted in their freedom and had a wild and wonderful time at the annual Rendezvous.

This book grew out of my Master of Arts–Thesis. Noted historian and writer Doctor Leroy Hafen at Brigham Young University suggested the subject. The cover painting is by Gary Carter of West Yellowstone, Montana. The cover layout by Michael Whitworth.

Shay Spaulding did most of the sketch illustrations. Photo credits include: Margaret Hawkes Lindsley; Bonneville Museum, Bonneville County Historical Society, Idaho; Washington State University; H.J. Warre–National Archives of Canada; and the Bureau if American Ethnology.

Margory Wilcock read the early manuscript. Sharalee Dyer Welch helped with early word processing. My wife Patsy remembered items I had forgotten and urged me on to finish it.

But the bulk of time and computer expertise is from Doctor Ray Couch at Ricks College, Idaho. Arranging text, footnotes and illustrations is an art form.

ABOUT THE AUTHOR

I grew up on the western border of Wyoming, about fifty miles south of Jackson Hole, in Star Valley. This valley was first settled by Mormons seeking refuge from polygamist hunting sheriffs. The Wyoming–Idaho line divides the valley and there is a town on each side of the line. The Wyoming community was first called "Liberty;" the one in Idaho was named, "Freedom." So as the story goes, if marshals hunting polygamists came from Idaho, the men could escape to *Liberty* in Wyoming. And if they came from Wyoming they could escape to *Freedom* in Idaho. Polygamist marshals must have been occupied elsewhere because it never happened. In fact, in my young thinking, nothing had ever happened in that part of Wyoming. I was wrong.

A hundred years before the Mormons, there was history aplenty going on in the Rocky Mountain valleys. Trappers were contending with each other and the Indians for valuable beaver skins. These trappers explored every stream cascading from the Continental Divide and became known as Mountain Men. Mountains like the Rockies were unheard of in the East. Star Valley and the other mountain valleys were called "holes" and were scenes of coming and going and hunting and trapping—of loving and fighting and freezing and dying.

I like history. At Brigham Young University I found like-minded friends when several of us obtained our Master's Degree in Western American History. I was fortunate that Leroy Hafen, author of many books and the editor of the Mountain Man Series, was my advisor. Exposed to his enthusiasm I came to appreciate the trappers as the vanguard of western explorers. However, choosing a subject for a master's thesis in the fur trade was a challenge because early history of the West is "source starved." Early trappers and explorers came from the ragged edges of society and lacked the ability or the inclination to write their own stories. Yet it is these *first hand* stories that are the foundation of accurate history. Even major actors on this scene like Jim Bridger couldn't write. He signed his name with a "mark" of two crossed lines. Other leaders, such as Johnson Gardner, Etienne Provost and his partner Leclarc also signed their names with a mark. If these major actors couldn't sign their own names, it is no wonder that the rank and file of trappers were illiterate. In the mountains, except for clerking, writing and reading weren't prerequisites for leadership or anything else.

One trapper, however, did write. In fact, he wrote in beautiful flowing script. His name was Daniel Trotter Potts. At twenty seven years of age he was older, educated, and from a genteel background. In contrast to the many trappers who couldn't sign their names, he sent long letters home. He came from the noted Potts family of Valley Forge, Pennsylvania. The Potts were well known and "well connected." Two of his letters were sent to "Dr. Lukens," perhaps of the Lukens Steel Co. which developed plate steel for engine boilers and launched the age of steam.

As a trapper each year he sent lengthy letters back to the settlements that were a capsule history of that year's trapping and exploring the Rocky Mountains. When he had finishing writing a letter, he folded a sheet of paper around it to make an envelope. Then he addressed it, paid .25 cents postage and gave it to the traders to carry back to St. Louis. There his letters were posted in the mail and forwarded up the Mississippi and Ohio Rivers to Pennsylvania.

For many years the letters were lost. The discovery of the Potts letters is a story in itself. They emerged in parts and portions first from old newspapers then from actual manuscripts that Potts had written from the Mountain Rendezvous.

I was able to handle these original old letters. It was exciting. That is the closest a student of history will ever get to his subject. This book is an expanded and updated version of the thesis I wrote in 1964.

The West and the Rocky Mountains were just being explored when Daniel Potts wrote his letters. There were no accurate maps. So for convenience I often use political boundaries that didn't exist at the time of the story. For example, I use Wyoming, Montana, Utah, and Yellowstone Park to aid the reader locate where the action is. Also, some chapters begin with a date and location.

ABOUT THE BOOK–LOST LETTERS FROM AN UNKNOWN TRAPPER

In 1827, two letters written by a fur trapper in the Rocky Mountains arrived at the *Gazette and Daily Advertiser* in Philadelphia. They contained curious and sensational news about the Far West. The letters, printed by the Gazette in serial form, were a scoop for the paper. News from the far West was in short supply. They were reprinted by other newspapers, then typical of much that is printed in newspapers, they were forgotten.

About a hundred years later the letters were rediscovered. They were a cache of information from an unknown time and so were a delight to historians. But, there were problems. The copies were not originals and only existed in newspaper form. And the author was unknown. Without more information and some knowledge about the author, they were only piece-meal history, and not a primary source.

However, some clues about the author were apparent from the text. The man was educated and a good writer. He identified himself as a member of the famous Ashley-Henry expedition which departed up-river from St. Louis in 1822. He was not a braggart, and reported in a terse matter-of -fact style about traveling up the Missouri, then the Big Horn and finally the

Wind River in Wyoming. There in present Dubois, Wyoming, in 1823-24, he wintered with the Crow Indians. The following summer with his companions he crossed over the Continental Divide into the heart of the Rocky Mountains. He was an observant and careful man. He correctly defined, in one terse sentence, the sources and flow of seven large western rivers.

The real prize was his 1827 letter. While recounting his adventures of the past year, this writer penned the earliest first hand description of Yellowstone Park. With or without its original author, this letter was exciting history! So newspapers and historians printed excerpts from this "Yellowstone letter" without knowing who wrote them. Then happily, two observant researchers puzzled out the author's name.

While searching *The National Intelligence* of Washington, D.C., Mr. Donald M.. Frost chanced on a letter by this phantom author which had first been published in the *Philadelphia Gazette* and was signed "D.T. P." Then, in the head note of an extract of the letter it declared the author was a "D. T. Potts" of Montgomery County. This name was confirmed for Donald Frost by another researcher from a different source. Miss Stella Drum, of the Missouri Historical Society found a "D. Potts" on an account book of Smith, Jackson, and Sublette. Searching further, Donald Frost found in *The Potts Family* [Cannonsburg Penn. 1901] a brief biography of "Daniel Trotter Potts." The biography read that Potts was "a lad of excellent habits and sound principles. When he reached manhood, anxious to see life and the country, he went west." So now the mystery trapper had a name! The next development was an unexpected piece of good luck.

The year 1947 was the 75th anniversary of Yellowstone Park. This event was heralded in publications throughout the country. Two living descendants of the Potts family, Mrs. Anne Rittenhouse and her sister Kate Nixon lived in Washington D.C. These ladies were granddaughters of William Potts, a brother to Daniel's father Zubulun. Fortune smiled. Anne Rittenhouse was reading an article about Yellowstone in the March 9th issue of the *Washington Post* when she saw an assertion that a "Daniel T. Potts" was *"the first news reporter of the Rocky Mountains."* It so happened that as the eldest member of her family, Mrs. Rittenhouse, along with her sister Kate Nixon, had a box of old records among which were original copies of Daniel Potts's letters, written from the Rocky Mountains. These ladies immediately contacted the National Park Service and happily informed them that the original manuscript of the famous, *first description, of Yellowstone*, was still in the family! This was a historian's dream–an authentic primary source, previously unknown, of an exciting incident from an unknown time.

The ladies added to the excitement when they revealed that besides the "Yellowstone Discovery" letter they had two more. One was dated "Rocky Mountains, July 7th 1824," and the other "St. Louis, October 13th 1828." Altogether it was an extraordinary find. So, the Park Superintendent, it's Museum Curator, and its Naturalist huddled, then cheerfully offered the ladies $100.00 for all three letters. When their generous offer was accepted, they obtained the letters and quickly locked them in a safe.

Money well spent. The letters fill gaps in the record and slightly crack open the window on the edge of prehistory in Western America. Penned on-the-spot, the Daniel Trotter Potts's letters are some of the earliest eye witness reports of exploring the Rocky Mountains.[1]

---

[1] Following their acquisition by the Park they were first published in *Yellowstone Nature Notes*, [Yellowstone Park, Wyoming], Sept. 1947, pp. 50-56. Donald M. Frost, gave the letters a pivotal role in his *Notes on General Ashley, The Overland Trail and South Pass* [Barr, Massachusetts: Barr Gazette, 1960].

In this book, unless the meaning is confusing, the spelling and grammar are Potts's. All Potts's letters are in the appendix with the original spelling. When italics are used in quotes from letters they are from this author, [Jerry Bagley].

A RARE FIND

In the basement of a three story stone building, fifteen paces from the entry door, stands a green, combination-locked, vault. The stone building is at Mammoth Hot Springs, Wyoming and its basement is the archives where rare manuscripts regarding Yellowstone Park are stored. The green vault is the sanctum sanctorum where the most valuable documents of all are kept.

In this safe are three manuscript letters. The letters are first incased in acid retardant paper, then laid flat into a grey envelope and placed in a box. The box is placed on the shelf of the green safe and the door is locked. The Park Archivists protect these letters as if they were crown jewels.

For Yellowstone Park they are crown jewels. The letters were written one hundred and seventy years ago by an explorer of the Rocky Mountains named Daniel Trotter Potts. And the prize jewel is a letter written by Potts that is the first eye-witness account of Yellowstone National Park. Potts wrote it after returning from Yellowstone, at the Rocky Mountain Fur Trade Rendezvous of 1827, held at Sweet Lake. Let's go back there . . .

The Sweet Lake Rendezvous of 1827

Trapping, killing and skinning animals is fowl dirty work. It stinks. Anyone who has skinned a beaver, mink or weasel knows how truly bad it smells. And the skinner quickly smells like the skin. In fact, this is good for his craft for as he takes on the smell of his prey, he is more successful in catching them. This line of work is mostly done by men on the course edge of society–men used to a rough and rugged life.

Daniel T. Potts didn't qualify. His ancestors were gentry folk with occupations that didn't make them stink. Unusual for his time and doubly so for a trapper, Daniel could *write*. And at the Sweet Lake fur trade Rendezvous of 1827 that was what he was about to do.

The mountain trade Rendezvous was in full swing at the southerly edge of Sweet Lake in Utah. One year previous Daniel Potts had written the earliest description of this Lake:

> In the first valley as you approach from the head of the river, [Bear River] is a small sweet lake, about 120 miles in circumference, with beautiful clear water, and when the wind blows has a splendid appearance.[2]

Now, a year later on July 8, action had picked up and the scene at Sweet Lake looked like this:

Smoke curled up from a hundred campfires then fanned into the clear atmosphere. Sweet Water Lake shimmered in various shades of turquoise. A few days previous, James Bruffee and Hyrum Scott had arrived with a long pack train of supplies. The train had left St. Louis April, 12, with forty-six men and $22,447.14 worth of trade goods. And the packers were paid $110.00 each for a year's service. Now, trappers and Indians had arrived with their furs to trade.

The summer Rendezvous was the key to success for the traders and an exciting party for trappers and Indians. Beaver pelts were best when the weather was cold, so they were trapped in early winter and early spring–just before the creeks froze up and just after they thawed. There wasn't time to explore the country, trap beaver, pack the furs out to St. Louis, then buy supplies and hurry back to explore and trap again. With the Rendezvous System the men could remain in the

---

[2] Sweetwater is drinkable water. It was named Sweetwater Lake in contrast to Great Salt Lake which lays westward just over the range. It was utterly unsweet and undrinkable.

mountains to explore and trap. The traders packed in goods from the East and exchanged them for furs at this annual gathering. Then the traders pressed the skins into compact bales and packed them back to St. Louis. This year it was all happening at the south end of Sweetwater Lake. Business and fun, they were buying and selling and having a party. A generic and classic Rendezvous description was dictated by James Beckwourth:

DANIEL WRITES A
LETTER FROM THE RENDEZVOUS

the absent parties began to arrive, one after the other . . . Shortly after, [arrived the traders], Accompanied with three hundred pack mules, well laden with goods and all things necessary for the mountaineers and the Indian trade. It may well be supposed that the arrival of such a vast amount of luxuries from the east did not pass off without a general celebration.

Then in one breath, Beckwourth describes the fun:

Mirth, songs dancing, shouting, trading, running, jumping,

singing, racing, target-shooting, yarns, frolic with all sorts of extravagances that white men or Indians could invent, were freely indulged in.[3]

And to lubricate the Rendezvous, Beckwourth says, "The unpacking of the medicine water contributed not a little to the heightening of our festivities."

Medicine water was alcohol flavored with molasses, pepper, and sometimes, gunpowder. Then it was diluted with water. As the men became more drunk, they were less fussy about the mix.

According to the observer, Cornelius Rogers, Alcohol was sold at $4.00 a pint. Some men would spend a thousand dollars in a day or two, [about $20,000 in 1999 money] and very few had much of their year's wages left when the Rendezvous broke up.[4]

It was the most exciting event of the season. For a year the

---

[3] Delmont Oswald, ed., *The Life and Adventures of James P. Beckwourth*, as told to Thomas D. Bonner, [Lincoln: University of Nebraska Press, 1972], p. 107. Packed to the mountains in small barrels, alcohol was then diluted with water, and spiced up with extra flavor. Molasses, pepper, and gunpowder were choices. As the men became more drunk, additional water could be added. Though frowned on by the government, liquor became an increasingly vital ingredient in the trade. The profit was good, it added to the party and lubricated trade. The Indians, unaccustomed to any liquor, were especially enlivened by the brew.

[4] Whisky, rum, or whatever alcohol concoction available, was priced according to supply. Demand was ever present.

men had been without fresh supplies from the East. And in small groups they had been searching mountain streams for beaver. They had been isolated, cold, and ever in danger from Indians bent on robbing them or worse. Now safely gathered with friends, they relaxed and became outrageous, rollicking, wild men. With their squaws and Indian friends they squandered their furs and had a spree. They compared adventures, played games and traded. At the Rendezvous they could trade beaver skins for gun powder, lead and knives. There

Trading Sugar For Beaver Furs

were beads and blankets, sugar and tobacco, beaver traps and Indian goods. Also, colored ribbons, brass tacks, cock bells, and bright cloth–the trader had them all. Beaver skins were the same as money. Some trappers threw away a thousand dollars in a few days–their whole season's work.

One man, however, stayed sober. And for a time, he left the party. His name was Daniel Trotter Potts. He enjoyed frivolity with his mountain friends, but his background wasn't so ragged as theirs; he was educated and could write. This was a bit unusual, And he wanted to send some letters home. Except for clerking, writing skill was unnecessary for a mountain man. But Daniel was eager to report the year's adventures to his friends and family–and glad he had the skill to do it. Also, Potts, coming from a business-minded family, wanted to tally up his earnings.

To avoid creasing the paper he held the pages loosely. In this country, paper was valuable like gold and harder to come by. He got the paper and a bottle of India ink[5] from the trader Hyrum Scott. Walking up to a low knoll overlooking the lake, he sat next to a pack box, spread the paper out on its smooth surface, and began to write.

Respected Brother[6] Sweet Lake, July 8, 1827

A few days since, our trader arrived by whom I received two letters, one from Dr. Lukens and the other from yourself. . . .Shortly after writing to you last year *I took my departure for The Blackfoot Country, much against my choice.*

Blackfeet Indians didn't have black feet.[7] However, they

---

[5] "India ink" is a product made of lamp black mixed with a binding agent and molded into cakes or sticks. In this form it could easily be transported to the Rendezvous then mixed with water for use. The tip of a large feather made a fine *quill pen.*

[6] This letter was one of several addressed to Robert T. Potts, a wealthy merchant in Philadelphia. His other pen pal, "Dr. Lukens," has not yet been identified, but he may have some connection to Lukens Steel Mills of Pennsylvania. The previous year, at the Rendezvous of 1826, Potts had planned to go southwest to California with Jedediah Smith but for reasons unknown he went north to Yellowstone, and made history.

[7] The literal translation of the native name is "black footed people." However the origins of the name are unknown. It is an irony that the Shoshoni-Bannocks, who were enemies of the Blackfeet, have a

had a black spot in their hearts for white men—and American trappers nurtured this anger. Heading into the teeth of Blackfoot Country, the fur hunters in 1826 had gone north from Cache Valley, then crossed over the rim of the Great Basin to Snake River. Trouble with the Blackfeet was immediate. Daniel Potts continues.

> . . . we crossed Snake River or South fork of Columbia at the forks of Henry's & Louis's forks [north of Idaho Falls, Idaho] at this place we was Dayly harrased by the Blackfeet . . . .

Daniel Potts loved unexplored country about as much as he disliked these Indians. Bad relations with the Blackfeet stemmed from an incident with Lewis and Clark on the Marias River in 1806, when a band of Blackfeet ran into the Americans, then attempted to rob them. The Americans responded with fight and in the fray that followed two Indians were killed and their horses and weapons taken by the whites. Now, even though twenty years had passed, the angry Blackfeet had not forgotten their loss.

Relations were so poor that the Americans didn't know for sure who the Blackfeet were. They often called any raiding party Blackfeet. There were actually three tribes: The Piegan, the Blood, and the Siksika. They were politically independent but spoke the same language, married each other and fought together. To the American trappers, the words, fighting, torture and Blackfeet were all the same. Skirmishes with these Indians made exciting camp fire tales that grew better with the telling. One of the best Blackfeet tales involves John Colter and is vividly told by Bradbury. Colter and his trapping partner were

---

Reservation near Blackfoot River. However, the two are apparently not connected. The origin of this name may stem from Shoshoni Indians getting black feet by walking across burnt prairie.

surprised and surrounded while trapping the Jefferson River in a canoe. After killing his partner the Blackfeet,

> seized Colter, stripped him entirely naked, and set to consulting on the manner they would put him to death. They were first inclined to tie him up as a mark to shoot at; but the chief interfered, and seizing him by the shoulder, asked him if he could run fast? Colter . . . was well acquainted with Indian customs, he knew that he had now to run for his life, with the dreadful odds of five or six hundred against him, and those [were] armed Indians; therefore cunningly [he] replied that he was a very bad runner, although he was considered by the hunters as remarkably swift. The chief now commanded the party to remain stationary, and led Colter out on the prairie three or four hundred yards, and released him, bidding him to save himself if he could. At that instant the horrid war whoop sounded in the ears of poor Colter, who, urged with the hope of preserving life, ran with a speed at which he was himself surprised . . . . He ran nearly half way across the plain before he ventured to look over his shoulder, when he perceived that the Indians were very much scattered, and that he had gained ground to a considerable distance from the main body; But one Indian, who carried a spear was much before all the rest, and not more than a hundred yards from him . . . he exerted himself to such a degree, that the blood gushed from his nostrils, and soon almost covered the fore part of his body . . . Colter, who, although fainting and exhausted, succeeded in gaining the skirting of the cotton wood trees, on the borders of the fork, through which he ran, and plunged into the river. Fortunately for him, a little below this place there was an island, against the upper point of which a raft of drift timber had lodged, he dived under the raft, and after several efforts, got his head above water amongst the trunks of trees . . . . Scarcely had he secured himself, when the Indians arrived on the river screeching and yelling, as Colter expressed it like so

many devils. [8]

Colter lived to tell the tale. But what a tale! He was naked, barefoot and at least seven days journey from Lisa's Fort. Stories like this gave trappers nightmares–and confirmed their grim estimates of Blackfeet character. No wonder Daniel Potts would rather go to California, but such was not to be.

Daniel and his companions had edged over the rim of the Great Basin into Snake River Valley. It was the largest valley in the Rocky Mountains and it strung along Snake River from the Tetons in Wyoming to modern Boise, Idaho. Near the two forks of Snake River the valley floor was flat like a table. The only trees were a fringe by the river, the rest was sage brush–some of it taller than a horse. But they could see the surrounding mountains.

The Tetons

When they got north of Idaho Falls the men looked to the East and were struck by the sight of three steep mountains. They were the Tetons. Its likely that some of the men had heard of these mountains from Andrew Henry. He had wintered in the shadow of the Tetons on a foiled trapping venture back in 1810 and afterwards the north fork of Snake River was called "Henry's Fork." The Astorians, returning from the mouth of the Columbia in 1812, called these remarkable mountains the "Pilot Knobs." But French Canadians, noting their shapes, dubbed them "the Three Teats" or in French –*Tetons*, and that name

---

[8] Bradbury, John, *Travels in the Interior of America*, [London, 1817], pp.18-21. Bradbury's tale is not first hand. But it's a good story and represents Blackfeet vs. trapper relations.

stuck.[9]

In the Rocky Mountains, a region crowded with lofty crags, the Tetons stood out as extraordinary landmarks. Potts could have called them the Pilot Knobs or the Tetons but customary to his sweeping topographical descriptions, he lumps them with the whole range and calls it "a large rugged mountain." From the forks of Snake River they went,

> up Henry's or North fork which bears North of East thirty miles and crossed a large ruged Mountain which separates the two forks.[10]

They went over the low break in the Teton Range.

---

[9] In 1819-1820, Donald Mackenzie may have led his trapping band near the Tetons. A letter from Alexander Ross to Peter Skeen Ogden suggests this: "We then visited Mr. Mckenzie's [Mackenzie's?]wintering ground of 1819-20 and the grand river [Snake River?] beyond the *trois butes*."
[10] *Potts's letter Robert Potts*, 1827.

THE FIRST ACCOUNT OF
YELLOWSTONE PARK

Trailing over the Teton Range, lodgepole trees were so thick they brushed the horses packs. These Lodge Pole Pines were straight, narrow, and tall, perfect to hold up Indian lodges they were named for. Fortunately, the pass was low and gradual—the high rugged Tetons were 20 miles south. They continued on an easy grade and dropped down on Lewis's fork of Snake River. To the south, in a valley soon to be named Jackson's Hole, the Three Tetons rose almost vertical and were mirrored in a glacially cold lake.

Mountains were landmarks, so Daniel kept track of them. But the flow of rivers was even more important. Animal, Indian, and trapper trails followed rivers courses. Sailors had explored numerous river mouths–where they spilled into the sea, but how the rivers got to the sea, and which inland river belonged to which ocean mouth was speculative. In 1826, much about the West was a guess.

So Potts observed carefully, talked to other men, and formed his own opinions. Then he took a stab at identifying the rivers, and was pretty good at it.

From Jackson's Hole they continued north to the origin of Snake River then up and over a mountain divide. But Potts noted it wasn't just a divide. It was the Continental Divide which sent water to different oceans. Large rivers began here and wound their way down to larger rivers and then the ocean.

In a remarkable paragraph Potts put it all together for his brother Robert.

> from thence [we went] East up the other fork, [the South Fork and main branch of "Snake River"] to it's source which heads on top of the great chain Rocky Mountains which separates the water of the Atlantic from that of the Pacific. At or near this place heads the Luchkadee or

California fork, [Green River which empties into the Gulf
of California], Stinking fork [Shoshone River], Yellowstone [River], South forks of the Missouri, [Madison
Jefferson, and Gallatin], and Henry's fork [of Snake River]
all those head at an angular point . . . .[11]

Potts found it natural to get the lay of the land and the flow
of rivers while he was walking or riding his horse. With no
man-made constructions competing for his attention, the rivers
were the main attraction. He makes a remarkable sweep of
western geography in the above paragraph. It is noteworthy he
knew where he was–on the highlands of North America, where
numerous rivers originate. By knowing where rivers started and
ended, he displayed a better knowledge of the West than
leading cartographers of his day. Numerous seaman had
explored the river mouths–where they dumped into the ocean.
And this had been accurately engraved on maps. But seaman
and cartographers only speculated about the origins of these
streams.

Yellowstone Lake and Geysers

They were high in the mountains, the air was clean and the
sky blue. From the Continental Divide Potts soon saw
Yellowstone Lake. Daniel's is the earliest known description,

---

[11] *Potts's letter to Robert Potts, 1827.*

"The Yellow-stone [River] has a large fresh water Lake near its head on the very top of the mountain which is . . . as clear as crystal."[12]

But there was more to see than the lake. Something was happening near its southwest shores—it looked like smoke. Was there a tribe of Indians camped in front of them? Daniel and the others were cautious, this was Blackfeet country.

In numerous places on the edge of the lake Potts could see pure white smoke puffing into the atmosphere. It contrasted remarkably against the dark green trees and the deep blue water. On a clear day in high Wyoming they could see for miles. The Yellowstone Plateau was flat compared to nearby mountains. Was it smoke? Or was it steam? They headed in that direction.

It was steam. Numerous hot springs were strangely hissing and puffing. And these were only a hint of the thermal wonders in the region. There were hot, bubbling mud pots, deep, blue hot pools, steam vents, spurting fountains and thunderous explosions. As he tells it,

on the South borders of this Lake is a number of hot and boiling springs some of water and others of most beautiful fine clay and resembles that of a mush pot and throws its particles to the immense height of from twenty to thirty feet in height The Clay is white and of a Pink and water appear fathomless as it appears to be entirely hollow under neath. There is also a number of places where the pure sulphur is sent forth in abundance . . . .

one of our men Visited one of those whilst taking his recreation there at an instant the earth began a tremendous trembling and he with difficulty made his escape when an explosion took place resembling that of Thunder. During

12 *Ibid.*

our stay in that quarter I heard it every day.[13]

Pretty exciting stuff! Anyone who has witnessed a geyser blasting water and steam high into the air understands Daniel's astonishment.

This written statement from Potts is the earliest eye witness report of the largest thermal area in the world. Later, Park naturalists would count more than ten thousand hot water · features in Yellowstone, *more than all the rest of the world combined*. And thermal features were not the only wonders of this region.

Arguably, the northwest corner of present Wyoming has more beauty and natural wonders than any region of similar size in the world. It is high in the mountains and straddles the Continental Divide. At this elevation, winter snows are captured then gradually melts in warmer months, flowing into small streams that start major rivers. The Missouri, the Green, the Snake the Big Horn and the Yellowstone begin their cascade from the Rocky Mountains here. To the south, mirrored in a series of beautiful lakes, are the Tetons.

Others had already described the Tetons, but this statement from Daniel Potts is the first known description of the Yellowstone Park area. It happened in 1826. [Daniel's hand written letter describing Yellowstone is below on page 18, and a transcription is in the appendix.]

---

[13] Potts's Yellowstone description is in his letter to Robert Potts, 1827.

The Falsehood of Colter's Hell

Commonly, it has been supposed that John Colter discovered Yellowstone Park. For almost fifty years the Park and "Colters Hell" were thought to be the same place.[14] That is a falsehood. The "Colter in Yellowstone" myth will be covered with more detail in Chapter VIII, however it will be briefly touched here.

Actually, in 1807 John Colter discovered a thermal area on the Shoshone River that fur trappers named "Colter's Hell." But, when the Yellowstone Park area became known, with its more extensive hot springs, some historians got the two mixed up. And they wrongly assumed that "Colter's Hell" was Yellowstone Park.[15]

---

[14] See Burton, Harris, *John Colter*, [Bison Press, Lincoln, 1993], pp. 88-92.

[15] John Colter's biographer, Burton Harris, explains that attaching "Colters Hell" to Yellowstone is a "modern invention." He quotes Father De Smit, Joe Meek, and other contemporary sources placing "Colter's Hell" on the Stinking River [It runs near Cody Wyoming and the name was later changed to Shoshone River.] Colter never claimed he saw the thermal activity in Yellowstone. His journeys near the region are controversial and not documented by a first or even second hand source. There is a dotted line on the Clark Map marked, "Colter's Route." Here are a variety of scenarios regarding it.

Harris suggests that Colter did get into Yellowstone, and perhaps to explain why he didn't report the hot springs, suggests he missed the main trail, and didn't get to the shores of Yellowstone Lake. Dale Morgan in *Jedediah Smith and the Opening of the West*, p. 419 suggests that Colter didn't see Yellowstone Lake or its thermal features at all, but instead saw a composite of Shoshone Lake and Lewis Lake. "Slim" Lawrence, who collected the Jackson Hole Museum, suggested to the author that Colter may have looped around Brooks Lake, [near Togwatee Pass] but never

Though his presence in Yellowstone is doubtful, John Colter did have remarkable experiences during and after his trek with Lewis and Clark. As the expedition was returning down the Missouri, Colter, who had performed his duties well, obtained a discharge to join two trappers on a beaver hunt. A year later Colter had quit these two and was paddling down the Missouri. Then, at the mouth of the Platte, he met a keel boat and fur trading company coming upstream headed by Manuel Lisa. He joined them and went back to the mountains.

Lisa's company had more than a casual relationship to the Lewis and Clark Expedition. Besides Colter, three other Expedition men had signed on. They were George Drouillard, John Potts, [no relation to Daniel] and Peter Wiser. Also, Reuben Lewis, [Meriwether Lewis's brother], became an active partner in 1810. And even William Clark, Lewis's co-captain, had a share in the venture. Lisa gathered men with experience on the upper Missouri, and men who otherwise might compete with him, then formed an organization called The Missouri Fur Company of St. Louis.

He guided his boat up the Missouri to the Yellowstone River then up the Yellowstone to the mouth of the Big Horn. Here, Lisa set the men to building a post. This restless leader of Spanish ancestry soon dispatched men out to invite friendly Indians to trade at his post. Among the men he sent out were Edward Rose, Peter Wiser, "Shamplaine," [Jean Baptiste Champlain] and Colter.

The routes and itineraries of these men are only faintly known. However, Reuben Lewis pretty well cancels Colter out

---

crossed the Divide to the Snake River and Columbia drainage. J. Neilson Barry maintains that south of the Big Horn, no single location on the Clark Map can be positively identified. So its anyone's guess.

as a Yellowstone discoverer. Reuben wrote a letter to his brother Meriwether describing lands south of the Three Forks. He wrote that not Colter, but Peter Wiser and Baptiste Shamplaine had fresh knowledge of the lands near present Yellowstone Park. They had gone south up the Madison River, crossed the Divide and dropped down on the beaver rich Snake River drainage. In a letter dated April 21,1810, written from the Three Forks and sent down the river with Colter, Reuben says,

> The return of your old acquaintance Coalter, [John Colter] gives me an opportunity of addressing you a few lines . . . . Mr. Shamplain tells me that Martin [marten] abound in the mountains dividing the waters of the Spanish River as it is called or what is supposed to be the Rio del Nort, from the waters of some of the Southern branches of the Collumbia on a River falling in to the gulf of California which he thinks most probable. Beaver abound in the same country but it lies so high that it is all most perpetual snow. The upper branches of the Collumbia are full of beaver and the rout by the middle fork or Madisons River is short without mountains it is about 5 or 6 days Travel to an illigable place for a fort on that River where the Beaver, from the account of Peter Wyzer, is as abundant as in our part of this country, Buffalow and game of every kind in great abundance . . . I . . . shall indeavor to get Mr. Shamplain to give me a sketch of the South and S E of this place which I think may be very much relied on as he is a young Man of observation & forward it by the first boat . . . .[16]

There is a significant point to be learned from this letter. *If John Colter had been over the Continental Divide and on the Snake River drainage, Reuben would have told Meriwether to question Colter about it face to face, instead of quoting Wiser*

---

[16] Fred R.Gowans, *A Fur Trade History of Yellowstone Park: Notes, Documents, Maps* [Orem, Utah, Grizzly Publications, 1989] p. 105.

and Shamplain and writing all this detail regarding their travels and reliability. This would have been easy since *Colter was the mailman who delivered the letter to Meriwether.*

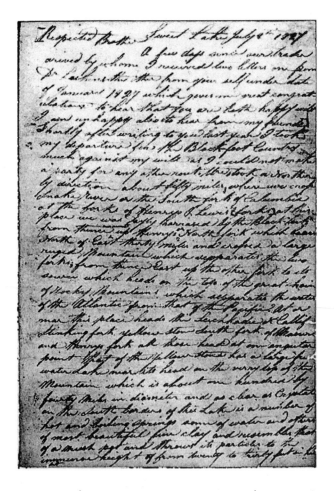

The earth began a tremendous trembling and an explosion took place ... he with difficulty made his escape." [Potts's Yellowstone Letter]

Colter's tie to Yellowstone and lands west of the Continental Divide is mostly myth. But his goings and comings happened

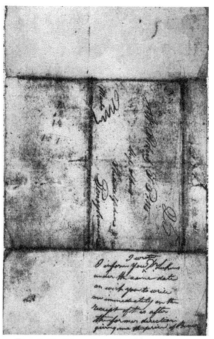

Daniel's Handmade Envelope

before 1811, and more will be said about him later. Let's get back to Daniel Potts and more certain history.

Potts Saw More Than He Wrote

Daniel Potts was a curious and observant man. And during his "stay in that quarter" he likely saw more of Yellowstone than he wrote about. Remarkable sites are not far from each other, summer made traveling easy, and there was ample time for exploring before the fall hunt. He penned the account at the Rendezvous several months later and by writing of painted mud pots, fathomless hot springs, hollow sounding crusted ground, and the exploding geyser, he pretty well covered the varieties of hot springs in Yellowstone.

He also recorded multiple river origins and the Continental Divide. That was important. Then, compressing the fall hunt and trip back to Cache Valley into thirteen words of one sentence he finishes: "From this place by a circuitous route to the Nourth west we returned."

Potts wasn't alone on this journey, but since no other name is known, he might as well have been. Others of the party were likely fascinated by unexplored country and strange sites. But the only report about it comes from Potts. His terse statement describing steaming mud pots, geysers and river origins is not doubted by historians and sets Daniel Trotter Potts as the first known man in Yellowstone.

At the Rendezvous he withdrew from the drinking, gaming, and trading long enough to write this letter about mountains, rivers and geysers, He dated it "Sweet Lake, July 8, 1827," and addressed it to his brother Robert. On High Street, in Philadelphia, Robert Potts had a store that was doing well. And while Daniel's letter to brother Robert was mostly about geography and adventure, he had business on his mind. Writing on the back of his folded envelope, Daniel informed him of his real concern: trade goods cost too much. He also told Robert of a second letter he had written to their friend, "Dr. Lukens,"which gave the current price of goods. And he requested that his brother write immediately giving him the price of beaver.

By a happy accident the original copy of Daniel's letter surfaced in 1947, one hundred and twenty years after he wrote it. The letter exhibits his fine writing and the envelope is especially interesting–being a folded sheet of paper. Perhaps a string held it together as there is no evidence of glue. Postage from the Rendezvous at Sweet Lake Utah to Philadelphia was .25 cents. And this postage cost is simply written with a pen in the corner–there were no postage stamps in the mountains.

There is Poor Prospect of Making Much Here

Daniel went to the mountains for adventure and to seek his fortune. In five years he had only achieved the first; and the proceeds from 1826 were especially discouraging. For one thing, a trapper's most valuable asset was horse–and he had lost three. Hungry Ute Indians had killed two for food–one was a favorite buffalo runner worth four hundred and fifty dollars. But lost horses wasn't the only problem, the Blackfeet had been a constant annoyance. Before the fall hunt they attacked at the forks of Snake River. On the return from Yellowstone Potts narrowly escaped after running "plumb in the face" of a large party. And they got bolder. Just before he arrived at Sweet Water Lake these Blackfeet brazenly attack the Rendezvous itself. He had earlier written, "A man in this country is not safe neither day nor night, and hardly ever expect to get back." The other challenge to making money came from white men—trade merchandise *did* cost too much. Potts declares both problems in one terse sentence. "There is poor prospect of making much here owing to the evil disposition of the Indians and exorbitant price of goods."

Compared to a man's wage in Philadelphia, where he might make a dollar or less a day, Potts was earning big money. But money made trapping furs was an illusion. He *could* catch a lot of valuable beaver but the wealth slipped through his hands to the traders.

There certainly was a lot of money to be made in the

mountains, but not from trapping. Other men had tried and failed. The hard working and honest Andrew Henry broke trail for all the others but still didn't get it together. There were tricks to the trade. General Ashley spent five years and went deeply in debt before he got it all right. About this same time Jedediah Smith took Henry's place as Ashley's partner. He had paid his dues on two ill-fated journeys searching for beaver south and west all the way to California. That didn't work. But when he and two partners, Jackson and Sublette, bought out Ashley and became the traders—then raised prices their first year—they found success. The money was in *trading*.

By then, Daniel Potts had learned the game too. The secret was, you made money not by trapping the beaver, but by trapping the trappers. The real profit was in exchanging highly marked up trade goods for beaver skins, then packing the skins to St. Louis and selling them with another mark up. When the new traders, Smith, Jackson, and Sublette, raised prices in 1827, it prompted Potts to illustrate "the exorbitant price of goods" in a letter to his friend, Dr. Lukens.

Some items he listed were,
powder, $2.50 per lb.
coffee, $2.00sugar,$2.00
blankets, $15.00

horses $150 to $300. and some as high as $500.[17]

Daniel was flirting with the idea of being a trader himself. There were too many middle men between him and the market. He had been doing the hard work but the traders were calling the shots. They were setting the prices on both the merchandise and the furs.

---

[17] For the full list, see the letter of 1827 in the appendix.

So he listed mountain prices in his letter to Dr. Lukens, told his business-minded brother about the list, and requested that he write him "immediately regarding the price of fur." Potts was in his thirties—old for a mountain man—he had come west for adventure and to seek his fortune. It was time to put a little more attention on the "fortune."

Moreover, starting a business wasn't new to Daniel. Contrasting with most trappers, he was educated and grew up near Philadelphia–not on the fringe of the frontier. And his family and friends were rich.

The family owned steel and grain mills and had associated with people of influence for generations. In 18th Century Pennsylvania it was popular to be a Potts.

So how did a well bred man came to be among wild Indians and uncultured whites in the Rocky Mountains? That is what the rest of the book is about.

He came from Valley Forge, Pennsylvania.

VALLEY FORGE, THE POTTS FAMILY, AND GEORGE WASHINGTON

PENNSYLVANIA, 1777

In 1777, General George Washington was having a bad winter. The Continental Congress had installed him to lead the Colonial Army, but it didn't give him enough provisions and pay. Basic military supplies were so scanty that Benjamin Franklin seriously proposed going back to the bow and arrow! Wintering in Valley Forge his men were cold and hungry–they often went two or three days without bread. Fortunately there was a grain mill nearby. The mill was powered by Valley Creek and owned by the Quaker, Isaac Potts. The Potts family were numerous in Valley Forge. They were generally Quakers, were influential, and prosperous. The family had owned a variety of mills powered by Valley Creek. They sawed wood, milled grain and had owned the forge from which the valley got its name. The forge was located at the mouth of Valley Creek in a deep rugged hollow. Here pig iron was wrought into iron bars then sold to other manufacturers. Iron making had been associated with the Potts family for generations.[18] For many years they were the largest and most successful iron-masters in the American Colonies.[19] The Revolutionary War kept all of the

---

[18] There is rich and varied history in the name, *"Valley Forge."* From an early date water powered forges and mills were built to take advantage of the fall in Valley Creek. It grew into a large operation; by 1764 as much as fifty-one tons of pig iron were hauled there annually and "forged" into iron bars then sold to manufacturers. In 1757 John Potts purchased a forge, a saw mill and three tracts of land from the estate of Steven Evans. In 1786 eighty-five tons of pig iron were used. John apparently enlarged the iron-works which from that time forward were called Valley Forge. The forging , saw mills, and grain mills were associated with the Potts family for several generations. *The Potts Family*, p. 241.

[19] John Potts in 1752 purchased almost 1000 acres at the confluence of Montgomery Creek and the Schuylkill River where he laid out the town "Pottsgrove" later "Pottstown." He operated mines, furnaces and forges in

mills busy–as long as they had raw material to process and the British didn't burn them out.[20] The colonial army needed iron for cannon but during the winter of 1777 a more pressing need was bread for the hungry soldiers. Isaac Potts was the man! His grain mills "were large and in good repute for the quality and quantity of flower they produced." His success and wealth was witnessed by the large, stone Potts mansion house–the house that George Washington used for his headquarters!

Potts Mansion House

Pennsylvania and Virginia. *The Potts Family*, p. 243.

[20] One Potts family historian writes that iron wasn't wrought during part of the war because the British burned the "old forge" down two months before the Continental Army camped there. Isaac nonetheless owned large grain mills and the stone mansion house which was likely built from iron profits. James, Mrs. Thomas, *Memorial of Thomas Potts Junior*, [Cambridge, 1874]. P.28

Isaac was a Quaker and minister of the gospel. Being a peace loving Quaker he at first did not approve of his house and mill being used for military purposes. But he changed his mind after a surprising discovery that General Washington was a prayerful man.

The Potts in this story may have been Isiaac or it may have been Daniel Potts's father Zebulan. The descendants of both men claim the honor. But whichever, it helped Washington. He got the house. Briefly, here is how it went:

> In 1777, while the American army lay at Valley Forge "
> . . . a Quaker by the name of Potts had occasion to pass through a thick wood near head-quarters . . . approaching with slowness . . . [he saw] the Commander-in-chief of the armies of the United Colonies on his knees in the act of devotion to the Ruler of the universe! At the moment when Friend Potts, concealed by the trees, came up, Washington was interceding for his beloved country."[21]

Though sincere Quakers, Both Isaac and Zebulan had "originality of mind and independence of character. It often led them beyond the rules of the drab coat and broad brim." Isaac

---

[21] *Ibid.* p. 222. The evidence that Zebulan and not Isaac chanced on Washington at prayer is from Zebulan Potts's granddaughter. She writes that one of Zebulan's trips to Washington's camp "became a national incident and is commemorated on a special U. S. stamp marking the hundred and fiftieth anniversary of the birth of Washington. The stamp was taken from a picture of Washington at prayer at Valley Forge with a broad brim hatted man [a Quaker] coming through the woods . . . " *letter from Anne G. Rittinhouse to Yellowstone Park Library Association* January, 1948. Anne Rittenhouse was in possession of the Daniel Potts letters and sold them to Yellowstone Park.

believed that "there was but one Christian Church . . . and that true Christians of every denomination should unite and harmonize."

Zebulon Potts, Danial Potts's father and closely related to Isaac, was essentially a gorilla for the American Army. Before the war he was constable of Plymouth Township, then during the conflict he raised a company to fight with Washington. He also scavenged clothes and food for the ill equipt army. The Quakers stuck to their creed and dismissed Zeb for joining Washington. But he was unrepentant and continued helping the Revolution.

Meanwhile the British were well aware of Zeb's war efforts and tried to catch him. A newspaper later reported that,

> Many forays were made by mounted Redcoats to the Potts home, [it was only a day's ride from their garrison in Philadelphia], often to be thwarted by admiring neighbors of the patroit. By night, with stones tossed on the roof of his house, they awakened Zebulon to the danger of nearby enemy patrols. On one occasion the witful colonist hid under an empty flour barrel in his kitchen to foil his would-be captors.[22]

---

[22] *Times Herold*, November, 19, 1965, [Norrisburg Penn.].

Zebulan was the first Sheriff of Montgomery County and its first state senator. With Martha Trotter he fathered ten children. The youngest was born eighteen years after his father's activities as a spy for Washington. They named him Daniel Trotter Potts and he is the prime character of this book. Contrasting with others of his kinfolk, Daniel forsook being a miller and sought his fortune in the mountain west.

The record doesn't tell much about him personally. His only description comes from the Potts Family Genealogy which says that Daniel was the fourth and last son of Zebulon and Martha Trotter Potts and was born July 18, of 1794. And, "born and raised on a farm, he was a lad of excellent habits and sound principles. When he reached manhood, anxious to see life and the country, he went west." Wasting few words, this statement identifies the man, his parents and points his direction.

Daniel's Mother, Martha Trotter Potts

Though his letters depict the Rocky Mountain West with detail, they tell very little about Daniel himself.[23] Rather than describe

---

[23] One of the only references to Daniel's life before going west is from the tax records. In 1816 he paid $1.00; in 1817 he paid in kind, 2 horses

himself he told his experiences—some were adventures, and some were hairy escapes. But mostly he wrote about new mountains and rivers and the beauty and wonder of it all. The only clues to Daniels's likeness are this picture of his mother, Martha Trotter Potts.

Daniel Potts Goes West

A second reference about Daniel Potts is from a head-note of *The Gazette and Daily Advertiser of* Philadelphia. Describing his letter from "Sweet Lake" with its earliest description of Yellowstone, the paper reads:

> The letter comes from a native of Pennsylvania
> who, activated by a spirit of romantic adventure,
> has left a good mill in Montgomery County, to
> wander in the wilds of the west.[24]

---

and .90 cents; in 1818, 2 horses, 2 cows and .90 cents; in 1919 he is listed as "removed." This is the year he went west.

[24] *The Gazette and Daily Advertizer* [Philadelphia], October 19, 1827. Daniel Potts's home was near Valley Forge, Pennsylvania. The valley got its name from the large forge on Valley Creek which was established by John Potts. He also established the town of Pottsgrove which became Pottstown. In *The Potts Family*, [Cannonsburg Penn,1901], is this description of John Potts, born in 1710: "John Potts, like his father was an enterprising business man, and for many years was the largest and most successful iron-master in the American Colonies, operating mines, furnaces and forges . . . ." During the American Revolution, a descendant, Isaac Potts, owned the mill and a large stone house which was used by George Washington as his headquarters through the winter of 1777-78 .

It is likely that the "Sweet Lake" letter of 1827 was furnished to the paper by Robert Potts so he also furnished the head note regarding Daniel's leaving a "good mill." Daniel Potts could have worked at Isaac's grist

So during his first 27 years he was a farmer and a miller. And from his writings and family background it is apparent that these early years were graced with education and gentility. The Potts family was well known. It was popular to be a Potts.

He left Pennsylvania and arrived in Illinois in July of 1821, and "tarried there until midwinter." He doesn't describe his activities there, but does say that he was "taken with a severe spell of rheumatism which continued with him for about two months"[25] –not a good omen for a man leaving civilization to

---

mill, a saw mill, or a steel mill. Numerous milling operations were powered by the swift current of Valley Creek in Valley Forge. And it was common for men of the Potts family to be millers. At least two letters were written to a "Dr. Lukens," likely related to The Lukens Steel Company [still operating in 1997]. Lukens Steel invented the process of making plate steel used to make boilers for steam engines. Daniel Potts was well connected for he regularly corresponded with Dr. Luken. In 1824, he wrote a letter to Thomas Cochlen, who also owned a steel mill. It isn't certain what kind of mill Daniel Potts worked in, but the family had worked iron for years. Perhaps he went west with the dream of making quick profits in furs then using the money to go into the steel business with one of these men.

[25] Daniel T. Potts, letter to Robert Potts, dated "Rocky Mountains, July 16, 1826", hereafter called , *Potts Letter, 1826.* For his first two years in the mountains Potts wrote two accounts, the first is the letter of 1824 to Thomas Cochlen. The existing manuscript document is a copy hand-written to Anne Thomas of Plymouth. The second account of these two years is a longer letter to his brother Robert written from the Rendezvous of 1826. These two documents are almost the only contemporary record of the Ashley-Henry thrust into the Rocky Mountains. The Ashley-Henry men were the first American parties to maintain a foothold in the Rockies. Others had proceeded them but were run out by the natives and harsh conditions. To preserve a base in the mountains they needed a large enough party for defense and access to supplies. They soon learned to live like the Indians, [and often with the Indians].

Daniel wrote three letters [we know of] to his brother Robert, one to T. Cochlen and one to Dr. Lukens–almost as many to friends as family.

trap in icy streams. But fortunately, he recovered and proceeded to the Missouri River, lyricly called "The River of the West," and more descriptively, "The Big Muddy." Daniel first saw the Missouri at St. Louis where it joins the Mississippi. St. Louis and the Missouri River were gateways to the West.

In St. Louis Potts entered "immediately" into the service of Henry and Ashley. He started up the Missouri River in a keel boat under the command of Henry on April 3, 1822.[26] Potts had evidently responded to an advertisement submitted by Ashley to several Missouri newspapers:

> To Enterprising Young Men –the subscriber wishes to engage ONE HUNDRED MEN, to ascend the river Missouri to its sources, there to be employed for one, two, or three years. For particulars, inquire of Major Andrew Henry, near the Lead Mines, in the County of Washington [who will ascend with, and command the party] or to the subscriber at St. Louis.[27]

St. Louis was the largest town on the frontier primarily because of the fur business, and few lived in the town whose well being wasn't in some way connected with the river trade. Daniel left Pennsylvania with beaver hunting as his objective and proceeded as a natural course directly to this town.

---

[26]*Ibid.*

[27]Frost, *Notes,* p. 65. Ashley, in 1822, was the highly respected Lieutenant Governor of Missouri. A self-made man, he rose to prominence in the upper Louisiana Territory along with the man who was to become his partner, Andrew Henry. The two had known each other as early as 1805 when Lieutenant Ashley served as witness for Andrew Henry's short-lived marriage. Ashley's constant interest in projects of an enterprising nature and the high value of animal skins doubtless prompted him to join with Henry in a fur trading venture. By September 9, 1821, the partnership was in full swing forming plans and making purchases.

It is worthy of note that Ashley in his St. Louis advertisements put a premium on "*enterprising young men.*" Many expeditions before them had not sought this attribute in their recruits. Ashley, though inexperienced in the fur business, came up with new methods that changed the trade. In a nutshell, instead of relying on Indians to bring in the furs he instituted the Mountain Trading Rendezvous and injected *private enterprise and the profit motive* into fur hunting. With self interest to spur them, his trappers thought of themselves as traders and "enterprising young men." It put an American flavor on their efforts and contrasted with the British program which used the men almost as servants.

These enterprising young Americans avidly searched out beaver streams and were the first whites to effectively discover the Rocky Mountains. And they left their names on rivers, mountains, passes and towns of the West. Note Weber's River, Bridger Lake, Smith's Fork, Hamm's Fork and Jackson's Hole. Also, Great Salt Lake, Cache Valley, Bear River, and Yellowstone Park were explored and their features named by these very men.

The Ashley-Henry roll included Jedediah Smith, Thomas Fitzpatrick, Thomas Eddie, Hugh Glass, Moses "Black" Harris, James Bridger, William Sublette and Mike Fink. The last may not have been so enterprising but was no less a colorful addition to the group. And there was Daniel Trotter Potts.

From one observer of this scene we have the following reminiscent account:

The animation created in St. Louis in the preparation for this great mountain expedition, will be long remembered by our citizens who were dwellers here at that period. Armed and equipped fitly for desperate encounters with the Redman, or his genial spirit the grizzly bear, these men paraded the streets while putting the last finish to the desperate preparations. Like the reckless crew of a man-of-war about to cruise against an enemy's squadron, they indulged deeply in the luxuries they might never again realize. The generous impulses which mark the character of such brave men, were extensively developed before their departure, and again in succeeding years when small parties returned, laden with the fruits of toil and privation, to taste again the luxuries of civilized life.[28]

St. Louis thrived on skin hunters.

---

[28] From the *Missouri Saturday News,* see Morgan, *William Ashley*, p. 7

PULLING AND POLING UP THE MISSOURI

ST. LOUIS, 1822

In St. Louis, beaver skins were the same as money. Most who lived in St. Louis profited from the furs that came down the river. Situated at the forks of the Mississippi and Missouri, St Louis was the natural terminal and jumping off place. That the Big Muddy was the road to the West was known by any Americans who cared--from the humble trapper to the President. Jefferson himself had instructed Leuis and Clark to follow this stream during their appraisal of his Louisiana Purchase. And their return in 1806 prompted other men to go after the riches in fur they said were there. Veterans of this Journey of Discovery roamed the town both bragging and telling the truth about "shining mountains" with un-trapped beaver streams. Ambitious men schemed to exploit this new fur frontier.

Andrew Henry knew the mountain streams were rich with beaver. He also knew if they could overcome cold weather, wild animals and thieving Indians, they could make a fortune. He had first hand experience in the Rockies. In 1811 he was on upper Columbia waters and trapped in the shadow of the Tetons. And they were Rocky Mountains indeed! He also built a post on a fork of Snake River which was thereafter named for him. But his party was pushed out. They needed more men and supplies. With Ashley's help in 1822 he had them.

It seemed a good partnership. Ashley was experienced in borrowing and business and Henry knew the mountains. So together they advertised for a hundred men–and then hired some more. Daniel Potts tells us there were a hundred men on his boat that left St. Louis on April 3. It was commanded by Major Henry himself. On May 8, Ashley launched a second boat captained by Daniel More. This was a bad luck decision because it hit a snag and was swept under with a cargo worth

$10,000. The significance of this loss in modern terms depends on the exchange formula, but if a man could clear $1.00 per day above expenses–a fair wage in 1820–it would take more than 25 years for him to pay off the loss.

A keel boat was about 65 feet long and 15 wide. Designed especially for river travel, it had a flat bottom and a capacity of 25 tons,. Actually, in design it was only one step up from a raft. There were several means of propulsion, and all but one were hard work. First, their were oars. In slow deep water they worked. When the water was shallow more power was required. So boatmen methodically worked poles against the river bed and pushed the boat up stream. But if the current was faster they resorted to the hardest work. They tied a long rope or cordelle to the mast, then the boatmen got out, grasped the other end of the rope and pulled. They dragged the loaded craft along, wading through shallow water, clamoring over rocks and slogging through mud. The only ease they got was when the wind was blowing in the desired direction, but mostly it was hard exhausting work. Boatmen were tough–in a class by themselves.

Everyone on board shared in the bone-bending work except the hunters who ranged along the banks seeking meat for the cook pots, Both Daniel Potts and Jed Smith were said to be hunters. And both had been to school. Education made life easier.

The first incident Potts deems worthy of mention while going up river was his arrival at Cedar Fort. Called Fort Recovery by Chittenden, it was located at the lower end of American or Cedar Island a mile below the present city of

Chamberlain, South Dakota.[29] Potts says that they arrived there in mid July. Daniel's memories of the place were not pleasant–he was hungry.

Hard Work, No Food and Desertion

Pulling and pushing the heavily laden boat was exhausting. And so was ranging through the country in search of game. The men doing this labor day after day needed a lot of food. But in 1822 the lower parts of the Missouri were destitute of big game on which Henry depended. They were compelled to chew on anything edible. Daniel says:

> we were reduced to the sad necessity of eating anything we could catch as our provisions where exhausted and no game to be had, being advanced five hundred miles above the fronteers, we were glad to get a Dog to eat and I have seen some gather the skins of Dogs up through the camp, singe and roast them, and eat heartyly[30]

A few days without food sapped the spirit of the "enterprising young men." Groups of them deserted and started walking back to the settlements for food. Potts included himself among the deserters. He declares that the food situation so discouraged him that "I was determined to turn tail upstream

---

[29] Hiram M.Chittendon, *The American Fur Trade* [New York: Rufus Rockwell Wilson, Inc., 1936], p. 927. The post was established in 1822 by the Missouri Fur Company which then included the prominent traders Pilcher, Charles Bent, Fontenelle, and Dripps. Chittenden mentions that the fort was called by both names with Cedar Fort perhaps being first. It possibly received the name of Recovery because it was built on the remains of the old Missouri Fur Company post which burned in 1810.

[30] *Daniel Potts to Thomas Cochlen*, written from the Rocky Mountains, July 1, 1824.

and bear my course down." He and eight others banded and left together. However, this attempt to return became a harrowing wilderness experience that tested him to the limit. After it, boiled dog skins or any other mountain fare wasn't a problem.

Without telling us how it happened, Daniel writes he was separated from his eight hungry companions and his gun at about the same time. His adding that he didn't even have clothes to his back indicates he was in danger from exposure. It also adds to the mystery of how he got separated from his friends. He recalled it vividly in a letter written two years later.

> now my dear friend how must I have felt, young Birds, frogs, and Snakes were acceptable food with me and not means of fire I in the course of a few days fortunately fell in with a party of Indians who treated me with great humanity and tarried with them four days and then fell in with a trader who conducted me within 350 miles of the frontiers he being able to give me but little aid, I tarried but three days when I started with privation consisting of only 3/4 of a pound of Buffalo suet [buffalo fat] and arrived at the frontiers in six days.[31]

Tracing his route, Daniel and his eight companions first left Ceder Fort and headed down the river. Then somehow he lost his knife, gun, and companions, [perhaps there was some foul play here]. Then, he luckily met up with friendly Indians who took him in.[32] It wouldn't be the last time Potts was helped out by Indians. Next he met traders who guided him within about 250 miles of his "frontier post," [likely Council Bluffs, Iowa]. Finally, traveling with scant provisions of two hands full of buffalo fat scavenged from a trader, he made his way down to Council Bluffs in six days,

---

[31] *Ibid.*
[32] *Ibid.*

Chittenden gives a description of Council Bluffs during the fur trade era,

> Council Bluffs, " . . . denoted where many trading posts have been built. It was one of the most important points on the whole course of the Missouri and was resorted to by traders from the very commencement of the fur trade on the upper river. The particular situation always known in those early years as Council Bluffs was 25 miles above the modern city of that name, and on the opposite side of the river about where the little town of Calhoun is now located . . . in 1804 Lewis and Clark held a council there with the Oto Missouri Indians. [hence the name, "Council Bluffs"?] In the course of the next fifty years probably twenty posts were established between this point and the mouth of the Platte, but all are difficult to locate precisely.[33]

After his long and lonely hike, Potts was cheered to meet General Ashley at the Bluffs and rejoin his expedition.[34] There was good reason; Ashley's boat had food! Perhaps he had heard from deserters that the men on the first boat were starving. And

---

[33] Chittenden, *The American Fur Trade of the Far West, pp.* 924-925.

[34] Ashley was commanding this boat because the *Enterprise* sent out May 8, 1822 ran into trouble. The Missouri River was always a challenge and ever changing. They were working against the current and with snags, floating logs, submerged stumps, and trees hanging out over the river from the crumbling bank, the *voyagers* had to be constantly alert. This last obstacle got the *Enterprise.* An overhanging tree caught the mast, the boat wheeled broadside to the current and was swept under. The cargo, $10,000 worth, went under in seconds. What a disappointment. Months of careful planning were foiled. It was bad luck for the partners and the men. They camped by the river and waited developments while Daniel Moore went down-river to tell Ashley the bad news. But typically, Ashley met this disaster with vigor–in 18 days he recruited forty-six man and had them pushing another boat load of goods up the river–with Ashley himself in command.

perhaps Ashley just didn't want to go hungry himself. At any rate, he departed from usual custom and included plentiful provisions of sea-bread and bacon. Daniel had eaten up his handful of buffalo fat and was famished. Meeting Ashley's boat was a godsend.

But traveling 350 miles on foot with only 3/4 pound of buffalo fat made his stomach unfit for a belly-full of sea-bread and bacon. Typical of many starving men who finally do get food, Potts ate too much too soon. And reported, "I was taken with a severe spell of sickness which all but took my life."

Desertion was common on crews going up the Missouri. If the leaders failed to provide adequate supplies and if game was not available, men looked to themselves for survival. So leaving the expedition and heading back toward the settlements was more than average behavior. Thomas James declares that of his company of 175 Americans starting up river with Manuel Lisa in 1809, only 10 remained at the Mandan Villages. All the rest had become "disgusted with the treatment . . . fell off in small companies and went back."[35]

Daniel's experience was similar. But he was glad to rejoin the company when this boat showed up with food and friends.

There was a remarkable new recruit on this boat. His name was Jedediah Strong Smith. He was less rough and raw than the others. But he was energetic and restless and in the next few years would travel farther and see more than any of them, making the round trip to California twice.

But for the present, Jed Smith, Ashley, Daniel Potts, and the rest of the crew continued up the Missouri and reached the

---

[35] Thomas James, *Three Years Among the Indians and Mexicans* [New York : J. B. Lippincott Co., 1962], p. 5.

mouth of the Yellowstone about the middle of October. Men from the first boat had been busily raising a fort. It was about a quarter of a mile above the confluence of the two rivers on the right bank of the Missouri. The post was a picketed enclosure with a log structure at each corner so rifleman could rake each side with shot if an enemy tried to climb the walls.[36] Ashley didn't waste time. After arriving he unloaded the boat then had the men push it off again heading down the Missouri for St Louis. It was much easier going downstream. Ashley wanted to hurry back and raise an outfit for the coming season. Henry was to stay and get the trapping going.

Until 1825 Ashley was known as "a man of credit." He was enterprising, industrious, busy and borrowing. He used credit to purchase goods which unfortunately were often lost from bad luck, then he turned around and borrowed again. He was a hard man to keep down, and he was learning. His creditors wanted him to succeed so they could be repaid. So they loaned him more.

Henry decided to winter at his Yellowstone post. He would try to keep some order among his inexperienced men, teach them to trap beaver and live off the land.

Strange Bedfellows On The Musselshell

The next river up the Missouri, on the same side as the Yellowstone, was the Musselshell. Either by common consent, or direction from Henry, the party split up. Daniel and 21 others moved up to winter where the Musselshell spills into the Missouri. The leader of the party, according to himself, was a

---

[36] Morgan, *Jedediah Smith,* p. 40.

Danish ex-sea Captain named John Weber.[37] Major Henry accompanied them part way, then with eight others he returned to the fort.

Daniel, in two letters, says he spent the winter with 13 men on the Musselshell. These men varied. Five are certainly known and were contrasting types. On the one hand is Daniel Potts, an educated man from a family acquainted with success. According to *The Potts Genealogy* he had "excellent habits and sound principles." Jedediah Smith was similar. He was a firm Christian, and was ever concerned about his standing with God. Smith was also ambitious, with deep wells of courage and fortitude. Balancing off these two was a trio of river boatmen named Mike Fink, Carpenter, and Talbot. From what we know of them they were tough, wild, undisciplined, and not religious. We will see later that the long winter of mismatched bed fellows in close quarters ended with a sensational tragedy.

Jedediah Smith went on a short hunt up the Yellowstone River before proceeding to the camp on the Musselshell. He arrived there after Daniel's party, either in late November or early December.[38] In one of the few pages of Jedediah's diary that have survived is the following account of the winter. At first he thought they would starve.

> We were generally good hunters, but at that time unacquainted with the habits of the Buffalo and seen none in the vicinity we supposed that they had abandoned the country for the winter. We therefore became somewhat apprehensive that we should suffer for want of provisions. When the weather had at length become extremely cold and the ice strong and firm across the River, we were astonished to see the buffalo come pouring from all sides

---

[37] *The Salt Lake Tribune* July 4, 1897, p.31.
[38] *Potts Letter to Thomas Cochlen, Rocky Mountain*, July 4, 1824.

into the valley of the Missouri and particularly the vast Bands that came from the north and crossed over to the south side on the ice. We therefore had them in thousands around us and nothing more required of us than to select and kill the best for our use whenever we might choose.[39]

Daniel's account squares remarkably with Smith's,

Here the game being very scarce, the prospect was very discouraging, though after a short time the Buffaloes flocked in great abundance; likewise the Mountain Goats; the like I have never seen since.[40]

Both men say they wintered in *cabins*. They were newcomers to the mountains and hadn't yet discovered the Indian tepee. Later many of them would appreciate the virtues of a hide lodge. They were snug and warm and being portable were much more adapted to the nomadic ways of trappers. Small cabins were also snug enough and warm enough if the men did their axe-work well enough. It took a good axe-man to fit the logs sufficiently tight to keep cold air from breezing in through cracks. However, by now some of the men were likely getting pretty good with an axe. Axes were designed for different tasks and ranked with the knife and rifle as needed tools. Main types are shown below. The one illustrated top left is an adz. It was used to chop away the top of a log or to hue out a dugout canoe. Because it was swung forward then between the standing man's feet it was called a "shin hoe."

Beneath it is an axe-hammer combination. Next,to the right, is a broad axe, used to flatten the side of a log.

---

[39] Sullivan, Maurice S. *The Travels of Jedediah Smith.* [Santa Anna; Fine Arts Press] 1934. pp.9-10.
[40] *Potts Letter to Robert Potts, Rocky Mountains*, 1826.

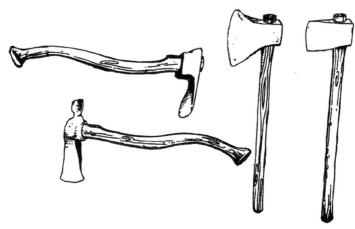

Tool of the Trade

Smith and Potts mention hunting buffalo for sport during the winter. Daniel relates the following hair-raising and foolhardy episode:

During the winter the Buffaloes came into our camp, one of which I was induced to charge upon by our company without fire arms, at first with a tomahawk only. After approaching very close, the Bull prepared for action with the most dismal looks, and sprang at me. When within one leap of me, I let fly the tomahawk, which caused him to retreat. After returning to our cabin, I was induced to make the second attempt, armed with a tomahawk, knife and spear, accompanied by five or six others armed. After traveling a short distance, we discovered the beast and in a concealed manner I approached him within fifty yards, when he discovered me, and made a rapid retreat, though, there being much fallen timber, I soon overtook him. First onset I put out one eye with the spear; the second failed in the other eye; on the third I pierced him to the heart, and immediately dispatched him.[41]

Mike Fink and his companions livened the winter with tales of their exploits both real and fabricated. Mike was of the breed, half horse, half alligator, which had been the dominant strain of men along the navigable rivers of America. Taverns the length of the Mississippi had heard him declare: "I am a Salt River roarer, and I love the wimming, [women] and as how I'm chock full of fight!" He was a tough boatmen of legendary exploits and a book has been written of myths inspired by his bravado.[42]

One ceremony performed frequently by Mike and his friend Carpenter was shooting a cup of whiskey off each other's head at seventy paces.

No one knows why Mike and his friends stayed up the river this winter. They were river-boat men, not hunters. Maybe there was no boat going back and they were not up to building a craft of their own. [It was all downstream, so a raft would have sufficed.] Whatever, the winter proved to be Mike's undoing, for in their cramped quarters nerves and tempers clashed. A deadly argument broke out between Fink and Carpenter apparently over a woman. The argument was patched up with varying success several times but came to head late in the spring.

---

[41] *Potts Letter Rocky Mountains*, 1824
[42] Walter Blair and Frank Meine, *Half Horse, Half Alligator* [Chicago: University of Chicago Press, 1956].

The river wasn't clear of ice until the 4th of April and on the 5th, the party broke up for the spring hunt. Potts and several

HARD WOOD
RAMROD

POTTS IS SHOT THROUGH BOTH KNEES
WITH A RAMROD.

others drew the assignment to hunt the Judith which fed the Missouri farther upstream. While going to their trapping grounds, Potts discovered the remains of two large camps of Indians, at least one of which had been Blackfeet. Daniel rightly assumed that it was "a remarkable escape of his scalp."[43] Their small party of thirteen would have been easy pickings for a band of Blackfoot warriors.

---

[43] *Potts letter to Thomas Cochlen, Rocky Mountains, 1824.*

Potts Has His Legs Shot Off–Almost

On the 11th of April a freak accident occurred that disabled Potts for the spring hunt, "and almost forever." For reasons unknown, an oak ramrod was in the barrel of a *loaded* gun. Either someone was cleaning the gun, or trying to remove a jammed ball with the rifle loaded. At any rate, it was stupid and careless. For the rifle was also primed and aimed in Daniel's direction. It fired and shot the wooden ramrod through both of his knees. With a bit of under- statement, Daniel declared the accident, "brought me to the ground."

His mates extracted the ramrod from his knees, bound him up, and gave Jedediah Smith leave to float him down to the fort on the Yellowstone. Only eleven men were left to trap in Blackfeet country. The rest, among whom were Mike Fink, Talbot, and Carpenter, had returned to the fort earlier.

The Death of Mike Fink, Carpenter, and Talbot

After arriving at the fort, Fink's and Carpenter's quarrel broke out anew but it was patched up once again. To display sincerity and cement their friendship, Mike proposed they shoot the whiskey-filled cup from each other's head as in times past. Carpenter accepted and they tossed a coin to see who would get the first shot. Mike won, but after the cup was filled Carpenter quietly told his friend Talbot that Mike planned to miss the cup and kill him. While he gamely awaited the shot, Mike leveled the rifle and made the most of his play. He paused and declared, "hold your noddle steady, Carpenter, and don't spill the whiskey, as I shall want some presently." Again he sighted down the barrel, pulled the trigger, and shot Carpenter in the center of the forehead. Then Mike set the gun down, blew the smoke from the barrel and said, "Carpenter . . . you spilt the whiskey!"[44]

Mike wasn't allowed to go unpunished. The accounts of retribution vary; however, the following is correct in essentials:

> But Talbot, who was Carpenter's fast friend, was convinced of Mike's treacherous intent, and resolved upon revenge whenever an opportunity should offer. Some months afterward, Mike, in a fit of gasconading declared that he had killed Carpenter and was glad of it. Talbot instantly drew his pistol, the same which Carpenter had bequeathed him, and shot Mike through the heart. Mike fell and expired without a word. [45]

Later this same year, after the post had been abandoned, a Blackfoot war party visited the fort and discovered the graves. They dug up the bodies to strip them of clothing but found them stinking and putrid. They abandoned the project and stuck with their leathers.[46] Now, only one of the trio was alive but no boatman or anyone else cared to punish Talbot for,

> Talbot was as ferocious and dangerous as the grizzly bear of the prairies. About three months after, Talbot was present in the battle with the Arikara in which Col. Leavenworth commanded, where he displayed a coolness which would have done honor to a better man. He came out

---

[44] Blair and Meine, *Half Horse,* p. 262.

[45] Morgan, *Jedediah Smith,* p. 49.

[46] Morgan, *William Ashley,* p. 44. Shirts or pants made of cloth instead of leather were considered a luxury by many trappers and Indians. See Osborne Russell's comment, note 80.

of the battle unharmed, but about ten days later while attempting to swim the Teton River he was drowned.[47]

The death of these three was reported in the *Missouri Republican* on Wednesday, July 16, 1823. The *Republican* may have received the report in a letter from Daniel Potts. He is one of the few writers who has come to light in Henry's party. Also, the ramrod-through-the-knees incident gave him plenty of spare time for correspondence. The newspaper version reads:

> By a letter received in town from one of General Ashley's expedition, we are informed that a man by the name of Mike Fink well known in this quarter as a great marksman with the rifle . . . was engaged in his favorite amusement of shooting a tin cup from the head of another man, when aiming to low, or from some other cause shot his companion in the forehead and killed him. Another man of the expedition [whose name we have not heard] remonstrated against Fink's conduct, to which he, Fink, replied, that he would kill him likewise, upon which the other drew a pistol and shot Fink dead upon the spot.[48]

The Arikara Massacre

While Henry and his not-too-congenial trapping band were making their spring hunt, Daniel convalesced at the fort. Meanwhile, Ashley was struggling up the Big Muddy this spring with two keel boats, the *Yellowstone Packet* and the

---

[47] Blair and Meine, *Half Horse,* p. 262.

[48] The death of Mike Fink and his companions has been the subject of much legend. There are at least five early published accounts with general agreement, and many more were written after 1850 that contain elements of the truth. The version that agrees best with known facts on the upper Missouri is told. Blair and Meine, *Half Horse,* p. 260.

Rocky Mountains. He left St. Louis on March 10, almost a month earlier than the 1822 departure.[49]

In quality, this year's recruits were a grade or so lower than the 1822 bunch. James Clyman remarks that most of the grogshops of St. Louis were searched to form a party that would make "Falstaff's battalion genteel in comparison."[50] Sometime before Ashley reached the fateful Arikara villages, he received an urgent message from Henry.

Jedediah Smith arrived in person to tell Ashley that more horses were needed on the upper Missouri. Horse flesh increased in price and scarcity with each mile from the frontier and Ashley might obtain some trading with the Sioux or the Rees [Arikara]. So with horses in mind, the General halted his boats at the Arikara village and proposed trade. This turned out to be a bad move.

Ashley was cautious and did the trading on a sand bar in the river--thus setting some distance between them and the questionable Ree. The business went okey the first day, but that was the end of it. On the second day an argument broke out when Ashley refused to exchange guns and ammunition for horses. Then one Aaron Stephens was caught and killed. He

---

[49] Morgan, *Jedediah Smith*, p. 50.
[50] Charles L. Camp ed., *James Clyman Frontiersman* [Portland: Champoeg Press, 1960], p. 7. The wry comment of Clyman is worthy of elaboration. Man-power was hard to find around St. Louis by 1823. An agent for the Missouri Fur Co. wrote the following: ". . . it is with great difficulty Mr. F. [Fontenelle] informs me to procure hands as so many boats has left this place this Spring . . . there never was such great demand for men . . . ." Morgan, *William Ashley*, pp. 8-9. Despite his comment, there were some very able men in Clyman's detachment. William Sublette, Thomas Fitzpatrick, David Jackson, Hugh Glass, Hiram Scott, and Edward Rose were aboard. All became notable Mountain Men.

was certainly in the wrong place and likely doing the wrong thing at the wrong time–with Indian ladies. It happened in the middle of the night. Out of these two incidents developed an explosive tension which brought one of the most severe massacres in the fur trade era.[51]

At daybreak any question about their good will was removed when one Ree drew close enough to yell out a trade offer: the exchange of Aaron Stevens body for a horse! The Arikara were always feisty, now their apatite was whetted, they were set for war. When the trappers refused to trade, the Ree yelled in defiance that Steven's eyes had been gouged out, his head cut off, and the rest of his body mutilated. Relations were ugly and so was the weather. A lightning storm came up and threatened the boats. These were critical moments for Ashley and his men.

The general was moored mid-river, some men were stuck on a sand bar with the newly bought horses, and they all were being raked by murderous gun fire from the well armed Rees. James Clyman never forgot his struggle to escape from the sand bar and then from drowning.

> You will easily perceive that we had little else to do than to Stand on a bear sand bar and be shot at . . . Their being seven or eight hundred guns in [the] village and we having the day previously furnished them with abundance of Powder and Ball . . . we made a breast work of our horses . . . they nearly all being killed . . . I, seeing no hopes of Skiffs or boats coming [to get him off the sand bar]. . . left my hiding place behind a dead horse, ran up stream a short distance to get the advantage of the current and conceiving myself to be a tolerable strong swimmer stuck the muzzle of my rifle in [my] belt . . . with all my clothes on but not

---

[51]Morgan, *Jedediah Smith*, p. 56.

having made sufficient calculation for the strong current was carried passed the boat within a few feet of the same one Mr. Thomas Eddie [saw me] but the shot coming thick he did not venture from behind the cargo Box and so could not reach me with a setting pole which [he] held in his hands . . . my first aim was to rid myself of all my encumbrances and my Rifle was the greatest . . . I next unbuckled my belt and let go my Pistols . . . I next let go my Ball Pouch and finally one sleeve of my hunting shirt which held an immence weight of water when rising to the surface I heard the voice of encoragemnt saying hold on Clyman I will soon relieve you This [from] Reed Gibson . . . and was but a few rods from me [in a skiff] I was so much exaused that he had to haul me in to the skiff where I lay for a moment to cacth breath when I arose to take the only remaing ore when Gibson caled oh, god I am shot and fell forward in the skiff I hauled the skiff up on the shore and told Gibson to remain in the Skiff and I would go upon the high land whar I could see if any danger beset us thair . . . I discovered sevral Indian in the water swimming over [some] of whom were nearly across the stream . . . he mearly said save yourself Clyman and pay no attention to me as I am a dead man and they can get nothing of me but my Scalp . . . I looked for some place to hide But there being onley a scant row of brush along the shore I concluded to take to the open Pararie and run for life . . . I saw three indians mount the bank being intirely divested of garments excepting a belt around the waist containing a Knife and Tomahawk and Bows and arrows in their [hands] They made but little halt and started after me . . . having the start of some 20 or 30 rods we had apparently an even race for about one hour when I began to have palpitation of the heart and I found my man was gaining on me . . . I turned to the right and found a hole washed in the earth some 3 feet long . . . and perhaps 2 feet deep with

weeds and grass perhaps one foot high surrounding it Into
this hole I droped and persuer immediatle hove in sight and
passed me . . . .

He hunkered down in his hole until the Ree were well
passed. Then Clyman displayed his wit and personality. When
he saw that his pursuers were standing together about a quarter
mile away. He stood up to catch their attention and,

I made them a low bow with both my hand[s] and thanked
god for my present Safety and diliveranc . . . But I did not
remain long here Wishing to put the gratest possible
distance between me and the Arrickarees . . . .[52]

While Clyman was running for his life, Ashley and the two
keel boats were being raked with gun fire from the Arikara
village higher on the bank. With little opposition from the
anchored boats the Arikara were shooting at will. And with no
experience fighting Indians, and everything against them, the
trappers were scrambling to get away, hiding behind trade
goods on the boat and fairing poorly on all counts. Daniel Potts,
who had only learned of the battle after Ashley called for relief,
summarized the carnage:

. . . this spring . . . a third boat was ascending the river and
was attacked by Rickarays Indians and was . . . defeated
withe the loss of 15 killed and 16 wounded,–indians only
two . . . . [53]

The Americans had to get out from under the Ree guns. So
they weighed anchor on one keel boat, chopped the cable on the
other, and drifted downstream. Clyman by now had made it
back to the Missouri and "chanced to look at the river and here
came the boats floating down stream . . . The boat was laid in

---

[52] Clyman, *Journal of a Mountain Man*, [Missoula, 1984] pp. 11-14.
[53] *Potts Letter, 1824.*

and I got aboard." Once safe on board his attention immediately went to his fallen buddy.

> I spoke of my friend Gibson when I was informed he was on board I immediately wen[t] to the cabin where he lay but he did not recognize [me] being in the agonies of Death the shot having passed through his bowels I could not refrain from weeping over him who lost his lifee but saved mine He did not live but an hour or so and we buried him that evening . . . Eleven [men were left] on the sand bar and their Scalps taken for the squaws to sing and dance over.[54]

The current soon moved them from the range of fire. Ashley let one boat drift back to Fort Atkinson to give the alarm, while with the other he went downstream only to the mouth of the Cheyenne. He needed reinforcements and needed them in a hurry. His best hope was Henry's band camped higher up the Missouri. Henry needed horses and Ashley needed men, it was hard to keep up.

Ashley looked for a man to carry an express past the hostile Arikara and up the river to Henry. It was a dangerous mission, who would go? Of his crew, the boatmen had no stomach for fighting Indians, and about 30 of his fighting trappers had been killed or wounded by the Rees.

At this point one man stepped forward and according to his biographer, it was the pivotal point in his life.[55] Jedediah Smith volunteered to take another man, sneak past the Rees and get help from Henry. When he successfully completed this mission it marked him for early leadership in the Rocky Mountain brigades. Actually, he was a logical choice. His trip as a

---

[54] Clyman, *Journal of a Mountain Man*, pp. 11-15.
[55] Morgan, *Jedediah Smith*, p. 57.

messenger down river from Henry gave him familiarity with the route and he may have been one of the few able-bodied men of spirit remaining. But he did it, that was the main thing.

Upon arrival at Fort Henry, Jedediah must have painted the Arikara massacre in glowing colors for Daniel wrote:

> It so imbroiled our blood that we unanimously volunteered our service to reinforce an give them battle which we did with the aid of three hundred Regulars and one thousand Soux Indians and defeated them without the loss of one man, in this engagement about seventy Rickarays lost their lives and evakuated their vilage . . . [56]

Though Daniel volunteered with the rest, because of his injured knees, he was sensibly left behind. Twenty others remained with him to protect the fort and supplies. With the remainder, Henry hastened to the aid of Ashley. The combined forces dispersed the Indians and destroyed their village. However, contrary to Potts's statement, it was not much of a victory. In truth, Ashley was severely drubbed in one of the worst massacres of the fur trade. It took six companies of infantry under Colonal Leavenworth from Fort Atkinson with their Sioux auxiliaries to run the Arikara off. The Ree still won the better part of the battle; they wisely fought then ran away. And the horses Ashley so badly needed were killed in the crossfire.

After the Arikara had scattered, Henry with thirty of his men began the long march back to his post on the Yellowstone. Daniel relates that the returning party was fired on by "Mandan and Groosvant" Indians "in the dead hour of the night." Two were killed and the same number wounded.[57]

---

[56] *Potts Letter, 1824.*
[57] *Ibid.*

Earlier in the year, high on the Missouri, and about the same time as the Arikara massacre, Henry lost four additional men. The known deaths now totaled around nineteen with about as many more wounded. This steady killing of trappers was a blow to the company who needed every man they could get, and it was bad for morale.[58] The men were getting battle-wise, and battle weary.

Hugh Glass—A Tough Trapper

Before reaching the fort at the mouth of the Yellowstone, members of the Henry party participated in one of the most famous episodes of the fur trade. In dramatic aspects, the known facts of the story compete with the most fancy yarns ever fabricated in the West.[59] It's the type of story Jim Bridger might have concocted at the Rendezvous in the mountains–but Bridger likely kept this *true* story to himself. It wasn't one of his brighter moments.

Before the entire saga played itself out, Potts wrote an abbreviated version in his Letter of 1824,

> [O]ne man was also tore nearly all to peases by a White Bear [Grizzley Bear], and was left by the way without any gun who afterewards recover'd[60]

---

[58] Four men were killed on the Upper Missouri when Henry attempted to reinforce the detachment in that area. Also lost were 4 horses, 30 traps on sets, and 122 traps in cache. It happened ten to fifteen miles north of Smith's River above present Great Falls, Montana. Hugh Johnson, *Sworn Statement at St. Louis, July 13, 1824*. Reprinted in Morgan, *William Ashley*, p. 72. See also *Potts Letter, 1824*.

[59] Philip S. George Cooke, *Scenes and Adventures in the Army* [Philadelphia; Lindsey and Blacisto, 1857], p.151.

[60] *Potts Letter, Thomas Cochlen, Rocky Mountains 1824.*

Daniels story is abbreviated, but important historically, as we shall see later. The man who was "tore nearly all to peases," and afterwards recovered was Hugh Glass. Glass had joined the Ashley-Henry expedition in 1823. And he had been wounded in the battle with the Rees. He was called "an old man" as early as 1824 and other circumstances indicate he was older than the average "enterprising young men" of the 1822 party.[61] After the fifth day of marching, while returning from the Arikara battle, Glass was leading the column in search of game. Clyman gives the following account:

> amongst this party was a Mr. Hugh Glass who could not be restrained and kept under Subordination he went off the line of march one afternoon and met with a large grizzly Bear which he shot and wounded, the bear as is usual attacked Glass. He attempted to climb a tree but the bear caught him an hauled [him] to the ground tearing and lacerating his body in a feareful rate by this time several of our men were in close gun shot but could not shoot for fear of hitting Glass, at length the beare appeared to be satisfied and turned to leave, when two or three men fired the bear turned immediately on glass and give him a second mutilation.[62]

---

[61] From a modern point of view Glass was not old. He was in his thirties. But he may have seemed an old man to Bridger who was in his teens. Teenagers think that way. Morgan, *Jedediah Smith*, p. 96

[62] *James Clyman p. 18.* also *Deposition of Hugh Johnson*, St. Louis, January 13, 1824, in *Morgan William Ashley*, p. 72.

HIGH GLASS
WAS MAULED BY A GRIZZLY
BEAR.
THEN LEFT ALONE TO DIE
BUT HE WOULDN'T

One man was tore all to pieces by a grizzley,
left alone without a gun, and yet recovered.

When the party finally killed the bear, Glass was in terrible condition. His body was lacerated all over and his wind pipe torn open by the bear's three inch claws. Since it was impossible to move him, and a delay might bring disaster upon all, Henry decided to pay a couple of men to remain with him until he died. It didn't look like Glass could last much longer when the main party struck out again up the Grand River toward the Yellowstone Post.

Second-hand sources give the dubious honor of staying with Glass to John S. Fitzgerald and a young man of seventeen, James Bridger. For five days they camped near the wounded man who hovered on the threshold of death. At length, growing fearful for their own safety and knowing that the old fellow couldn't last much longer, they gathered up his knife, rifle and ammunition, then hastened to catch the larger party. On arrival they reported that Glass was dead and buried, and he was for the time being listed as another casualty of the year's activities.

In their favor, Bridger and Fitzgerald sincerely thought he would die, [certainly without a knife and gun he would die, but they needed to take them to prove Glass was dead. If they left them with Hugh the main party might think they had abandoned Glass also].

But they figured wrong. Though badly mauled by the bear, and now deserted, Glass didn't want to die alone in the wilderness. And when his would-be protectors ran off with his rifle and tools he was angry. This anger and a gritty will to survive began to stir his remaining embers of life.

He dragged himself to a spring of cold water where limbs of a wild cherry bush hung overhead and for ten days he remained there regaining precious strength. At length, he determined to make his way to Fort Kiowa on the Missouri, a distance of about 100 miles.

Scarcely able to crawl, Glass painfully made his way down to the Big Muddy, his energy reportedly being supplied by anger and a desire for revenge. Anger was supplemented with real nourishment when he lucked upon some wolves dining on a buffalo calf. With a flint and steel, Glass started a fire, scared away the wolves, and chewed on the buffalo calf himself. Living on roots, berries, and whatever else he could find, after inconceivable suffering he at length reached Fort Kiowa.[63]

At the fort, Joseph Brazeai was preparing a party to ascend the river. Rather than miss the only boat back to his unfaithful guardians, Hugh, improved in health, joined the party.[64] This was the first attempt to ascend the river after the Arikara

---

[63] Morgan, *Jedediah Smith*, p. 99.
[64] *Ibid.*

massacre.

When they were within ten miles of the Mandan villages, the pirogue [a fancy French name for boat], put to shore for Glass to hunt. While moving along the river bank in search of game, he stumbled into a party of Rees who were part of the feisty village who ran away from Colonel Leavenworth and Ashley. Here Glass had a bit of good luck. The Arikara tried to catch him, but a trio of Mandan Indians on horseback saw the unequal match and snatched him away from the Rees. Undaunted from this brush with death, Glass continued by land up the river to Henry's Fort.[65]

Meanwhile Potts spent the summer getting his legs and knees to work again. Painfully he practiced stretching his leg muscles, then standing and finally walking a few steps at a time. He also may have tried to grow some corn. Information of the times was relayed eastward from Moses Harris:

> Major Henry's party planted some corn at the mouth of the yellow Stone, but the ground was so dry that it did not even swell or rot–there had not been sufficient rain the year past "to wet a man through his shirt sleeves."[66]

When Captain Henry arrived, he told them of a more serious calamity; more than twenty horses had been stolen by the Assiniboine. Henry had been holding council with the Assiniboine chiefs on board his boat when the Indian braves spirited away twenty four horses with saddles, blankets, and a quantity of pistols. The chiefs assured him that the horses were only borrowed to pack the plunder to a point up river where

---

[65] *Ibid.*, p. 100

[66] *Letter from Colonel Henry Leavenworth to Major General Alexander McComb, Fort Atkinson, December 20, 1823.* Reprinted in Morgan, *William Ashley*, pp. 68-69.

trading could take place, and departed for the appointed rendezvous. Once out of gun-shot range, the natives probably had a great laugh over the affair, for they considered the trading was over and done.[67]

Since they needed a base closer to the Rocky Mountains, the post on the Yellowstone was no longer suitable. Consequently Henry determined to move everything 125 miles up the Yellowstone River and build a new post to winter at the mouth of the Big Horn. By fall they had got as far as Powder River. Daniel's knees must have almost recovered, for he went on a short beaver hunt and had a scare from Indians.

> I was closely pursuid by a party of Indians . . . whom I took to be Blackfeet and narrowly made my escape by hiding in a little brush and they came so close that I could see the very whites of their eyes which was within five yards.[68]

That's close. Henry, after getting horses from the Crows at the Powder River, detached a party of trappers then proceeded up the Yellowstone to build his Big Horn Post. At the same time, Hugh Glass was relentlessly trailing them up river searching for the unfaithful bodyguards who stole his rifle and left him for dead. When he arrived at Fort Henry he found it abandoned. He knew that Henry and his men had gone up the Yellowstone, so he followed their trail. Though getting stronger by the day, he remembered his mission. He was still angry.

At the commencement of the new year a celebration was held at the newly built post on the Big Horn. They had a good dinner and were having a fine time when a strange visitor appeared at the gates. Hugh Glass returned as one from the

---

[67] Deposition of Joshua Griffith, St. Louis, January 12, 1824. Reprinted in Morgan, *William Ashley, pp. 71-72. See also Frost, Notes,* p. 120.
[68] *Potts Letter, Thomas Cochlen,* 1824.

dead. This stopped the party immediately. We can imagine the thoughts going through their heads when they saw Glass. When they decided he wasn't a ghost, they crowded closer to hear what he had to say.

Fitzgerald wasn't there. He had quit the trappers and gone back to Fort Atkinson. So Bridger was left to face the angry man alone. It may be from this incident Bridger got the superstitious vein that remained with him throughout his sojourn in the mountains. The chronicler tells us that Bridger could scarcely be induced to enter Hugh's presence.[69] There is little doubt that Jim supposed the bones of Hugh Glass were still back on the Grand River.

But Glass chose not to carry out frontier justice on young Bridger who lived to witness many more winters in the mountains. Philip St. George Cook, who published this version of the story in 1830, has the Bridger-Glass encounter as follows:

> Young man, it is Glass that is before you; the same that, not content with leaving, . . . to a cruel death upon the prairie, you robbed, helpless as he was, of his rifle, his knife, of all which he could hope to defend or save himself . . . I swore an oath that I would be revenged on you . . . . But I cannot take your life; . . . you have nothing to fear from me; go,–you are free,–for your youth I forgive you.[70]

But Glass continued after Fitzgerald. When he learned that Fitzgerald had gone to Fort Atkinson, he volunteered to carry dispatches there, accompanied by E. More, A. Chapman, Dutton and Marsh. The party proceeded to the source of the

---

[69] Charles L. Camp ed., "*The Chronicles of George C. Yount*," California Historical Quarterly, Vol II,[April, 1923] pp. 24-33.
[70] Philip S. George Cooke, *Scenes and Adventures in the Army* [Philadelphia: Lindsey and Blaciston, 1857], p. 151.

Powder River and from there down the Platte in a skin boat. Upon reaching the Black Hills, they ran into thirty-eight lodges of Arikara Indians and were invited to dinner. Before the meal was over, the Rees treacherously pilfered their guns and tried to kill them. His life once more hanging in the balance, Glass made good a miraculous escape, but Chapman and More were killed. However, when Hugh finally caught up with Fitzgerald he had joined the army and was protected by them. According to one version of the story, Glass obtained his rifle, gave the man a lecture, and told him to "settle the matter with your own conscience and your God."[71]

The Hugh Glass episode has been widely told and is accepted by most fur trade historians. There are numerous sources with general agreement. However, Jim Bridger's most recent biographer has disclaimed everything except that Glass was a great story teller. He bases this on the idea that of all of the sources, only one, James Clyman's, is contemporary. He is wrong. Potts was a contemporary, and in the most recent discovery of Daniel Potts' letters, the original thesis is supported.[72]

---

[71] See Morgan *William Ashley*, p. 77, Also see Morgan's helpful footnotes, p. 251. Camp, *Chronicles*, pp. 32-33, and Morgan, *Jedediah Smith*, p. 319.

[72] Cecil Alter, *Jim Bridger* [Norman: University of Oklahoma Press, 1962], pp. 38-43. Alter concluded in his first version of Bridger's life that there were errors in the Glass story and he down-plays the episode. However in his revised version [Columbus 1950], Alter takes the position that Hugh Glass invented the story, that he is a "frontier braggart," and instead of being pitied should be given credit as a "distinguished raconteur," [One who recounts stories and anecdotes with skill and wit]. Potts, however, was on the scene, and it is very unlikely that the man who "was also tore nearly all to peases by a white Bear and was left by the way without a gun who afterwards recovered" is anyone other than Hugh Glass. Every biographer has the right to hope that his subject takes the

While writing of Henry's return from the Arikara battle, in precisely the correct context of time and place, Daniel relates:

> one man was also tore nearly all to peases by a White Bear [grizzly] and was left by the way without any gun who afterwards recover'd.[73]

All of the essential elements of the story are here.

Glass continued working as a trapper until the winter of 1832-33 when he made a foray back into the Arikara country and his luck finally ran out. Here he and Edward Rose were killed and scalped. Johnson Gardner caught up with the murderers several weeks later and burned them to death. In one story Gardner was later captured by the Arikara and burned to death himself. It was a tough life, an eye for an eye.[74]

---

noble path and is the good guy. Alter was unfortunate this time.

[73] *Potts Letter to Thomas Choclin, Rocky Mountains*, 1824.
[74] Morgan, *William Ashley*, p. 287.

TRAPPING ACROSS THE ROCKY MOUNTAINS

BIG HORN AND WIND RIVERS, 1824, [WYOMING]

Daniel got his first taste of trapping in the fall of 1824. The hunt was a short one but long enough to get his feet wet. Wet and cold–if his knees were not mended yet at least the water would numb them. This hunt was carried out as they were trekking up Wind River to winter with the Crow.[75] Others in the party had experience trapping the previous spring, but this was Daniel's initiation into the profession. He had high hopes with good reasons.

The Business of Trapping

If a young man wanted opportunity and adventure the West was where it was. The high price of furs made opportunity and the Rocky Mountains were an adventure. There were good reasons for the high price of fur.

It got cold. In the 1800s, the main room of the house was the kitchen because the cooking fire was always going. Other rooms–often there was only a bedroom–were only visited at night when you crept into a bed piled high with blankets, feather ticks and furs. The chilly bed might be warmed up a bit with a large rock heated on the stove. Outside you wore a fur coat and in a horse drawn slay snugged under a buffalo robe. There wasn't any fossil fuel except coal and no central heating. The cook stove was stoked with wood.

In latitudes of America, England, and Europe, people stayed warm bundled in animal fur. Besides making coats and robes the fur was "felted" to make hats. Since fur was both

---

[75] *Potts Letter to Thomas Chonklin*, 1824.

useful and stylish, providing it was big business–the demand was enormous. Entrepreneurial men fought and schemed to get into the game. America was the fur supply house for Europe and the richest source was high in the Rocky Mountain West. Rich capitalists such as John Jacob Astor spent fortunes to get into the mountain fur business. They soon learned that fur wasn't free for the taking.

In the beginning the fur traders hoped that Indians would enthusiastically provide the skins in trade for factory goods and cheap trinkets. There is a story of Pacific Coast Indians trading

Rocky Mountains

thousands of dollars worth of sea otter skins for one steel chisel. That kind of tale would be repeated and remembered by the skin merchants. Actually, the Indians did want the supplies and they prized the trinkets, but a work ethic was not part of their lifestyle. They only chose to hunt when it suited them, so their production was unreliable. It gradually became clear to the traders that other fur-getting methods were needed. Since the potential reward was great, men of ambition and capital attacked the problem, and in fits and spurts they mastered the skin game.

For starters, they learned the Indians not only couldn't be relied on, but they were often hostile! So strong, self-sufficient bands of white men and m'etes[76] were formed, large enough to beat off angry Indians protecting their turf. These bands were supplied with the necessary quantities of traps, guns, blankets, coffee, sugar, knives and on and on. To get the fur, it took a lot of money. In Canada the British Northwest Company and Hudson Bay Company found success by *hiring* men to trap then selling them highly marked up goods. The Americans were more successful using free trappers, but like the British, the traders also sold highly marked up goods.

The actual going-to-the-woods and trapping didn't appeal to most entrepreneurs. Ashley only went when circumstances forced him to–when his operation would fall apart if he didn't. Trapping was done by young men. They needed to be sharp of eye, fleet of foot, healthy and tough. Only then would they have a running chance to survive cold weather and hostile Indians. Life and death often hinged on a single shot, then a "Green River" knife and if these failed, swift feet and good luck. Flexible morality was another good trait. Mountain Men have been called "a majority of scoundrels," and "a reckless breed of men." The stakes were high. It seemed that a man might earn far more as a skin hunter than farming or working for the going wage.

---

[76] M'etes were mixed blood, their fathers often from Europe and their mothers Indians.

The Beaver

The life blood of the mountain fur business was beaver. These shy, industrious animals inhabited the high mountain streams and during the colder months bore a fine pelt to keep themselves warm. In the early years of the 19th century, as the Rocky Mountains were first getting explored, there was extraordinary demand for beaver fur. It was fueled by a whim of fashion. Pressed flat, or felted, beaver had already been used to make a variety of hats. But at this time fuzzy top hats had taken over traditional silk hats as the going style. Tiny barbs on the hairs helped bind it together and gave beaver excellent felting qualities.

With both Europe and America as markets, demand was good and prices high. It is easy to see why young men were excited about trapping. At this time when the average worker would get from .50 cents to $1.00 per day, a beaver skin, depending on its place of sale, was worth from $3.00 to $8.00. And a man might trap ten or more a day. So the lure to "enterprising young men" was heady. After all, a man could get rich in this business![77]

---

[77] The worldwide trade of the beaver-pelts is summarized in Paul Chrisler Phillips, *The Fur Trade,* [Norman: University of Oklahoma Press [c1961], pp. 1, 3-14.]. For another view of fur-trade economics see Morgan, *William Ashley,* pp.119-136

Beaver didn't consider themselves hat material. They were doing their thing; chewing down trees, backing up streams, getting fat on bark and breeding more little eager beavers. Superbly adapted to its home and occupation, the beaver has large front teeth. He also has web feet, a broad flat tail and is a wonderful swimmer. A beaver can submerge for 15 minutes and surface a half mile away. In the summer it dines on fresh saplings and bark, and in winter it has the same diet but not as fresh. It usually chooses a location on a stream, near quaking aspen trees, and erects a sturdy dam of mud, sticks, and aspen.

Big teeth chopped trees for a home with a secret door, web feet, and a flat tail made him a great swimmer. Beaver hair had tiny barbs so it felted easily into hats.

The lake created by the dam is the beaver's security. If danger approaches, it can quickly dive under water. The beaver's long front teeth are both a tool and a peril. It either gnaws or dies. If the beaver doesn't keep its teeth worn down by constant tree chomping, its ever growing incisors would curve inward and eventually pierce its skull.

As mentioned, Aspen trees are preferred and any size are prey for this industrious woodsman. To fell a tree it gnaws around it until it falls. Contrary to efforts to make the beaver smarter than he is, the beaver doesn't choose the direction it wants the tree to fall. He only gnaws around it deeper and deeper until it starts to fall then scurries out of the way.

The aspen provides the beaver with nourishment and dam cribbing. Successive dams are built by families of beaver so that vast quantities of water are held in the mountains in pond after pond. This animal is natures way of slowing the rush of spring snowmelt and holding water in the mountains for the dryer months. For it's home the beaver forms a mound of mud and sticks with an underwater entrance. And except from the fur trapper, a beaver is safe.

Note the beaver's flat tail, large web feet, and the underwater entrance to its home. Beaver are truly remarkable. They fell trees, build excellent dams and construct safe dry homes. Their rich fur keeps them warm even under water!

A Mountain Man's Tools

Trappers were not equal. At least they entered the business unequally supplied. Their tools were dependant on what they could afford and the fortunes of their "trader."

Sometimes they got what they paid for, and sometimes they got whatever was available–regardless of the price. Fortunate trappers obtained quality equipment that was either new or repaired but usable. Less fortunate men drew shoddy gear that broke down in the rigors of the wilderness. Daniel Potts likely was well equipt at the beginning. However, we

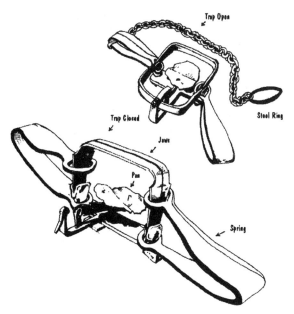

Each man carried six traps

remember that he lost his gun on the Missouri then was shot through the knees on the Musselshell River, [with his own gun that was faulty?]. In any case, if he had the best rifle of the time it was a percussion type made in St Louis by the Hawken brothers or other gun makers who copied them. The percussion had advantages over the earlier flintlock in being simple, waterproof and short. The hammer struck an explosive water proof "cap" that had been slid over a nipple on the breach. A flintlock, in contrast, had a flint stone on the hammer. When the trigger was pulled the hammer slammed this flint against iron, thus making sparks which ignited gunpowder in the pan which in turn sent a flame through a small hole in the breach to the main charge.

A HAWKEN RIFLE WAS THE BEST
It WOULD KNOCK DOWN ANYTHING (EXCEPTING A GRIZZLY BEAR SOMETIMES.)

A Hawken was shorter and stouter than a "Kentucky" flintlock, with a heavy barrel, and double triggers. The first trigger was to "set" the second one–then with a light touch the second would discharge the rifle. It was 50 caliber–large enough to down a buffalo, elk, or grizzly [but a grizzly was remarkably strong and sometimes put up a terrible fight even after being shot]. Another gun used in the business was the

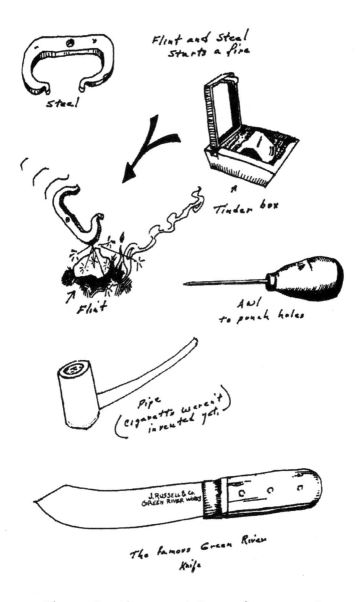

Flint and Steel starts a fire

Steel

Tinder box

Flint

Awl to punch holes

Pipe (cigarettes weren't invented yet)

J. RUSSELL & Co. GREEN RIVER WORKS

The famous Green River Knife

Items in a trappers "possible sack"

trade musket. It cost less and at close range still did the job. The value of skins depended upon their condition, place of sale, and your arrangement with the trader.[78] Daniel was fairly successful his first season. In spite of his injuries, he made $350 in the fall and spring hunts. And he hoped to make $1200 the following year.[79] These were high hopes but he was fired by ambition and boundless beaver. He acquired better tools as fortune permitted and in 1827 had a buffalo-running horse worth $450.00!

Let another trapper, Osborne Russell, describe a trappers clothes and tools:

> A trappers equipments in such cases is generally one Animal upon which is placed one or two Epishemores [buffalo robes] a riding Saddle and bridle a sack containing six Beaver traps a blanket with an extra pair of Mocasins his powder horn and bullet pouch with a belt to which is attached a butcher Knife a small wooden box containing bait for Beaver a Tobacco sack with a pipe and implements for making fire with sometimes a hatchet fastened to the Pommel of his saddle his personal dress is a flannel or cotton shirt [if he is fortunate enough to obtain one, if not Antelope skin answer the purpose of over and under shirt] a pair of leather breeches with Blanket or Buffalo robe a hat or Cap of wool, Buffalo or Otter skin his hose [stockings] are pieces of Blanket lapped round his feet which are covered with a pair of Moccassins made of Dressed Deer Elk or Buffalo skins with his long hair falling loosely over his shoulders completes his uniform. He mounts and places his rifle before him on his Saddle.[80]

---

[78] See William Ashley's account ledger for the Rendezvous of 1825 in *Morgan, William Ashley,* pp.119-129. Individual men, parties, prices and goods they purchased are listed.

[79] *Potts Letter to Thomas Cochlin,* 1824.

[80] Osborne Russel, *Journal of a Trapper,* p. 82.

Osborne Russell was in the Rocky Mountains six years later than Potts trapping the same streams. Fortunately for later enthusiasts he kept this remarkable journal. The "butcher knife" he speaks of was a Green River knife. More than any other tool, it was the symbol a trapper. The American brand name "Green River" became so important to trappers that English knife makers stamped it on knives they exported to America.[81]

"Green River" had nothing to do with Green River Wyoming even though the trappers spent so much time there. It pertained to Green River Massachusetts where this famous knife was manufactured. Russell doesn't mention that a trapper's leather clothes had no pockets, so he kept small items in his leather "Possible Sack."

Now we return to Daniel Potts, however he skipped scribbling anything about the fall of 1824. He could have recorded events, leaders and trapping parties, but he didn't, and consequently mystery surrounds the period. He only writes that he embarked for the fall hunt from the mouth of the Big Horn on the Yellowstone River. The only other source of information is Moses Harris whom Colonal Leavenworth quotes in a letter:

> [Henry] ascended the Yellow Stone river to the mouth of the Powder river. He was then prevented from going further with his Boat, by the rapids of the river. He there met the Crow Indians from whom he obtained 47 horses. With these he started a trapping party in a South Western direction towards the Mountains. He intended to start another party in a short time afterwards.[82]

---

[81] Russell, *Firearms, Traps and Tools, p.200.*
[82] *Letter, Leavenworth to McComb.* December 20, 1823.

Daniel was likely in the second group. They left the post that Henry's remaining men were building on the forks and continued up the Big Horn.[83]

They soon crossed the first range of Rocky Mountains Daniel had seen–the Big Horns. Though the mountains were impressive, he was more excited with the basin beyond. He lyricly described it as "a large and beautiful valley adorned with many flowers and interspersed with many useful herbs."[84]

The trappers proceeded up this valley and likely were the first white men to see "the world's largest hot spring." This hot spring, located near present Thermopolis, Wyoming is said to discharge millions of gallons daily at a temperature of 135 degrees. Daniel was enthralled with the spot and wrote its first description.

> At the upper end of this valley on the Horn is the most beautiful scene of nature I have every seen. It is a large boiling spring at the foot of a small burnt mountain about two rods in diameter and depth not ascertained, discharging sufficient water for an overshot mill, and spreading itself to a considerable width forming a great number of basins of various shapes and sizes, [formed] of incrustations of sediment, running in this manner for the space of 200 feet, there falling over a precipice of about 30 feet perpendicular into the head of the horn [Big Horn River] or confluence of the Wind River.[85]

---

[83] Dale Morgan thinks that Potts wrote his "remarkable letter" of 1824 from this post. See *Morgan, William Ashley*, p. 9.

[84] *Potts Letter, to Robert Potts*, Rocky Mountains, July 16, 1826.

[85] *Ibid.* That this is certainly the "worlds largest hot spring" is the opinion of locals. Its pretty big.

His earlier work as a miller prompted Daniel's remark about the volume of the spring. Growing up in Valley Forge, he was familiar with numerous water mills powered by Valley Creek.

Winter with the Crows–The Crow Tepee

Earlier in the season, Potts and his fellows had made arrangements to winter with the Crow. They were usually friendly to the Americans and could head them to trails over the Divide. Their wintering ground was at modern Dubois, Wyoming and it boasted uncommonly warm winters–for the

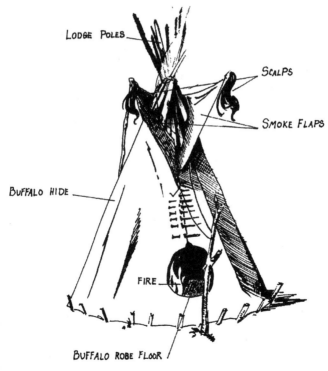

A snug but movable house.

Rocky Mountains. Potts wrongly attributed the mildness of the winter to "the immense number of hot springs." More accurately, constant wind from the plains and a "rain shadow" created by the Continental Divide cause the mild weather.

They lived in tepees. With a double liner on the lower wall, buffalo robes on the floor and fire in the middle the tepee is a remarkably livable shelter. At night they bundled in buffalo robes . Daniel was surprised at the comfort of his Crow tepee.

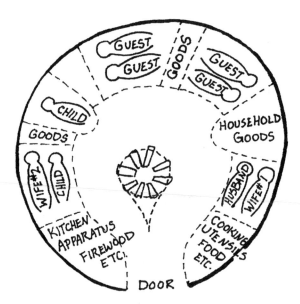

Crow Tepee Floor plan—room for
Everyone and Privacy For No One.

Extra care was taken to anchor the tent down. Shoshone Indians call this basin "the valley of the warm winds." And there is no doubt about it being windy. Potts's contemporary, James Clyman wryly observed in 1823, "Wind River is well named." A trapper wading in icy streams was sensitive to these things. But the Crow were fine hosts.

This tribe was called "erarapio", or literally, "kicked-in-their-bellies."[86] If this name seems offensive, it at least surpasses that of their river-dwelling cousins. The River Crows were known as "dung-on-the-river-banks." In the spring and summer the Mountain Crow roamed freely to the north and east with the other Crow bodies, but they returned to the Wind River in the land of the Wyoming Shoshone for the winter. Of the American Indians, the Crow were the favorites of the whites for reasons suggested by Warren Ferris:

> In their lodges, they consider themselves bound to protect strangers, and feast them with the best they can procure . . . Their women are, without exception, unfaithful, and offer themselves to strangers unhesitatingly for a few beads or other trifles. Jealousy is hardly known among them. Though the property of one proved to have had illicit connexion with another's wife by "crowic law," is immediately transferred to the injured husband.[87]

They had, however, what the trappers considered to be a serious moral defect; they were thieves. Their interest in this

---

[86] The Mountain Crows were divided into two unequal bands, the larger called Acaraho, Main Body, or "where-the many-lodges-are." The smaller branch was termed "kicked-in-their-bellies." Robert H Louie, *The Crow Indians* [New York; Farrar and Reinhard, 1935], pp.3-4. The author spent some nights in a tent in Dubois during the winter of 1986. It is warm enough if you can keep the wind from blowing the tent away.

[87] Warren A. Ferris, *Life in the Rocky Mountains*: p.303. It would seem that self interest would enhance morality.

ranged from hatchets to horses as Keemle relates:

> I was robbed by the Crows, a set of fellows with whom I
> had been all the winter, and treated with the greatest
> frendship, and made them many presents; but finding me
> alone they could not miss the opportunity & robbed me of
> everything even powder, lead & tobacco for my personal
> use.[88]

He adds that between 1824 and 1831 he was: "robbed a
third time and a fourth near the scene of the first," and that,

> the Crows, are thieves at home and abroad and spare no
> chance to rob us, but never Kill. This they frankly explain
> by telling us that if they killed, we would not come back,
> & they would lose the chance of Stealing from us. They
> have no Shame about stealing & will talk over their past
> thefts to you with all possible frankness & indifference . .
> . . They have a great many mules and horses. I suppose I
> have seen ten thousand horses & mules feeding at their
> Village.[89]

Crow Horse Stealing

With the Crow, stealing horses was as art. Some years
earlier, in 1812, Robert Stuart was leading "the returning
Astorians" back to the States with dispatches for John Jacob

---

[88] Quoted from Morgan, *William Ashley*, p. 252, footnote 252, from the
National Archives, Records of the Bureau of Indian Affairs, Letters
Received, Miscellaneous, 1831; also printed in full in *Abel, Charon's
Journal,* pp. 343-349. Keemle and Gordon of the Missouri Fur Company
had at some point gotten attached to Jedediah Smith's party coming to the
Crow wintering grounds. They wintered with the Ashley-Henry men
1824-25, but did not go further west with them the following spring. See
Morgan, *William Ashley*, p. 252.
[89] *Ibid.*

Astor. They had been shadowed by a band of Crow horse thieves for seven days. And they knew it. Near present Alpine Wyoming, to avoid crossing the big river, the trail followed down the *west* side of Snake River. In some places the river squeezed the trail up against the steep western mountain. On September 18, they were about five miles north of present Alpine. On the nineteenth they were up at dawn but the Crow had been up earlier. They came yelling through the camp and stampeded their horses, [the site is now beneath Palisades Reservoir]. Afterward, Stuart, now walking, had ample time to contemplate Crow horse stealing tactics and wrote it up in his journal,

> one of the party rode past our camp and placed himself on a conspicuous knob, in the direction they wanted to run them off: when the others [who were behind our camp], seeing him prepared, rose the war hoop, or yell [which is the most horribly discordant howling imaginable, being an imitation of the different beasts of prey] ; at this diabolical noise, the animals naturally rose their heads to see what the matter was —at that instant he who had planted himself in advance put spurs to his steed, and ours, seeing him gallop off in apparent fright, started all in the same direction, as if a legion of infernals were in pursuit of them.–In this manner a dozen or two of these fellows have sometimes succeeded in running off every horse belonging to our parties, of perhaps 5 or 600 men; for once those creatures take fright, nothing short of broken necks, can stop their progress . . . [90]

Now afoot, with baggage on his back, Stuart had plenty of time to think about Crow horse stealing expertise. However, this happened back in September of 1812 and is only retold to illustrate Crow thievery went way back.

---

[90] Robert Stuart, *On the Oregon Trail*, [Norman, Okla., 1953], p.102.

Before arriving among the generous and thieving Crow, Daniel was introduced to freezing mountain weather. He and his companions only knew that the Crow camp was somewhere up Wind River. With this scanty information, they struck off over the Owl Creek Range then got separated and lost.

In trapping, as in war, companions are often your margin of safety. Faced with biting cold weather, hostile Indians and hunger, a few more men with a few more balls, powder, and provisions were the difference between life and death. Earlier, when Daniel was lost from his party on the Missouri, he had a terrible time and almost starved. Now on the Owl Creek range, it happened again. He writes,

> at the commencement of winter we started for the Columbia Mountain to winter with the Crow Indians who are our only friends in this country here I got straid away from my company and fell in with Indians who were not Crows and traveled thirty miles from one hour by sun in the evening until midnight across the mountain through Snow up to my middle which frose my feet severely so that I lost two toes entire and two others in part from this I did not recover until late in the spring . . . . [91]

He was lucky the Indians weren't Blackfeet who would have taken more than his toes. They were likely "Snakes," or Wyoming Shoshone. Anyway, it was okay to lose toes–trapping in icy streams was hard on toes. It was an occupational risk that "came with the territory." While on the Oregon Trail some years later the adept historian Francis Parkman noted mountain men without toes, and described "old Rouleau, both of whose feet had been frozen and were amputated at the first joint of

---

[91] *Potts Letter, to Robert Potts*, dated from Rocky Mountains, 1824.

each foot." His Moccasins were appropriately shortened also.[92]
It was routine. And fortunately the Snake chief had a treatment
for Daniel's frostbitten feet.

> Here I am obliged to remark the humanity of the natives
> towards me, who conducted me to their village, into the
> lodge of their Chief, who regularly twice a day divested
> himself of all his clothing except his breech clout, and
> dressed my wounds, until I left them.[93]

Potts's care givers could have been the Sheepeater branch
of Shoshoni. They weren't pals of the Crow. Little more than
20 miles east of Dubois is a prominent flat topped mountain
called "Crow Heart Butte." The Shoshoni Chief Washikie is
reputed to have fought and killed a Crow brave on the butte
then ate his heart as a ritual of bravery. But the Shoshoni and
Crow seemed to bury the hatchet during winter and share the
"Valley of the Warm Winds." The two groups were likely not
more than 40 miles apart. It was a good place; besides being
warm, it boasted numerous herds of mountain sheep. These
were easily hunted on the snow free slopes ringing the valley.[94]

So far, Daniel's injuries included terrible damage from the
wooden ram rod shot through both knees a season earlier and
now frozen feet. But once again he mended. And when the pain
subsided he caught up with his companions and the Crows.
Along with his seven companions, the Crows also played host
to more of the Ashley-Henry men.

---

[92] Francis Parkman, *The Oregon Trail* [Garden City, NY: Doubleday and
Co., Inc. 1946]. p. 112

[93] *Potts Letter, to Thomas Conchlen, Rocky Mountains,* July 1824.

[94] Regarding the Crowheart Butte story, when asked about this incident
years later, the respected chief Washiki said: " young men do foolish
things." The Mountain Sheep are still there; it is one of America's largest
herds.

Jedediah Smith, with James Clyman, Thomas Fitzpatrick, and others of lessor note had proceeded to the Wind River by a more direct route than Henry's men. They were guided by a mulatto named Edward Rose, who's knowledge of the Crow language would be useful during the winter. Rose was part Black, but also part Cherokee and White. From what is passed down, he looked like an Indian, but was coyote ugly, with a brand on his forehead and the end of his nose chewed off in a fight. Fighting was his hobby. And he was brave to the point of idiocy. All this was big medicine to the Indians.

From Fort Kiowa, Rose led them almost due west and entered Big Horn Basin by way of the Schell River. According to their historian, James Clyman, the party spent the month of November in Big Horn Basin before proceeding over the Owl Creek Mountains and the Crow encampment on Wind River.[95] Here Henry's party, and eventually their chronicler Daniel Potts, were snugly tented up with the Crow.

Though neither Potts or Clyman mentions the other, it is apparent from what they say about wintering with the Crow that the two parties were together near present Dubois Wyoming.

Wind River came in from a canyon on the west. Every few miles along the river there was flat ground–space to set up a hundred or so tepees. And lots of red willow–useful for arrow shafts–fringed the river. Mountain sheep grazing the wind swept highlands provided excellent meat, wool and horns for tools. Sheep were important to their survival and pictographs of long horned sheep are still visible, scratched into the soft stone of Dinwoody Canyon. These show the natives held the sheep in great respect and may have even worshiped them. In daytime, the sun was usually shining but the damnable wind blew night

---

[95] James Clyman, *Journal of a Mountain Man*, [Missoula, 1984], p.24.

and day. Yet it was such a good winter camp that the Crow and Shoshoni managed a delicate peace to share the region–camping a day or week apart.

When Clyman arrived buffalo herds were strung along the river. And he reports "several grand hunts." In one they killed a thousand buffalo. He was taken by how the Crow could stand hardship and cold.

> I have frequently seen . . . dozens of them runing bufaloe on horseback for hours togather all their bodies naked down to the belt around their waists and dismount with but a slight trimble and many of them take a bath every morning even when the hoar frost was flying thick in the air and it was necessary to cut holes in the ice to get at the water.
>
> They put their children to all kinds of hardships and the femals in particular pack the littl girls and dogs when on march the whole employment of the males being hunting and war . . . [96]

Jedediah Smith and his band were grateful to meet up again with Henry's well supplied party. Smith was pursuing his trade with religious intensity. Come hell, high water, or deep snow–he was going over the Divide to the Columbia waters as soon as he possibly could . The crow reported that beaver were so plentiful there that trapping was unnecessary, you only needed to knock them in the head with a stick. Smith wanted to forge over the Divide without delay but needed to refresh their supplies first.

Fortunately, Henry's men plenty and to spare.

Some basic necessities were only available by boat and

---

[96] *Ibid.* p.25.

pack train from the east. They included gun powder and lead, traps,and knives. Other things were nice to have like tobacco, sugar, and blankets. And some items, like beads and colored cloth were needed for Indian trade.

The First Rendezvous?

The loss of his toes caused Daniel to walk carefully and slow during the winter; much of his time doubtless spent inside the tepee with his Crow hosts. By spring, however, he was up and around, and made a creditable hunt. As the snow melted and summer approached, Potts and his friends in Wind River country needed to get these furs safely down-river and once again restock their supplies. Having contacted Henry, plans were made for the various parties to get together [can we call it a rendezvous?] and exchange their peltries for goods they would need over the Continental Divide on the "Columbia Waters." Andrew Henry had brought the merchandise up from his dismantled post on the Missouri. These supplies would be traded to Potts and his friends for their furs, or packed for future trade deeper in the mountains. The object

A Trappers most used tool with a field-made stag handle and full leather sheath

was to obtain beaver skins–and the goods were for that purpose only. Getting the merchandise this far had been expensive and laborious. But one more push was needed to get them over the Continental Divide. For this, a meeting with his westward bound trappers was in order.[97]

So at some point, likely between the bend of Wind River and the mouth of the Big Horn, a meeting or rendezvous was held. It could have been the same occasion when Potts celebrated Independence Day with a friend. Typically, Daniel wrote letters at the rendezvous to be carried back east with the furs. His letter of 1824 is dated July 7–about the same as later rendezvous letters. There may have been nearly 50 whites and surely some Crow Indians at hand as their furs were exchanged for supplies from the Big Horn Post then packed for a push into the heart of the Rocky Mountains.[98] Daniel traded his beaver skins for $350.00 and he doubtless spent it all on goods to carry him through the next season.[99] Men who had been long separated entertained each other with stories and competitions. The reunion of isolated trappers was always an opportunity for fun. Potts and a friend celebrated Independence Day with a buffalo chase:

> I have celebrated the fourth of July by the persuit of a Bull Buffalo, two [of us] being on Horsback ran him about three

---

[97] The following winter on Cub Creek of Cache Valley the Weber party seemed to be well stocked with Indian trade goods. When Peter Skene Ogden was in the vicinity of their winter camp he learned that the Americans were trading muskets and powder to the Indians. Normally you didn't trade guns and powder unless you had plenty.

[98] There is no first-hand account describing the meeting of Henry's parties this summer, but they must have met. Henry obtained Potts's $350.00 in furs, gathered the mail, and got the report on South Pass. Daniel's letter of July 7 suggests the Rendezvous date.

[99] *Potts Letter, to Thomas Cochlen, Rocky Mountains,* 1824.

miles, came up along side, pourd in two broad sides. he took [to] the river and it not being foardable, he sunk to the bottome and the pursuit ended . . . .[100]

Except during melting snow run off the Wind River is fordable. So this chase and perhaps the rendezvous likely happened downstream in deeper water. The only Rendezvous sport that the genteel Daniel ever reveals is a buffalo chase. If he ever got drunk or dallied with Indian ladies he didn't brag about it. His only mention of drinking alcohol involved a political toast.[101]

Some features of later Rendezvous were apparent at this meeting. Furs were exchanged for supplies then packed for shipment. The men played games. Potts and a friend celebrated Independence Day with a buffalo chase. Typical of later Rendezvous, Potts wrote letters. With fresh trade goods, good friends and some Crow allies, a variety of entertainment was possible.

So this meeting of the Henry parties may have been a prototype of the famous trapper Rendezvous to come.[102]

---

[100] *Ibid.*

[101] *Potts Letter, Rocky Mountains* 1826

[102] The Rendezvous was the heart and soul of Ashley's success in the Rocky Mountains. The distance to civilization being so far, it was necessary that the trappers remain in the field and not return to St. Louis each year. They would need supplies and need to get their furs out of the mountains. Thus the Rendezvous provided for a place and time to meet and make the exchange. It also provided time for a party, to meet friends unseen for a year or more. Dale Morgan hints that the meeting of Jedediah Smith and his party on the Sweetwater which was proposed for June 1 but actually happened June 15 might be the prototype of later Rendezvous. However, I see the meeting of the Weber-Potts-Henry contingents to be more significant. Perhaps both get-to-gethers were natural events that mirrored marketing and necessity. For treatment of all the Rendezvous [except 1824, which is first suggested here], see Fred

Packed home with the furs was Potts's letter to his friend, Thomas Cochlen, of Pennsylvania. The letter would cause a good deal of speculation in the calm and less exciting eastern settlements. For Daniel wrote,

> A man in this Countrey is not safe neither day nor night, and hardley ever expect to get back. —this Countrey is the moste healthey in the world I believe: —A variety of hot springs, boiling Sulpher, and Oil springs, allso salts, salt Peter, and Volcanoes: petrifaction is astonishing; such as men, animels, fish, wood, and sea shells . . . when I have been hunting I have often thought of you and some others of my friends how you would glory in the sport. —White Bear [Grizzly], Buffalo, Elk, Deer, Antilope, and Mountain Sheep are our principle game.[103]

There was big adventure in the Rockies. This letter would excite his friends and concern to his family. One wonders where he saw his volcanoes and petrified men. Is this a tall tale? Potts is usually truthful. Perhaps he is re-telling stories of someone else. However, his report of hot springs hints of more spectacular curiosities he will see later on.

Before embarking on the Big Horn, Andrew Henry

Gowens, *Rocky Mountain Rendezvous*, [Provo, Utah, 1976.]

[103] *Potts letter, Rocky Mountains*, 1824. The letters of Daniel Potts are absent of startling and fictitious tales–except this one of petrified men and volcanoes. Perhaps he was quoted in error, perhaps not, however, the telling of tall tales was a prerogative of men who had been where others had not. Moses Harris was in a restaurant in St. Louis some years after his mountain travels and spoke of "this petrified grove in a restaurant whare a caterer for one of the dailies was present and the next morning his exacerbated statement came out saying a petrified forest was lately discovered whar the trees branches leaves and all were prefect and the small birds sitting on them with their mouths open singing at time of their transformation to stone," James Clymam, *Journal of a mountain Man*, p.23.

organized and prepared his combined parties for their push over the Divide into the heart of the Rocky Mountains. Henry had been in these mountains back in 1810. He knew there were plenty of beaver, but he also knew the risks in getting them. The challenges were Indians, bad weather, wild animals, and hunger. So he prepared his men with supplies, advice, and good leaders.

Jedediah Smith had led the first party through South Pass to Green River. And there is little question about his leadership skills. Perhaps his only flaw was *trying too hard*. He led the first Americans overland to California in 1826, then turned around and did it again in 1827. Their party ran into hostile Indians and suffered a massacre both times and most of that country was devoid of beaver.

After years of speculation, it seems the leader of the second group–men who trapped the Wind River, was John Weber.[104] Perhaps Weber had been in charge of one of the parties since wintering on the Musselshell in 1822-23.

Regarding Weber, from his son William, we learn that he was born in 1779 in the town of Altona near Hamburg, then a part of the Kingdom of Denmark. At an early age he ran away to sea and advanced to the rank of captain. The Napoleonic Wars persuaded him to come to America, and by July 29, 1807, he was living in St. Genevieve, Missouri. Both Ashley and Henry also resided there, so their acquaintance was likely. If this description is accurate, he could hardly be missed.

---

[104] There are two early accounts of Weber. One apparently by his son William was published about 1906 in the Jackson [Iowa] *Sentinel* or the *Bellevue Leader*. This was reprinted in Camp, "*The D.T.P. Letters,* pp. 24-25. The other by an old acquaintance of the Captain, J.C. Hughey of Bellevue, Iowa was printed in the *Salt Lake Tribune*, July 4, 1897, p. 31.

Captain Weber had sailed for six years as a Danish sea captain before coming to America. Nature had done well by him: he was a man of large and powerful frame, of erect carriage and graceful manner, his face indicated the superior intelligence behind it, he had a nose like a Roman Emperor and an eye as regal and pacing as that of an American eagle, the courage of a hero, and the staying qualities of a martyr.[105]

Following the trading and some last minute instructions, Henry launched the trappers toward the "Columbia Waters." Then he packed the furs and began the long voyage to the settlements.

Andrew Henry Leaves the Mountains

July of 1824, when Henry's boat descended the Big Muddy, marks the passing from the scene of a great Mountain Man. Andrew Henry was expected to shortly return to the Rockies, but he did not.[106] The constant struggle against turbulent rivers, treacherous Indians, and potential bankruptcy apparently soured him on the mountain trade.

Arguably, Henry was the first American to explore the Rocky Mountains. In 1810, as a partner in the old Missouri Fur Company, he built the first American post west of the Rockies.[107] This foray into Snake Country didn't bring him

---

[105] *Ibid.*

[106] Ashley hoped that Henry would join him even after the expedition was on its way. See, *William H. Ashley to William Carr Lane*, Fort Atkinson, October 29, 1824. Reprinted in Morgan, *William Ashley, p.* 98.

[107] For the story of the rediscovery in 1917 of Henry's Camp near present Drummond, Idaho, on the west side of the Tetons, see, Margaret Hawkes Lindsley, *Major Andrew Henry in Idaho* [n.p., c 1985], pp. 22-23.

much earnings, but he discovered streams and trails, and learned techniques he would use again in 1822. And he taught the others. Those who could stick with him became Mountain Men. Jedediah Smith, Jim Bridger, Hugh Glass, Daniel Potts, and John Weber learned their mountain skills from him. He was an active, in-the-field-commander who taught his men to live like Indians, depending on the hunt for food.[108]

Little is known about Henry other than his life in the mountains. Though some of his men became famous, and his partner got rich, Henry gave more to the fur trade than he received. Born in New York County, Pennsylvania about 1775, he later moved to Tennessee. By April of 1800 he was on the Missouri, and spent two years in St. Genevieve. Here he became acquainted with William Ashley who acted as a witness for him in a short-lived marriage. The girl was Mary Villars, and the union lasted two weeks. As with all of Henry's fortunes, only the bare bones of the story are known. The couple were formally divorced in October of 1807.[109]

But Henry gradually got a foothold in St. Genevieve. He acquired half interest with Francois Azor, dit Breton, in a lead mine. In 1807 along with Ashley, he was appointed 2nd Lieutenant in the cavalry company of the District of St. Genevieve. Then in 1809 he joined Manuel Lisa on a fur venture up the Missouri.

---

[108] Remember Potts's trials up the Missouri. See footnote 31.
[109] By 1824 Henry was married to a lady named Mary. No historical study of Andrew Henry has been made. References concerning his life are contained in Richard Edward Oglesby, *Manual Lisa and the Opening of the Missouri Fur Trade* [Norman: University of Oklahoma Press, 1963]; Thomas James, *Three Years Among the Indians and Mexicans* [Philadelphia and New York: J. R. Lippincott Company, 1962]. The more recent, *Andrew Henry* by Margaret Lindsley, is written as a novel in the framework of known sources.

It was on this expedition that Henry led a party from the Three Forks to Snake River and built a post. His name remains on the lake and principal fork of Snake River marking the path of travel, [Henry's Lake and Henry's fork of Snake River]. The party survived the winter but then split up and most of the men went east in 1811.[110] For more than ten years Andrew resisted the temptation to return to the mountains. Then under some inducement, he reconsidered and joined with Ashley in 1822. His experience working with men and trapping gave their partnership a jump start. For his part, in addition to boundless energy, Ashley had connections to buy trade goods on credit. Their outfit cost more than $20,000 so credit was a must.

The first two seasons of their partnership were filled with failure and disaster. With the keel boat sinking in 1822, the caches rifled at the mouth of the Yellowstone in 1823, and the continual loss of horses, Ashley and Henry were deeply in debt. On the trip back to St. Louis Henry was robbed once more.[111]

When he arrived home in St. Genevieve, Andrew learned that his wife, in order to pay the bills had put his farm up for sale.[112] He went through with the deal that a lesser man might have balked at. And he concluded it was time to stay closer to home and seek a more reliable occupation. Having been absent for 28 months, he hadn't been much of a husband.

But he quit at the wrong time. In 1824 the trappers crossed over the Continental Divide onto rich beaver streams of Green and Bear Rivers. This also marked the crossing from debt to riches. It wasn't that Henry didn't know about that rich beaver

---

[110] Oglesby, *Manuel Lisa*, p. 90-97, 115-116.

[111] Morgan, *William Ashley*, P.86

[112] Newspaper notice of the *St. Louis Enquirer*, August 30, 1824, full text in Morgan, *West of William H. Ashley*, p.87. At his death his estate was valued at only $150.00.

country, and Daniel Potts would have reassured his leader about the wealth to be taken. He enthusiastically planned to make twelve hundred dollars in the coming year.[113] However, no one knew better than Henry how quick fortunes were lost seeking furs. Perhaps with the load of furs from Wind River country, Henry was able to turn the assets and liabilities of the company over to energetic William Ashley, and he went back to mining lead—no windfall profits but less occupational hazards."[114]

Trapping or Trading?

The departure of Henry marked the closing of one era and the opening of another. Henceforth the emphasis would be on trapping instead of trading with Indians. Nathaniel J. Wyeth recounted the change in 1833:

> About 12 years since Mr Wm H. Ashley engaged in the Indian trade [trying] by various means to obtain furs. At the time he was engaged in this undertaking he was bankrupt, but was a person of credit,[115] which enabled him to get the requisite means. His first attempts were predicated upon the possibility of trading furs from the Indians in the interior for goods. In this he was not successful, and in the event became much reduced in

---

[113] *Daniel Potts Letter, Rocky Mountains*, 1824

[114] There is no indication that Andrew Henry acted dishonestly with Ashley, or "left him holding the bag." About the only reference to his character comes from a contemporary who said that Henry "admits everything with his humor as well as his honesty and frank manner and without beating around the bush." Oglesby, *Manuel Lisa*, p. 91

[115] Ashley had both credit and political influence: he was Lieutenant Governor of the new state of Missouri. It is ironic that Henry departed at just the wrong time. At his death his estate was only $150.00. White and Gowens, *"Traders and Trappers"* part 2, pp. 60-61.

means, and credit, but in the course of this business perceived that there was plenty of Beaver in the country to which he had resorted for trade, but great difficulty to induce the Indians to catch it. After many trials of trading voyages *he converted his trading parties into trapping parties*. In the first establishment of this business he met with all the usual difficulties incident to new plans but still made something. About this time a Mr. Gardner one of his agents met a Mr. Ogden, clerk of the H. B. Co. in the Snake Country at the head of a trapping party. Gardner induced the men of Ogden's party to desert by promises of supplyes, and good prices for furs. The furst thus obtained amounted to about 130 packs or 13,000 Ibs. worth at that time about $75,000. The following year Ashley sold out to Smith Sublette & Jackson for about $30,000 and left the business, after paying up his old debts, [he was] worth about $50,000[116]

There were three reasons for Ashley's financial turnaround of 1824: First, instead of relying on Indians, his own men did the trapping. They waded the streams and set traps he had supplied them with. Here it was a matter of emphasis; the mountain men always trapped as they traded.[117] But now they *focused* on gathering their own beaver skins from the Green, the

---

[116] Nathaniel J. Wyeth, *The Correspondence and Journals of Captain Nathaniel J. Wyeth 1831-6: A Record of Two Expeditions for the Occupation of the Oregon Country*, with Maps, Introduction and Index . . . edited by F. G. Young [Eugene, Oregon: University Press, 1899; Sources of the History of Oregon, v. 1, 3-6], pp. 73-74.

[117] Richard Edward Oglesby, *Manuel Lisa and the Opening of the Missouri Fur Trade*, pp. 58-64: Lisa's parties lived by trade and off the land, traded and trapped furs, and made the Crows their allies in the winter of 1807-1808. The connection with Andrew Henry is very obvious: his was the last signature to the *Articles of Agreement - St. Louis Fur Company*, 1809 [September 20,1809] [p p. 202-208] and was an investor and field commander in this company [pp. 99-125, passim].

Bear, and other streams that fed the upper Missouri and Columbia Rivers.

Second, Ashley's men became openly predatory on their Canadian and British counterparts. They challenged the pricing systems of Hudson's Bay Company and wooed away many French-Canadian, mètes or Iroquois trappers. And these men brought with them stocks of furs that otherwise would have gone to Hudson Bay Company.

Third, once success was established and he was prospering financially, Ashley sold out for top dollar with the agreement that the new partners would purchase supplies from him! This enriched him handsomely. Ashley paid off his old debts,[118] and was able to spend more time in his favorite enterprise, which was politics.[119]

Back in the mountains, Ashley's men were able to remain in the field and rely on the rendezvous system for supplies. To learn survival they copied the Indians. Their teachers were the

---

[118] Clokey, *William H. Ashley*, p. 134, writes that Ashley was in debt between $75,000 and $100,000, generally concurring with Wyeth that Ashley was "bankrupt." But that was before the sudden and complete change in his fortunes as a result of the 1824 fur-trapping season and the sale of the enterprise.

[119] In the absence of Governor McNair, Missouri Lieutenant Governor Ashley had been deeply involved in the highly charged partisan politics of Missouri as an ally of Senator Thomas Hart Benton [see Clokey, *William H. Ashley*, pp. 122-127]—Ashley ran for governor in 1824 and was soundly defeated [pp. 127-131]. After the loss, he tried to position himself to succeed William Clark as Superintendent of Indian Affairs when Clark sought appointment as Surveyor General [p. 136]. Ashley was also involved in St. Louis city politics as an ally and friend of Mayor William Carr Lane [p. 136]. Finally, after several false starts, he organized a formidable campaign for the U. S. Congress, won election and served from 1831 to 1837 in the House.

Crow and Shoshone with whom they wintered, married, and stole horses. By "going Indian," Ashley's men came to think of the mountains as their home. And they banded with these friendly tribes against their enemies.

Daniel enjoyed his stay with the Crow on Wind River. In fact, his description of the river might be the earliest.

The Wind River is a beautiful transparent steam, with a hard gravel bottom about 70 or 80 yards wide, rising in the Rocky Mountains running E.N.E., finally north through a picturesque small mountain after it discharges through this mountain it loses its name [and is called the Big Horn River].

The Wind flowed eastward while Daniel was headed west. He wrote his intentions and the risk:

We are about to embark for the Columbia waters [the west side of the Continental Divide] where I expect to remain for two years at least. A man in this Country is not safe neither day nor night, and hardly ever expect to get back[120]

---

[120] *Daniel Potts to Thomas Cochlen,* dated Rocky Mountains, July 1, 1824.

THE "COLUMBIA WATERS"

S hortly after July 7th 1824, Potts bade farewell to friends going east and with his companions he headed over the Continental Divide to the "Columbia Waters."[121] The men who had explored this country earlier in the spring pointed out the sights of this valley to newcomers. There was one of particular interest on the Popo Agie.

It was an *oil spring*. This curiosity elicited responses from many western travelers; Daniel's report was the first written:

> There is also an Oil Spring in this valley, which discharges 60 or 70 gallons of pure oil per day. The oil has very much the appearance, taste and smell of British oil.[122]

Potts was corroborated by later Mountain Men in his analysis of the spring. It became a universal practice to describe

---

[121] *Potts Letter, to Thomas Cochlen, 1824*. Potts's term, "the Columbia waters," had several uses in the fur trade. The mouth of the Colombia River was on maps of the Pacific coast but its inland coarse was yet unknown. Regions west of Salt Lake were also unknown and poorly represented on maps. According to prevailing cartographic tradition, there was a large branch of the Columbia, the Multnomah, somewhere west of the "Rio Colorado of the West" draining into the Pacific Ocean. Since Daniel was aware that Green River drained into the Gulf of California, it is apparent that his party had previously planned to trap in the Northern Great Basin, an area which they mistakenly thought drained into the Columbia. Later, "Columbia waters" meant any water draining into the Columbia, and included the Snake, Teton, Salt and Grays Rivers, or any of the creeks feeding these streams. On his foray into Blackfoot Country Potts wrote they crossed the Snake River at "the South fork of the Columbia at the forks of Henry's and Louis's forks of Snake River." Weber refers to the "Columbia Waters" as the best trapping grounds. *Salt Lake Tribune*, July 4, 1897. Ashley, with Provost as his source, says that Weber's band wintered in 1824 on the "head waters of the Columbia." Morgan, *William Ashley*, p. 116. They were yet unaware of the Great Basin and didn't know Bear River emptied into Great Salt Lake.

[122] *Potts Letter to Thomas Cochlen, 1824.*

the substance exuding from it as "like British Oil."[123] Put to a similar use as its namesake, the oil was used by trappers to lubricate their skin and salve their wounds. It was also doubtless used to soften and preserve their leather saddles and bridles. Flowing freely from the ground, it was pretty handy stuff.

Not all of the later trappers utilized the spring in this manner however. The chronicler Osborne Russell relates how his band set the spring on fire. The blaze continued until all the available oil was consumed, producing "a dense column of thick black smoke."[124] In a valuable, recently discovered map by Jedediah Smith, the spring is properly placed near present Lander, Wyoming.[125]

South Pass, 1824

Following directions of their Indian hosts and likely a well worn trail, Potts's party left the oil spring and proceeded up the valley to South Pass.

The earliest accounts of this grand gateway to the West were of Indian origin. In 1812 a Shoshone Indian had informed Robert Stuart and the Returning Astorians of a "shorter trace to the South," of the trail taken by Wilson Price Hunt and the

---

[123] British Oil, is a "A rubefacient liniment containing linseed oil, oil of turpentine, oil of amber, juniper oil, and petroleum". *Webster's Unabridged Dictionary.*
[124] Russell, *Journal of a Trapper*, Aubrey L. Haines, ed.[Portland: Champoeg Press, 1955], pp. 57-58.
[125] Morgan and Wheat, *Jedediah Smith's Maps,* See Fremont Wilkes Smith Map. Early oilmen, taking advantage of the obvious, drilled Wyoming's first oil well in this vicinity in 1884. *Official Wyoming Road Map*, Wyoming State Highway Commission, 1962.

Overland Astorians in 1810. Hunt had threaded his way through the mountains by going up the Wind River, over Union Pass, through Jackson Hole and over steep Teton Pass. However, this "shorter trace" described by the Shoshone is the first reference to a much easier route that is actually a gap in the great chain of Rocky Mountains.[126]

While wintering with the Crows in 1823-24, the Ashley-Henry parties pumped their native hosts for information about westward routes, Then Smith led a band west up Wind River and attempted a mid-winter crossing of the Divide near Union Pass. They failed. There was too much snow. They returned to the Crow camp tired and chilled–but they persisted. With some ingenuity better directions were obtained by making a sand map. Clyman authored both the map and this account:

> I spread out a buffalo robe and covered it with sand, and made it in heaps to represent the different mountains [we were then encamped at the lower point of the Wind River Mountains], and from our sand map with the help of the Crows, we finally got the idea that we could go to Green River, called by them Seeds-ka-day. We undertook it in February . . . .[127]

The Indians headed them right for South Pass, but it was still tough going. They were traveling through blowing snow in the high-mountain desert country. And their constant companion was that wonderfully cold Wyoming wind. Mormon hand-cart companies would later meet disaster here. The Smith-Clyman party seems to have missed the easiest route.[128] But they suffered their way through.

---

[126] Philip Ashton Rollins, *The Discovery of the Oregon Trail* [New York: Eberstadt and Sons, 1935], p. 84.

[127] Camp, *James Clyman,* p. 33.

[128] Frost, *Notes,* pp. 35-37.

It remained for Potts's party to find the natural route that was used twenty years later by great caravans of westering pioneers. Not being in such a hurry as Smith, Potts's group stayed a bit longer in the warm Crow tepees and crossed the Pass in the summer. Evidently, communication improved for Keemle reports that a Crow chief told them, that a pass existed in the Wind River Mountains, through which he could easily take his whole band upon streams on the other side. He also represented beaver so abundant upon these rivers that traps were unnecessary to catch them–they could club them with sticks.[129] The Americans savored this news.

Since Potts and his company did not leave Wind River Valley until July, they had ample time to find the regular trail over South Pass–probably with some Crow Indians as guides. Daniel writes, "From this valley [Wind River Valley] we proceeded by S.W. direction over a tolerable route to the heads of the Sweet Water." The head of Sweetwater is very near South Pass. They trapped as they traveled and Daniel collected over three hundred and fifty dollars worth of furs in spite of his lost toes. If his companions, with their toes intact, did as well the entire Wind River Valley including the "tolerable route" over the Divide was explored.[130] At least some of the party visited the high rolling prairies of South Pass and sent news of

---

[129] Solitaire, "Major Fitzpatrick, the Discoverer of South Pass," *St. Louis Weekly Reveille*, March 1, 1847. See also LeRoy Hafen and William Ghent, *Broken Hand* [Denver: Old West Publishing Co., 1831], Appendix.

[130] Daniel Potts writes of the immense number of hots springs in this valley and wrongly assumes they are the reason for the mild winters. There are numerous thermal sites in Fremont County Wyoming. From this and other details he describes, it is apparent that the entire valley was explored this season. *Potts Letter to Robert Potts*, 1826.

this gateway through the Rockies back with Henry and the eastward bound furs.[131] For the St. Louis press reported that:

> By the arrival of Major Henry from the Rocky Mountains, we learn that his party have discovered a passage by which loaded waggons can at this time reach the navigable waters of the Columbia River. This route lies South of the one explored by Lewis and Clarke, and is inhabited by Indians friendly to us.[132]

South Pass can easily be missed because it has little resemblance to a mountain pass. It is as Potts says, more of high rolling prairies than a mountain pass. On either side mountains are absent. But now that it was known, the most vexing problem to western travel was removed.

After leaving the oil spring, Potts and his fellow hunters had proceeded directly towards the wide opening in the mountains. Daniel, the only chronicler, gives the essentials of the journey:

---

[131] *Potts letter to Robert Potts Rocky Mountains, 1826. Arkansas Gazette,* Arkansas Post, Arkansas Territory, November 16, 1824. Reprinted in Frost, *Notes,* p. 126. See also footnote #132, which follows. By the spring of 1824 it is evident that the entire valley or eastern slope of the Wind River Mountains had been explored by trappers; For example, Potts describes Thermopolis Hot Springs where Wind River emerges from the canyon and as he says, "loses it's name"–and becomes the Horn [or Big Horn] River. And on the way to South Pass, they visited the oil spring near Lander then took a "tolerable route" to the head of Sweetwater River. After which they crossed South Pass which Daniel describes as " high rolling prairies." Others of his party would have trapped and explored other streams and other areas.

[132] Dale Morgan in *Jedediah Smith,* pp. 154, 155, attributes this news to Thomas Fitzpatrick of Smith's party, who returned to the settlements by way of the Platte. He possibly takes cue from Camp, *James Clyman,* p. 30. However, Henry likely brought the news of the discovery of the pass in 1824. Compare Morgan, *William Ashley,* p. 93.

From this valley [Wind River Valley] we proceeded by S. W. over a tolerable route to the heads of SweetWater, a small stream which takes an eastern course and falls into the north fork of the Great Platt, 70 or 80 miles below. *This stream rises and runs on the highest ground in all this country* The winters are extremely [cold], and even the summers are disagreeably cold . . . .After crossing the above mentioned stream, we took a more westerly direction over *high rolling Prairies* to a small branch of a considerable river, known to us by the name of Seet Kadu, and to the Spaniard by Green River, and is supposed to discharge itself into the Bay of California. This river has a bold running current, 80 or 90 yards wide, & bears a S.E. direction. It falls from the Rocky Mountains in many small rivulets, on which were considerable beaver.[133]

This may be the first record of a crossing that tells the route from the east—the path that thousands of pioneers would later use.[134] In 1812, Robert Stuart and his straggling band of "Returning Astorians" were the first whites to traverse South Pass from the west.

From the "high rolling prairies," Daniel says the party went west to the Little Sandy which is a branch of the Seet Kadu or

---

[133] *Potts Letter To Robert Potts,* Rocky Mountains,1826. Here Potts first describes the significance of Green River to the fur gathering business. My italics are added to highlight Potts description of South Pass and his knowledge that he is on the Continental Divide.

[134] Though Henry's party were in Green River Valley in 1811, and headed east, there is no evidence that they knew of South Pass. The Astorians, in crossing the Continental Divide, had known of the pass and intended to use it, but in order to avoid Indian trouble they stayed above the main trails. Jedediah Smith and his party were first to cross at this latitude from east to west but it is difficult to know where their trail was. See James Clyman, *Journal of a Mountain Man,* [Missoula, 1984], p. 30.

Green River. By now the party had crossed the trail of Jedediah Smith's contingent who had been trapping Green River since March.

Smith and Fitzpatrick had split their party of eleven and agreed to meet on the Sweetwater in early June. When Smith failed to appear, Clyman and Fitzpatrick went down the river to ascertain where it might be navigable. Fitzpatrick then split off and was to follow a few days behind Clyman–after joining with Jedediah Smith. Clyman went ahead and camped at the mouth of the Sweetwater . . . and waited. After waiting eleven days for his companions, James Clyman "began to get lonely." He counted his short supply of lead balls–only eleven, and decided to start walking east to the settlements. In one of the great solitary hikes of the fur trade, Clyman walked all the way down the Platte to Fort Atkinson on the Missouri. Suffering from loneliness, hunger and fatigue, when he finally saw the American flag he "swooned immediately."

When Jed Smith did show up at the rendezvous point he commissioned Fitzpatrick along with Stone and Branch to "get the furs out of the mountains the best way they could." They followed the Clyman route, narrowly missing him at one point and finally reached Fort Atkinson "in a more pitiable state" than him.[135]

The sources are silent concerning any meeting of the Smith and Potts contingents during the year 1824. It is obvious that men under Jedediah Smith did not know that Henry had provided for a mode of marketing the furs of Potts and his fellows. If this information were known, it is not likely they would have risked a valuable load of furs and three men on a journey down the Platte. Prior to their hike that river was an

---

[135] *Ibid.*, p. 34.

enigma to the trappers.

Perhaps it was late July when Daniel Potts and his party reached the Seet Kadu. This name, freely spelled and pronounced, is of Crow Indian origin. The Spanish name for the stream was Rio Verde–probably a recognition of the effect the water had on flora bordering the river. For hundreds of miles the Green River passes through arid country generally parched and brown. The green borders of the river are a striking contrast to the general landscape. This stream became well known to all trappers because more Rendezvous were conducted near its banks than any other spot in the mountains.

Typically Daniel was astonished at the Green River Peaks and Wyoming's tallest mountain.

> This valley, like all others I have seen in this country, is surrounded by mountains, those to S. W. and N. . . . is the highest I ever saw, and perhaps the highest in North America. It stands rather detached and majestic, beginning abruptly towards the E. and terminating toward N.W. Its tops are the repository of eternal winter. In clear weather its appearance is truly sublime and reflects the brilliancy of the diamond in its various colours.[136]

Crossing the Green, the party continued southwest toward the next range of mountains. Winding out of the Green River drainage, the caravan "had very good traveling over an inconsiderable ridge."[137] Though ignorant of the geography, they soon descended into the *Great Basin* and "fell on a considerable river, called Bear River."

---

[136] *Potts Letter, Rocky Mountains*, 1826. Gannet Peak is 13,804' high.
[137] The "inconsiderable ridge," is probably Blacks Fork.

Bear River and Cub Creek in the Great Basin

For the Americans, Bear River country and Cache Valley became the heart of trapping operations during the fur trade. After 1824 they wintered there and cached their furs and trade goods, [hence the name, "Cache Valley"].[138] Daniel and Jedediah Smith considered it to be their "home" in the mountains. On four occasions the trappers collected in this part of the Great Basin for the annual trade fair. The region is of such importance as to warrant a glimpse into its past.

Most likely, Potts and his companions were the first Americans to visit Bear River since 1811. In that year a band of Astorians were returning to the settlements under Robert Stuart. The party had been searching for the Bear, which was called by them "Miller's River," after their guide.[139] Joseph Miller, along with four other men, had spent the previous season trapping the area. The others were John Hoback, Edward Robinson, Jacob Rezner, and one Cass.[140] The first three mentioned constituted a group of the most hardened gentlemen to ever cock a trap. In fact, Washington Irving tells of "mysterious speculations, and dark surmises," suggesting that in a starving time they ate the man named Cass,[141] –when desperate they took desperate actions. After being robbed three times by Indians, they were found in a pitiable state fishing on Snake River by the

---

[138] A "cache" is a storage of furs or equipment in an underground pit. The pit or hole was dug in dry ground, filled with the items the trappers wanted to protect, then carefully covered with dirt and concealed.

[139] Rollins, *Oregon Trail*, p. 129.

[140] Washington Irving, *Astoria* [New York: R. F. Fenno, 1900], Chapter 31. His full name is Martin H. Cass. There are so many different editions of *Astoria* that citing certain pages is meaningless. In this study I will cite only the chapter involved.

[141] *Ibid.*, Chapter 52.

Returning Astorians.

Miller by 1812, was fed up with mountain life, "his curiosity and desire of traveling thro' the Indian countries being fully satisfied."[142] When the Astorians came along, he consented to guide them east through the mountains to the settlements. And he thought they might find a short cut through Utah country rather than take the rugged trail over Teton Pass, and down into Jackson Hole. That path then crossed Snake River, then led up a narrow trail through Hoback Canyon in Wyoming. However, it was Blackfeet war parties, more than difficult geography that impelled them to try a route farther south.[143] Their plans were thwarted by bad luck and another tribe of Indians–the friendly but thieving Crow.

When he reached the upper waters of Bear River, Miller was disoriented. He had not seen this particular section of the stream. Here a band of Crow Indians began to harass the party. In an attempt to elude them and get their bearings, they detoured north through present Star Valley Wyoming.[144] Upon

---

[142] Rollins, *Oregon Trail*, p. 113.

[143] *Ibid.*, p. 128.

[144] The Stuart party were the first whites known to pass through present Star Valley, [formerly Salt River Valley] Wyoming. The area was a natural route from Bear River to Jackson's Hole and later became a favorite of the trappers for its well-stocked streams and fine pasturage. Warren Ferris appreciated the flat ground that was comparatively free of animal burrows. Here he could "run" buffalo without fear of breaking his horses legs. Interesting thermal sites, the "boiling kettles" were examined by Ferris near present Auburn. Ferris, *Rocky Mountains*, p. 53. The valley is unequally divided by the west boundary of Wyoming and drained by Salt River. This name is derived from the numerous deposits of salt on the tributaries of the river. It appears both as rock salt and in white snow-like deposits from springs. General Ashley no doubt took some samples of rock salt from Thomas' Fork in 1826. Morgan, *William Ashley*, p. 153. Osborne Russell mentions how the trappers would travel long distances

reaching Snake River near present Alpine, the men easily recognized it as the stream they called, "Mad River." Unfortunately, a few miles north of the confluence of Snake and Salt rivers the Crows caught up with them. Then early in the morning, the Crow party stole all of their horses.[145] So the returning Astorians were forced to head out the next morning for Green River, South Pass, and the settlements *on foot*.

Despite being fed up with the mountains, Miller and the Returning Astorians were impressed with Bear River and declared it was "abundantly stocked with beaver of the largest and best quality they had ever seen."[146]

The next visitors to the river were British. They were men of the mighty North West Company from Canada. It was Englishmen who christened the stream with its present name. The North West Company had early been the chief British contender for this territory. Buying out Fort Astoria during the War of 1812, they succeeded in obtaining a seaboard base for their already far-flung operations. Then a bevy of great explorers from this company explored and mapped the Great Northwest while it was still the disputed territory of four

---

to gather this mineral at present Stump Creek. Russell, *Journal*, p. 12. This last stream received its name from Emil Stump, who along with William White, built a salt works in present Tigee. They hauled wagon loads of the stuff to Montana gold fields in the 1860's, selling it for as much as sixty cents per pound. Writers Project, W. P.A., *Wyoming, A Guide to Its History, Highways and People*, [New York, 1941] p. 396.

[145] For a description of the horse raid, see footnote #90. The section of Snake River flowing through Grand Canyon got the name "Mad River" from the overland Astorians who explored it from the Hoback to its rapids. They were disappointed in not being able to travel down it by boat. Irving, *Astoria*, Chapter 31. The site where the horses were stolen is presently under the man-made Palisades Lake. Perhaps near Edwards Creek.

[146] Rollins, *Oregon Trail*, p. 86.

nations. Alexander McKenzie had been "first by land," across the continent, six years before Lewis and Clark[147] A man with a similar name, Donald Mackenzie, took the first British brigades to Bear River in present Utah. The English called it "Snake Country" after the Indians who inhabited the area and who's tribal sign was a snake or serpentine motion of the hand. It may have stemmed from the in and out weaving of their grass shelters. One name of the Shoshone was, People-Who-Use-Grass-or-Bark-for-Their-Lodges. Snake River was part of Snake Indian country and was likely named for them also.[148]

Though he was now working for the British, Donald Mackenzie had been an Astorian. When Astoria fell to the British he joined the North West Company. Like Eteinne Provo and a few other fur traders, Mackenzie was fat. But he wasn't slothful. He brought energy and new ideas to the Nor'Westers. He didn't wait for Indians to bring furs to the post then ply them with trade goods. Instead, like the Americans would later do, Donald led brigades of his own men into the field trapping. And in 1818 he personally led a contingent of men to Bear River.

After Mackenzie, Michel Bourdon captained the Snake Country brigade in 1822.[149] The upper portions of Bear River were trapped twice by this contingent, but they were yet to see

---

[147] McKenzie was first to cross the continent north of Mexico.

[148] Or, it is possible the reverse is true, that the Indians were named for the river. History from non-written sources is speculative.

[149] Bourdon had been on the first Snake Country excursion with Donald Mackenzie in 1818-19. David E. Miller, ed., "Peter Skene Ogden's Journal of His Expedition to Utah, 1825," *Utah Historical Quarterly*, Vol. XX [April, 1952], p. 166. Donald Mackenzie wrote a letter from "Black Bear's Lake", September 10, 1819. Alexander Ross, *The Fur Hunters of the Far West*. Edited by Kenneth Spaulding [Norman: University of Oklahoma Press, 1956] p. 153.

the lower stretches of the stream. This information comes from Peter Skeen Ogden, a later Snake Country captain. William Kittson, Ogden's right-hand man, declares that the river received its name, "Bear River," from the great number of those animals on its borders."[150]

The Great Northwest at the time of Ashley's intrusion was jointly occupied by the United States and England. Following the War of 1812 and the abandonment of Astoria, the British became firmly entrenched and were reaping bountiful harvests of beaver skins. Not surprisingly, the English tried to take most of their furs from Snake Country—the region that might become part of the United States. Simpson, the factor at Fort Vancouver, made plans to *over trap* the Snake Country, thereby establishing a "fur desert" as a buffer zone between them and the Americans.[151] This, he believed, would discourage free enterprising American trappers from penetrating and also discourage pioneers from settling there. Unfortunately for his plan, Snake Country was so large and rich with beaver that it resisted over trapping. Also, American trappers under Ashley charged into the Snake country, lured away English hunters with better prices, and threatened to beat the British to every stream. Protocol and rules of fair play broke down in the mountains. The law of the wilderness was *might makes right*, and these rival parties on the same turf set the stage for conflict.

Potts and his fellows reached Bear River in the fall of 1824

---

[150] David E. Miller, ed., "William Kittson's Journal Covering Peter Skene Ogden's 1824-1825 Snake Country Expedition," *Utah Historical Quarterly*, Vol. XXII [April, 1954], p. 128.
[151] Snake Country was trapped by Donald Mackenzie from 1818 to 1821. Michel Bourdon evidently led the brigade in 1822, followed by Finan McDonald in 1823 and Alexander Ross in 1824. See Morgan, *Jedediah Smith*, pp. 115-125.

and began trapping. Daniel was impressed by the beaver rich streams and the beautiful scenery. This spot became his home in the mountains. His description of the course of Bear River does Potts credit as a keen observer of mountain geography.

> we fell on a considerable river, called Bear River, which rises to the S. in the Utaw Mountains, bears N. 80 or 90 miles, when it turns short to the S.W. and S. and after passing two mountains, discharges itself into the Great Salt Lake. On this river and its tributary streams, and the adjacent country, we have taken beaver with great success. Since the autumn of 1824, you have no doubt heard, and will hear by the public prints, of the furs brought in by Gen. Ashley, which were the product of our toils. The first valley as you approach from the head of the river, is a small sweet lake, about 120 miles in circumference, with beautiful clear water, and when the wind blows has a splendid appearance. There is also to be found in this valley a considerable sour spring near the most northerly swing of the river. The valley is scantily supplied with timber, as is the case with most of the low grounds of this country.[152]

The Weber party first encountered Bear River at the western Wyoming border. That fall they doubtless explored most of its course in present Idaho. A memorable feature was the *sour spring* which became famous in trapper and immigrant literature as "Soda and Beer Springs."[153] Later visitors declared the beverage to be as close an approximation to beer as could be found in the mountains.

When cold weather sealed over the streams with ice, the party sought a warmer place to winter. Having followed the

---

[152] *Potts Letter, to Robert Potts*, Rocky Mountains, 1826.
[153] Potts' description is the first mention of the famous Soda Springs that I have found.

river around its broad loop, they collected on Cub Creek near present Richmond, Utah, where they set up tents and shelters.[154] Early Mormon settlers report seeing old stumps and wood piles in this area.[155]

However, the winter months were not a period of idleness for the men. They fought, traded with the Indians, and explored.[156] While scouting the region they made an exciting discovery. The long-time legend of a salty inland sea was about to be confirmed.

Who Discovered Great Salt Lake?

Perhaps the earliest known hint of Great Salt Lake was given by Baron Lahontan, who pushed west from the upper Missouri in 1689. He came upon a band of Indians he calls Mozeemlek "who's principal river empties itself into a Salt Lake 300 leagues in circumference."[157] Almost a hundred years

---

[154] General Ashley was told by Provost in 1825 that Weber's band had wintered on the "South waters of the Columbia." Provo didn't know about the Great Basin–where the streams flowed inland–away from the ocean. The true courses of all the mountain streams were unknown at the time–except the Missouri. Leuis and Clark had followed it in 1803-06. See footnote #156 below.

[155] Alter, *Jim Bridger,* p. 58.

[156] The casualty reports indicate that "Thomas, a half-breed was killed by Williams." Letter from Smith, Jackson, and Sublette to General William Clark, published in Morgan, *Jedediah Smith,* pp. 337-343. The event no doubt gave Thomas's Fork of Bear River its name. Presently U.S. Highway 89 leads up Thomas's Fork from the Bear River-Great Basin drainage to the pass at the south end of Star Valley. Salt River drains this valley into the Snake and then the Columbia.

[157] Quoted from Dale Morgan, *The Great Salt Lake,* [Indianapolis: Bobbs Merrill Co., 1947], p. 44.

later the famous Dominquez-Escalante expedition made a near-miss of seeing the lake. In 1776 the party was seeking a land route from Santa Fe to Monterey. After coming as far as Utah Lake, they learned from the Indians that there was an "other lake with which this one is connected . . . [and] . . . its waters are noxious or extremely salty." If this Spanish party had pushed on another 30 miles they would have been the first white men to discover Great Salt Lake.[158]

After this near miss by the Dominguez- Escalante expedition coming from the south, for 47 years contingents of whites from the north also failed to see the lake. British and American parties did go as far as Bear River, but they failed to follow it one or two more days to Salt Lake.

In the fall of 1824 a party from Taos, New Mexico, nearly discovered the lake. Etienne Provost and one LeClerc led a band of beaver hunters to the Utah Lake area. Here this expedition came to an untimely dispersal after meeting a tribe of Snake Indians whose chief was known as "Bad Gocha," or bad left-handed one. This wily chief invited the intruders to smoke and council only after they laid aside anything made from metal. He professed it bad medicine to smoke the pipe with metal objects near. [Gocha knew what knives and guns were made from.] At any rate it was a ploy–once the council was in session and the calumet of peace was being passed, at a signal, the Indians rose up, whipped out knives concealed in their robes, and took to killing the whites. Provost was one of the few who escaped. The proximity of these whites to Salt Lake suggests they heard of the big lake to the north and

---

[158] Herbert E. Bolton, *Pageant in the Wilderness* [Salt Lake: Utah State Historical Society, 1950], p. 186.

perhaps saw it.[159] Provost's group weren't the only ones to *almost* discover Salt Lake in 1824.

This summer Peter Skeen Ogden was leading the first white men into Ogden's Hole. On May 5, Ogden wrote,

> . . . our Course this day was west over a fine Plain Covered with Buffaloes & thousands of Small Gulls the latter was a Strange Sight to us I presume some large body of Water near at hand at present unknown to us all.[160]

Ogden had guessed right but instead of following Bear River to the lake they turned left and trapped Logan River and Blacks Fork. So apparently, the first white man to see Great Salt Lake was one of Weber's band later this same year.

As the story goes, speculation arose among the men wintering on Cub Creek as to the course of Bear River. There were good reasons for speculation; the "San Buenaventura River," leading from the mountains to the Pacific Ocean, was a prominent but unconfirmed feature of early maps of the West. Also, the Indians had likely told them of an unusual salty lake to the south. So they speculated: Was it part of the salty ocean? Did Bear river flow to the ocean?

Whatever the questions, a bet was made to determine the course of Bear River and young Jim Bridger was chosen to take a trip down river and settle the affair. Jim's biographer claims that he made the trip because his prowess was at stake.[161] It had only been a season since Hugh Glass had turned up to cast reflection on Jim's courage and honor; perhaps he was

---

[159] This occurred either on Provo River or Jordan River. If on the latter, the party no doubt saw Great Salt Lake. Ferris, *Rocky Mountains*, pp. 308-309.

[160] *Ogdens's Snake Country Journals*, 1824-26. P.44.

[161] Alter, *Jim Bridger*, pp. 59-60.

attempting to reestablish himself. Whatever the case, from this time on, Jim Bridger's reputation as a mountaineer was not challenged. The report of his reputedly solitary trip comes from Robert Campbell, in a letter to G. K. Warren, United States Government Geographer. The letter was written in 1857 following a meeting of Campbell, Jim Bridger and Samuel Tullock.

> A party of beaver trappers who had ascended the Missouri with Henry and Ashley found themselves in pursuit of their occupation on Bear River in Cache [or Willow] Valley, where they wintered the winter of 1824 and 1825; and in discussing the course which Bear River ran, a bet was made between two of the party, and James Bridger was selected to follow the course of the river and determine the winner. This took him where the river passes through the mountain, and there he discovered the Great Salt Lake. He went to its margin and tasted the water, and on his return reported his discovery. The fact of the water being salt, induced the belief that it was an arm of the Pacific Ocean . . . .[162]

Thus, the great inland sea was effectively discovered and soon made its way onto maps of the West. It was a curiosity and a prominent landmark. After the myth that it was "an arm of the Pacific Ocean" was dispelled, it was called "Grand Lake." Daniel Potts seems to be first to call it "Great Salt Lake" in his letter of 1826.[163]

---

[162] G. K. Warren, "Warren's Memoir," *Pacific Railroad Reports*, XI, p. 35. Reprinted in Alter, *Jim Bridger*, pp. 59-60.

[163] Ashley calls it "grand lake or Buenaventura" in his Narrative of 1825. Morgan, *William Ashley*, p. 118, and "Grand Lake" in the *Missouri Advocate and St. Louis Enquirer*, March 11, 1826. Reprinted in Morgan, *Ibid.* pp. 140-141. It is called "Great Lake" in the *Missouri Herald and St. Louis Advertiser*, November 8, 1826. Reprinted in Morgan, *William Ashley*, pp. 153-154. Potts used the term "Great Salt Lake" three times

As earlier mentioned, Peter Skeen Ogden headed the British brigade in 1825. He was hand picked to lead the Snake Country operations and wipe out its beaver. It was pretty well understood by both British and Americans that when the Northwest was formally divided, lands south of the Columbia River would be American. So destroying Snake Country made sense on two counts. First, they might as well strip American streams of beaver first, and second, with its fur riches gone, Americans would be slower to settle it, thus making a buffer zone between the countries.

Snake Country captain, Peter Skeen Ogden

Ogden was well chosen. And though born in Quebec of loyalist parents he got his name on a valley and city in America–Ogden Utah. He was stout, tough, stubborn, smart, and it is said, could manhandle any two of his party at the same time. He also had a rambunctious sense of humor and was a good leader. His Hudson Bay bosses hoped he could whip the unruly métis in line. These mixed bloods traveled with the company but were often free trappers and were becoming more trouble every year. In Ogden's view, they were dishonest, unreliable, and lazy and for a price were prime for desertion.

---

and "Great Lake" once in his letter of 1826.

These part-Iroquois were led by "Old Pierre" Tivanitagon whose name is still on"Pierre's Hole," the beautiful valley west of Jackson Hole and the Tetons. Another leader was Ignace Hatchiorauquasha, who was understandably called John Grey, [You try to pronounce his Indian name!].

These men knew the other side of the story. The British were treating them unfairly. Generations of mixed blood métis had resulted from white trappers and their Indian brides. But the British treated them like serfs–they were kept in debt to the company and were payed little more than the Indians. Many of these mixed bloods were smart and proud. They may have been prideful of Indian heritage, but they were several generations from their Indian grandmothers, and more white than Indian. And they wanted white mans prices for their furs. Ogden was right, they *were* primed for desertion. [164]

But Ogden had even more challenges than his Iroquois Métis. The year previous, Jedediah Smith had chanced onto a party of Iroquois and métes marooned near Blackfoot River. They offered their furs for an escort back to camp. Jedediah happily obliged them and for good measure accompanied them and their leader, Alexander Ross, all the way back to Flathead Post on the Columbia. He was an unwanted guest, for it allowed Jed and his band to snoop on the British operations. In just a few weeks they picked up knowledge the British had spent years learning. Snake Country expeditions had made the British familiar with much of the geography of the Rockies–information that was sorely needed in the American camp. All this was accomplished in spite of Ross's explicit instructions "not to

---

[164] John Jackson, *Children of the Fur Trade, Forgotten Métes of the Pacific Northwest.* [Missoula,1996].

open up a road to the Americans."[165]

The English were well aware of the American threat to their business. Their answer was to have Ogden meet Ross's incoming brigade, re outfit it, then immediately take it back into the field with himself in command. And trap all the beaver in Snake Country.

Meanwhile the wily Jed Smith hung around the post while Ogden got the brigade fitted out then packed up and followed him back to Snake Country.[166] Peter Skeen Ogden and Jedediah Strong Smith were the best field captains of the trade during this decade. Maybe they learned from each other. Ogden was smart, focused, persistent and tough. Smith was just as smart and tough and was also fired by religion and free enterprise.

Ogden didn't know it yet, but in addition to his other challenges, he was about to crash head on into Americans more predatory than Jed Smith. Fortunately for our history, Ogden kept a journal, for no first hand American account has come forth. His diary is in Hudson Bay Co. Archives and records rivalry the Company didn't want. After succeeding the North West Company in 1821 their program was to continue existing policy of taking all the furs possible from *south* of the Columbia and destroying Snake Country. Through no fault of Ogden the plan was about to come apart. When his brigade reached Cub Creek, from Indian sources, Ogden received disturbing news.

> The Snakes . . . inform us that a party of 25 Americans wintered near this & are gone in the same direction we had

---

[165] The clash between British and American trappers is detailed in the next chapter.
[166] Jedediah Smith's winter among the British is recorded by his biographer. Morgan, *Jedediah Smith,* pp. 128-142.

intended going if this be true which I have no reason to doubt it will be a fatal blow to our expectations . . . .[167]

Ogden had been reluctant to have Jedediah Smith follow him to Snake Country–but he couldn't do anything about it. That still another American party [Weber-Potts and their pals] was in the Snake Country was a surprise to him–the year of 1825 was sizing up bad.

The direction of the rival hunters was not all Ogden learned–these intruders were already trading with the Indians. Four of this party of Snakes had recently acquired guns from the Americans.

these Indians had 4 Guns [Barnets] & altho' one had 1802 marked on the lock & another 1817 Still they were in good order & appeared as if they were taken out of the Store only a few days Since nor were they wanting in ammunition having procured it from the Americans.[168]

This reference to the famous "Northwest" gun is of considerable interest. The gun was also called a London Fusel,

---

[167] "Ogden's Journal," *Utah Historical Quarterly*, p. 171.

[168] The reason the guns had varying dates of manufacture is suggested by their scarcity in St. Louis. In a letter from Thomas Hempstead to Josiah Pilcher of the Missouri Fur Co. we learn: "I sold to Gen. Ashley all the Guns I brought down of the new ones with Dick's broken brich [breech] one I wished to keep those you had to have them fixed as you wished, but he would not take the others without them, and I thought it was best to make the best of a bad bargain and let them go at what B charged us, neither could they be fixed in time for us as, that expedition [Ashley-Henry] had evry blacksmith shop and Gunsmith in town employed." Reprinted in Morgan, *William Ashley*, p. 9. Ogden does not say the guns were purchased from the Americans, but this is obvious, for all four guns could hardly be in such "mint" condition if they had been traded by Indians from the British expedition the year before. Also, these Indians had just recently been among the Americans.

or Hudson Bay Fuke. It was a favorite with the Indians and was also used by many white trappers. Guns for Indian trade were of a particular type and the Barnet, made in London, became the prototype for all trade guns. It was first obtained by Hudson Bay Fur in 1821. Ogden would be expected to show interest in the fact that the Americans were also trading Barnets to the Indians and that the arms were like new, just out of storage.[169]It meant the Americans were busy gaining the alliance and trade of the Indians *with fresh trade goods*–far away from their home base in St. Louis. Since the Weber party had guns and ammunition sufficient to share with the Indians, it also indicates that Henry sent considerable goods over the mountains. Traders usually didn't exchange powder and weapons unless they had plenty.

---

[169] All trade guns were light in weight, often short of barrel and cheaply constructed. Commonly they were gauged to shoot a one ounce ball, .66 caliber or 16 gauge. Called a fuke, London fusil, or a Northwest Gun, the Barnet was of English make, and built especially for the American Northwest by a London firm. They were also called "Northwest guns." Barnet was a prominent name in guns for three hundred years. Hudson's Bay Company first purchased them in 1821. The North West Co., the Mackinaw Co., The American Fur Company, and the U.S. Indian Trade Office all distributed Barnet trade guns in the early 19th century. On March 21, of 1804 the Superintendent of the Indian Trade Office wrote to Thomas Waterman of Philadelphia and ordered 100 "real Northwest guns by Barnet or Katland." Carl R. Russell, *Guns in the Early Frontiers*, [Los Angeles: University of California Press, 1957], p. 112.

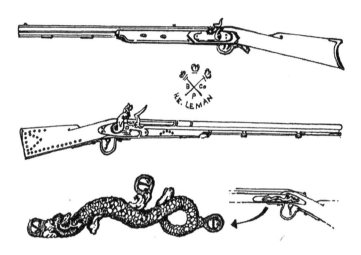

Top, Hawken type rifle.
Bottom, inexpensive trade musket with
serpentine and brass tack decorations.

Peter Ogden lamented the fact that the Americans were
trapping down Bear River ahead of him. The smaller creeks had
been frozen over in the early spring forcing Weber's men to
trap along the immediate vicinity of the Bear. On the 8th of
May, Ogden indicates considerable vexation:

> but few traps in the Water the Americans have taken nearly
> all the Beaver they are a Selfish Set they leave nothing for
> their Friends we act differently.[170]

In light of Peter's errand to destroy all the furry creatures
in Snake Country this statement is hypocritical. But for Peter
Skeen Ogden, the worst was yet to come.

---

[170] "Ogden's Journal," *Utah Historical Quarterly*, p. 173.

Gardner and Grey for America and the M'etis

It was no small point of pride that America had beaten the mighty British in the Revolution. Patriotism was trumpeted by all classes of Americans. They believed it was their destiny and duty to move west to the Pacific and fill up the country; democratic institutions held out a glorious future for the young nation. And patriotic feeling was not lacking on the frontier. Political speeches were given and toasts drunk at any suitable occasion in the mountains. And a suitable occasion might arise whenever there was liquid for the toast. The fur frontier felt a special keenness in promoting Americanism. It was here that partisans of either side, in the War of 1812, met to contend ownership of the Northwest.

A Conference following the Treaty of Ghent had provided that the territory be jointly occupied by the United States and England for twenty years. This didn't solve anything and only shoved the decision ahead to a later date. It left the region free game for anyone. As a consequence of being thousands of miles from the frontiers the skin hunters felt little need to be fussy about legal restraints, laws were unenforceable, and the wealth of the country was up for grabs. So when the American Johnson Gardner bumped into some of Ogden's dissatisfied M'etis or Iroquois and learned they had collected a pile of furs for Hudson Bay Company, he intervened and pointed out some virtues of free enterprise. The story comes from the victim, Peter Skeen Ogden.

Ogden wrote that on Sunday, the 22nd of May, one of his trappers came into camp accompanied by two freemen. The latter had deserted Hudson Bay Company at Flathead Post in 1822. Since then they had been members of "a party of 30 men who were fitted out by the Spaniards & Traders on the Missouri . . . ." They had spent the winter in the Utah area attached to

Etienne Provost's party that was mostly wiped out by a wily band of Shoshonis. When Ogden asked about geography to the south, they said "it was only fifteen days' march to Taos in New Mexico." That seemed pretty close to Mexico–he was far south of British lands. But he was more concerned with competition than geography. The number of Americans in the area was alarming. There were three separate parties who were momentarily unaware of each other's presence. At least two of the groups had joined by Monday.[171] Both came calling at Ogden's camp.

John Grey
Father Nicholas Point, Courtesy Historical Photograph Collections,
Washington State University Libraries.

---

[171] Ibid., pp. 179-181.

First, Provost and his band "from the Spanish settlements" ambled in.[172] This meeting went well enough, but the Americans who came in the afternoon were another story. They were assertive and predatory. Peter had been assigned the Snake Country Brigade to keep the independent Iroquois and M'etis in line. He was smart and tough, but when this second band led

YOUNGER BRIDES WERE COMMON

John Grey's Wife
Father Nicholas Point, Courtesy Historical Photograph Collections,
Washington State University Libraries.

by the pugnacious Johnson Gardner burst into his camp, he was surprised, unprepared, and unable to stanch the flow of his dissatisfied men to the Americans. The historic clash of the American and British parties took place at Ogden's camp at the site of present Mountain Green, Utah.

Johnson had already teamed up with Ogden's Iroquois. John Grey, a M'etis of mixed blood and a leader of the Iroquois was *eager* to quit the British. Led by Gray, the Iroquois were

---

[172] Ibid., p. 181.

shopping for better prices. Hudson Bay Company had a monopoly and controlled both the price of goods they sold and furs they bought. Also, the M'etes couldn't have been unaware that free enterprise offered American trappers a chance to accumulate wealth. So the argument was pretty simple; "If the Americans will pay more for our furs, why not take it?" And the Americans *were* offering more! They boasted of giving $3.50 a pound for fur! [$5.00 per skin]. This was *eight times* more than the British were paying! And compared to British prices, American trade goods were cheap.

With Grey leading out, twenty three valuable British hunters went over to the American side. A sketch of Gray by Father Nicholas Point shows him looking more white than Indian. But though he looked like a Europian, he represented the M'etis, the trappers in the middle who's ancestry came from both sides.[173] A large portion of trappers were "children of mixed blood," or M'etis. In fact, French-Canadian trappers had been working the American streams from the earliest years. And French-Canadian was just another name for M'etis. They often had either French or English names because their Indian names were so formidable. For example, John Grey's Indian

---

[173] The first generation of hunters moved to the wilderness and took native wives. Their sons and grandsons often continued in the trade. See John C. Jackson, *Children of the Fur Trade*, [Missoula Montana, 1996]. John Gray was a decendent of William Gray who at seven years of age was captured in New England by Mohawks. Growing up with the tribe, he chose to stay with them and later became a chief. Thus John Gray was a M'etis or a mixed blood. He played a roll between the races during a large part of the fur trade as either a diplomat, skilled grizzly bear hunter or scoundrel, depending on the self interest and point of view of the observer. Gray's River, Gray's Lake, and Gray's Hole attest to his presence in the Rocky Mountains. Interestingly, Peter Ogden, the victim of this clash who lost his M'etis trappers and their furs, had a M'etis wife. Her name was Julia Tete Plate.

name was the tongue wrenching *Ignace Hatchiorauquasha*. Grey's influence in mountain history is witnessed by his name on Greys River, Greys Lake and Greys Hole.

But the deserting Métis or Iroquois posed a problem–how were they going to get their furs from Ogden's packs?[174] They decided on the direct approach and Johnson Gardner took the lead.

Spearheaded with an American flag, and motivated by patriotism, Manifest Destiny, and self interest, Gardner headed up a procession of American and Iroquois trappers and marched into the surprised Ogden's camp.[175] Twenty-five Americans and their Iroquois friends confronted Ogden "with colors flying" on the afternoon of May 23. They dismounted and assertively set up their own camp only 100 yards from the British. Then, losing no time, they promptly charged that the English were intruders on American soil. A first-hand account comes from the victim–Ogden.

> Monday 23rd. Remd. in Camp in expectation of the arrival of our absent party, early in the day a party of 15 men Canadians & Spaniards headed by one Provost & Francois one of our deserters, arrived, and also in the afternoon arrived in Company with 14 of our absent men a party of 25 Americans with Colours flying the latter party headed by one Gardner they encamped within 100 yards of our encampment & lost no time in informing all hands in Camp that they were in the United States Territories & were all free [whether] endebted or engaged & to add to this they

---

[174] The Iroquois respected Ogden as a leader and a man to be reckoned with, likely some had removed their furs the night previous to this confrontation. *Ibid.*, p. 183.

[175] Manifest Destiny was the concept that it was the destiny of the American nation to spread west and fill the continent. It was commonly believed by Americans of the time.

would pay Cash for their Beaver 3 ½ dollers p. lb., their goods cheap in proportion our Freemen in lieu of Seeking Beaver have been with the Americans no doubt plotting.[176]

After posting a "strikt watch," Ogden retired for the evening and slept poorly, exasperated at the Americans and his disloyal Iroquois. Morning came. As the sun rose Gardner again came calling at the British camp.

> This morning Gardner came to my Tent & after a few words of no import, he questioned me as follows Do you know in whose Country you are? to which I made answer that I did not as it was not determined between Great Britain & America to whom it belonged to which he made answer that it was that it had been ceded to the latter & as I had no license to trap or trade to return from whence I came to this I made answer, when we receive orders from the British Government we Shall obey, then he replied remain at your peril, he then departed & seeing him go into John Grey an American & half Iroquois Tent of one of my Freemen I followed him, on entering this Villain Grey said I must now tell you that all the Iroquois as well as myself have long wished for an opportunity to join the Americans & if we did not Sooner it was owing to our bad luck in not meeting them . . . he then gave orders to his Partners to raise Camp & immediately all the Iroquois were in motion & made ready to Start this example was Soon followed by others at this time the Americans headed by Gardner & accompanied by two of our Iroquois who had been with them the last two years advanced to Support & assist all who were inclined to desert.[177]

---

[176] Ogdens Journal, p. 181. According to Kittson, Ogden's clerk, the Americans were under "different heads," "bearing flags." This might indicate that parts of both Smith's and Weber's men were present. "Kittson's Journal," *Utah Historical Quarterly*, p. 137.

[177] *Ibid.*

With this success the Americans and villain Iroquois grew even bolder.

For Ogden and Hudson Bay Fur all this was an abrupt turn of fortune. What had been exclusive British trapping grounds yielding a fortune in furs was now infested with interlopers. But foolishly, he remained one more day in the area. On Wednesday, the 25th, two more men deserted and "they were immediately Surrounded by the Americans who assisted them in loading & like all Villains appeared to exult in their Villany . . . ."[178]

It was the last straw, Ogden ordered his remaining men to pack up and move camp. But as he swung onto his horse, Gardner accosted him one more time and pressed the issue home.

> Gardner Came forward & Said you will See us shortly not only in the Columbia but at the Flat Heads & Cootanies we are determined you Shall no longer remain in our Territory . . . our Troops will make you leave this Fall . . . .[179]

It is ironic that neither party was in the right. Both were interlopers on *Spanish* soil since the encounter occurred below the 42nd parallel. Gardner, with numbers on his side seized the opportunity, tempted the British trappers with higher prices and won them over. He also won their furs which ended up with Ashley. Though Peter Ogden claimed otherwise, most of these

---

[178] *I bid., p. 184.*

[179] *Ibid.* If it were not for Ogden these incidents would not be known. It is surprising that the Americans [including Potts], didn't exult more for the record.

hunters never returned to British service. The British were treated to a dish of Manifest Destiny, served up in Mountain Man style.[180]

The Rendezvous of 1825

After losing out in a bid for the governorship, General Ashley decided to go to the mountains with his caravan of supplies. With Henry quitting and the bankrupt state of the company, a "violent effort" was needed to recoup the enterprise and pay off his creditors. So he determined to take personal command and left the Missouri on November third. Ashley was yet unaware of the pleasing news that his men had collected bales of fur–much of it at the expense of the British. Leading the caravan on essentially the same route later made famous by the Mormons, he arrived on Green River, April 19, 1825.[181]

---

[180] It is surprisingly difficult to establish the identity of any American participants in this incident other than Gardner. Daniel Potts, the only writing trapper we know of in Weber's band, is silent on the entire affair. However no letter from Potts has surfaced for 1825.

Since there were "25 odd men," it might have been the entire Weber outfit. Though there is no mention of Jedediah Smith being present, either he or some of his party were there, for Ogden later relates: "I have already observed it was an unfortunate day Mr. Ross consented to allow the 7 Americans to accompany him to the Flatheads, *for it was these fellows that guided and accompanied them to our Camp.*" *Ibid.*, p. 181. My italics. See footnote #176, p.128.

If a letter from Potts is ever found dated from 1825 the event will doubtless be chronicled. His only statement concerning the period is, "On this river, [Bear] and its tributary streams, and adjacent country, we have taken beaver with great success," [Potts didn't mention that they had "taken" some of the beaver not from the streams but from Hudson Bay Fur].

[181] Ashley's Diary in Morgan, *William Ashley*, p. 106.

This country west of the mountains was just being explored by the Americans. It was heady times; they were making early maps on the edge of the unknown. Ashley threw himself into organizing his men for trapping *and* exploration. He was particularly curious about the course of Green River. So he immediately divided his men into four groups: Clyman was to hunt the upper Green, Fitzpatrick would go south, and Ham west. Ashley himself would go down the Green. Before separating, Ashley made preparations for the first certain mountain trade fair, the Rendezvous of 1825. He declared: "The Place of deposit . . . the cache of goods will be the place of randavoze [sic.] for all our parties on or before the 10th of July next . . . ."[182]

Since Ham was headed west, he was told to find Weber's men. The General charged him "to fall in with the two parties of men that were fitted out by me in the year previous, and who were then as I supposed beyond the Range of Mountains appearing westerly."[183]Ashley hoped to get all the parties together and exchange his supply goods for their furs.

Zacharias Hamm likely went up the canyon named for him [Hamm's Fork] and led his party down onto Bear River. Almost immediately they bumped into Weber's men.[184] It was a happy event for the skin hunters. Hamm told them Ashley was just

---

[182] *Ibid.*, p. 106.

[183] Ashley Narrative, H. C. Dale. *The Ashley-Smith Explorations, and the Discovery of the Central Route to the Pacific* [Cleveland, 1918], pp. 136-137.

[184] Ham had separated from Ashley on April 22 on Green River. On June 7, Ashley learned from Provost that: "Mr. Weber had wintered on the south Waters of the Columbia River and had heard of my being in the Country that he had gone over to the green river in serch of me-" Morgan, *William Ashley*, p. 116. This indicates Weber was the leader of Potts's group.

over the mountains with new supplies and maybe for some, he had letters from home. New trade goods, letters from home, and a good time with your friends, what more could you ask for? Each trapper would be imagining his buy list. "With some of these beaver skins I can buy a pile of Indian gewgaws, get a new knife, and replace the rifle I lost crossing Bear River ."[185] Beaver skins were the medium of exchange and spent the same as money.

The Rendezvous of 1825 has been considered the first mountain trade fair. The pattern was started in 1824 when the party of Weber, Potts, and Bridger met Henry and exchanged their furs for goods. After Ashley met his men on the Seedskeeder in 1825 its advantages were readily apparent and the tradition was firmly in place. The men looked forward to these great summer parties where men of every caste joined to squander a year's earnings. And the traders exchanged goods for valuable fur–the prize that kept the whole affair going.

The trappers first interest was to have a good time with friends. Hopefully, after the fun, there would still be some "hairy bank notes," left to buy tools for the next season. Gambling, gaming, drinking, and chasing after Indian squaws became features of the rendezvous system. However, drinking was absent in 1825. Ashley had forgotten to bring along any whiskey.

Ashley reported there were 120 men who gathered to

---

[185] Despite their value, it seems a lot of guns were lost. A rock-incrusted trade rifle in the Teton National Park historical museum at Moose Wyoming was found in the Grosventre River and x-rays show it loaded and ready to fire. The author found a double barreled percussion gun in Salt River, and a single barreled percussion near Snake River. J. B.

rendezvous on Henry's Fork of the Green.[186] Beckwourth, a mulatto who accompanied the General, telescoped the figure in his description:

> . . . he [Ashley] opened his goods and there was a general jubilee among all at the rendezvous. We constituted quite a little town, numbering at least eight hundred souls, of whom one half were women and children . . . all kinds of sports were indulged in with a heartiness that would astonish more civilized societies.[187]

Allowance must ever be made for Beckwourth's estimates. He was one of the fanciest spinners of yarns in the mountains. Sometimes his tales seem close to the truth but are shuffled into the wrong years. His memoirs were published, thus achieving for him immortality as a fur trade chronicler. While describing the Rendezvous, Beckwourth makes a rare mention of the Weber–Daniel Potts–Jim Bridger men,

> The General transacted a very profitable trade with our salt lake friends. He purchased all their beaver, of which they had collected a large quantity . . . .[188]

---

[186] The actual site of the Rendezvous has never been definitely determined. It was 20 miles from where originally designated. There are two possibilities: one being 20 miles up Green River, the other 20 miles up Henry's fork from Green River. This would be the natural choice, being much better supplied with grass and timber. Dale Morgan breaks down the 120 men into: 29 deserters from Hudson Bay Fur, 13 men with Etienne Provost, 7 trappers with Jedediah Smith's , 25 men in Ashley's caravan, 25-30 trappers with John Weber and 16-21 men unaccounted for–possibly free trappers under Gardner. See Morgan, *William Ashley*, note 208, p. 288.

[187] T. D. Bonner, ed., *The Life and Adventures of James P. Beckwourth*,Introductio and notes by Delmont Oswald. [Lincoln, University of Nebraska Press, 1981], p. 75.

[188] *Ibid.*

Ashley's ledger of 1825 sheds considerable light on the year's fur operations.[189] It also invokes questions. The transactions of Jedediah Smith, Johnson Gardner, William Sublette, "Old Pierre" Tivingtagtoten, [his Iroquois name isn't quite as tongue wrenching as John Grey's] and many others are listed but there is no name that directly refers to Weber's party. Daniel Potts, Jim Bridger, and John Weber himself are absent from the record. One stray figure of 3,100 pelts is considered by some to be the total furs of this contingent, but the full story will never be known until more of Ashley's account books are found.[190] Of the 120 men present, only thirty-seven are entered into the book. Using the figure of 3,100, the party of twenty-five would average 124 beavers each, making about $620.00. Actually, as in all walks of life, there was considerable difference in the productivity of trappers—and their ability to accumulate money. Some were more skilled and motivate, and less inclined to blow their year's earnings at the Rendezvous. It is doubtful, however, that Daniel Potts made the twelve hundred dollars he had hoped for in 1824.[191]

Following the business and fun, Ashley had men press the furs into compact bales and pack them on the horses. Beckwourth, our primary source for the Rendezvous, gives the details.

---

[189] Morgan, *William Ashley*, pp. 118-129.

[190] *Ibid.* Though the 3,100 pelt figure may be correct for the Weber party, there still must be more of Ashley's ledger that is lost. It is unlikely that he didn't trade with this party and record the transactions as he did with the others. Possibly Weber's men still had considerable of Henry's goods from 1824.

[191] Beaver averaged about 31 skins, and 52 pounds to the pack, or 1 2/3 pounds per skin. At $3.00 per pound, Ashley bought skins from the free trappers at $5.00 each. Morgan, *William Ashley*, p. 295. According to Ogden, Johnson Gardner offered $3.50 per pound to the British deserters. See footnote #176.

In about a week the general was ready to start for home. The packs were all arranged: our Salt Lake friends offered him the loan of all the horses he wanted, and engaged to escort him to the head of Wind River, one of the branches of the Yellow Stone. The number selected to return with the general was twenty men, including my humble self; thirty men were to accompany as a guard, and to return the horses we had borrowed.[192]

Daniel Potts, with some of his "Salt Lake friends," helped pack the horses then escorted "the humble Beckwourth," and Ashley over the Continental Divide. In spite of the mid-July date, the crossing was *cold*. Daniel remembers that "the ice froze near half an inch in a kettle."[193] His party escorted the General to a navigable point on the Big Horn, unpacked the horses, and returned with them to Bear River for the fall hunt.

A new star began his rise in the fur brigades this fall. William Sublette, who had previously been of Jedediah Smith's party, was chosen to lead the pack horses back to Bear River.[194] From this date, Sublette assumes ever increasing leadership among the brigades. Smart, ambitious, and long-legged, he made more money than any of the young men hired by Ashley and Henry. And when the occasion demanded it he walked all the way from the mountains to St. Louis. There will be more about this trek later.

Jedediah Smith had been chosen as Ashley's partner to replace Andrew Henry. He would direct operations in the mountains, while from St. Louis, the General would take care

---

[192] Bonner, *James Beckwourth*, p. 48.

[193] *Potts's Letter to Robert Potts*, 1826. Daniel and his cohorts knew the route and just backtracked their trip of the year before.

[194] John E. Sunder, *Bill Sublette, Mountain Man* [Norman: University of Oklahoma Press, 1959], pp. 60-61.

of the business end of the company. Likely Smith recognized the talents of Sublette, and tabbed him for assistance and leadership. Within a year, along with David Jackson, these two would be partners and sole "traders" to the Mountain Men. No record exists of John Weber's reaction to these developments, but from 1826 Sublette seems to be in command of the ex-sea captain's party.

Returning from Wind and Green River country the men commenced the fall hunt on Bear River, "its tributary streams, and the adjacent country."[195] Sometime this fall they were raided by Snake Indians. Peter Ogden recorded that thirteen men were killed, 180 traps were stolen and "guns, knives and other articles in proportion."[196] It was a hard life. The hostile natives kept them hopping.

When the streams froze they gathered in Cache, or Willow Valley which Potts called their "chief place of rendezvous and wintering ground."[197] These names for the valley were used interchangeably during the early years, but the first is more meaningful to the fur trade, and survives today[198]

The winter being more cold than usual, the parties decided

---

[195] *Potts's Letter, to Robert Potts,* 1826. This itinerary is sweeping enough to include Green River or streams of the Snake River drainage. Dale Morgan speculates that the party returning up Wind River may have continued west, [over Togwattee or Union Pass] dropped down into Jackson's Hole, discovering it for themselves and giving the "hole" or valley it's name. Morgan, *William Ashley,* p. 146.

[196] *Ogden's Journal,* pp. 173.179-180.

[197] *Potts Letter to Robert Potts, Rocky Mountains,* 1826.

[198] *Ibid.* Mountain men would dig a bottle shaped pit in dry ground and "cache"or bury supplies or furs for retrieval later.Each season they doubtless "cached" their stuff in Cache Valley. French words attest to the influence of the M'etis.

to move their camp down to Great Salt Lake Valley.[199] Two camps were set up—one at the mouth of the Bear and the other on the Weber. Potts and his captain were presumably on the latter. The winter months were made lively by a horse robbery conducted by Bannocks. According to Jim Beckwourth, eighty of their mounts were spirited away. After participating in a foray of retribution, Jim relates returning to camp and finding the place surrounded by a village of two thousand five hundred warriors, of the Snake tribe, who were "perfectly friendly" having recently made peace with the Americans.

From the same source we learn that the trappers numbered seven hundred "with wives and children."[200] If this number is correct, there was polygamy in Utah before the Mormons. According to British reports, there were only one hundred Americans in Snake country.[201]

Circumnavigating Great Salt Lake

With the opening of the spring hunt, the two encampments on Weber and Bear Rivers split into smaller brigades to work as many streams as possible. An intensive plan was initiated both to trap *and explore* the Rocky Mountains. Daniel does not mention which area he hunted, but from intimations in his letter of 1826, it was somewhere in northern Utah. He was thoroughly familiar with this region, and wrote even more detailed reports of the lands adjacent to Great Salt Lake. It was all new country, and he learned as much about it as he could.

---

[199] *San Francisco Bulletin*, October 29, 1858, p. 2, col. 3.

[200] Bonner, *James Beckwourth*, pp. 60-61.

[201] Letter of George Simpson to the Hudson's Bay Company. Reprinted in Morgan, *William Ashley*, p. 305.

Four men, likely in Sublette's contingent, were detached for an unusual mission. Following its discovery by Jim Bridger, Great Salt Lake had occupied a high place on the trapper's list of things to see. This spring, most of the men would have had this opportunity, but a more careful examination was needed. In the trapper's minds, there was still a possibility that it might be an arm of the sea, or at least be connected to the ocean by the fabled "Buenaventura River." After all, *it was salty*! But a reconnaissance of the lake was needed to settle the issue. So four men were chosen to paddle around it in a "skin boat." They were to look for the mouth of the Buenaventura River and see if this salty lake was connected to the salty Pacific Ocean. It was the first time that white men launched a boat on this inland sea.

As with other sensational western events, time has generated more candidates for this episode than the patchy record allows. Mountain trappers were not known for telling the truth, and succeeding years added to their achievements. "The older they got the better they were."

However, from various histories, the following four men may have been on the trip: James Clyman, Moses "Black" Harris, Henry Fraeb, and Louis Vasquez. Judging from his excellent report of the west side of the lake, Daniel Potts, is another possibility.

No matter which men made the "coasting," at least there is general agreement on what they saw. The narrative of this voyage, included in many sources, said: they coasted the lake, suffered greatly from thirst on the western side, and found no outlet. In spite of this latter report, Ashley clung to the old hope of a Buenaventura River in his report of Salt Lake. He reported, "they did not exactly ascertain its outlet, but passed a place where they supposed it must have been."[202]

Daniel does not claim to be one of the four, but his graphic and detailed description of the inaccessible shores of the lake makes you wonder if he skipped that detail.[203]

> The G. S. Lake lies in a circular form from N. E. to N. W. the larger circle being to the S. It is about 400 miles in circumference, and has no discharge or outlet, it is generally shallow near the beach, and has several islands, which rise like pyramyds from its surface. The western part of the lake is so saturated with salt, as not to desolve any more when thrown into it. The country on S.W. and N.W. is very barren, bearing but little more than wild sage and short grass. The S.E. and E. are fertile, especially near the outlet of the Utaw Lake and Weber's river. The former is about 30 yards wide at its mouth, the latter from 50 to 60, and very deep.[204]

Potts was completely familiar with the geography of Utah Lake and its large salty sister to the north. Much of this detail could only be learned from first-hand experience.[205]

Following the spring hunt and reconnaissance of the lakes, Daniel returned to Cache Valley for the annual trade fair.

---

[202] *Alexandria Gazette*, Alexandria, Virginia, Thursday, December 28, 1826. Reprinted in Frost, *Notes*, pp. 137- 138.

[203] Frost, *Notes*, p. 44

[204] *Potts Letter to Robert Potts*, Rocky Mountains, 1826. Potts writes that lands southeast and east of the lake are fertile. This is where the Mormons settled and made "blossom as a rose." It is now Salt Lake City.

[205] If Daniel was a member of the "coasting" party, he missed a footnote in history by not saying so.

The Moving Rendezvous of 1826

General Ashley came to the mountains for the last time in the spring of 1826. The original plan was for Jedediah Smith to deliver the supplies. He left St. louis November 1, 1825 with $20,000 worth of trade goods. However, Smith got snowed in on the Republican Fork and needed more mules. After getting word of their plight, Ashley secured additional mounts and caught up with them April 1, at Grand Island. Before entering the Great Basin, the General dispatched Smith and "Black" Harris to make contact with the trappers. The trade goods and horses took precedence so everyone walked except Ashley. The trip was hard on his men. They had nearly starved back on the Missouri River before finding buffalo at the head of Grand Island. A fair amount of them–25 or 30–deserted. Also they took a new route in 1826. They took the north branch of the Platte to present Casper Wyoming, then followed the Sweet water to South Pass and over to Green River. A newcomer was with them–Robert Campbell. He was a man of talents who clerked, kept records and soon gained stature among the fur brigades. He remembered that Ashley,

> sent off Smith and Harris to the Trappers in the Mountains, to arrange in advance for a rendezvous, which was about twenty miles North of Salt Lake in Utah, called Cache or Willow Valley at Haines [Ham's] Fork, near [the future] Fort Bridger, the Trappers came out to meet us. There were about from 60 to 75 of them. We were also joined by fifteen lodges of Iroquois, who had left the Hudson Bay Company, and joined Ashley at Cache or Willow Valley. They had met Ashley the year before, where they had made a satisfactory traffic of their peltries with him. They

brought in plenty of Beavers . . . .[206]

So from Campbell we learn that 60 or 75 men met Ashley at Hamm's Fork. Also, fifteen lodges of M'etis or Iroquios hooked on. These were the same that had deserted Hudson Bay Co. the year previous–still perhaps led by John Grey. Then they proceeded to Cache Valley and arrived about May 25. Jim Beckwourth vividly remembered Ashley's entrance into the valley:

---

[206] Campbell Narrative, quoted in Morgan, *William Ashley*, p. 145.
Varying and secondary sources have made the site of the 1826
Rendezvous conjectural. Newspaper accounts credited to Ashley indicate
that at least some of his caravan reached Great Salt Lake. These accounts
say Ashley "went to the station of the party which he had left beyond the
mountains, . . . thence descended a river, believed to be the
Buenaventura, [actually Bear River] about one hundred and fifty miles to
the Great Lake." The same source speaks of "The lake which terminated
the expedition westward, . . . " *Alexandria Gazette*, December 28, 1826.
See Frost, *Notes*, pp. 137-138. Also in Morgan, *William Ashley*, p. 153.
The caravan evidently arrived in Cache Valley around May 25, and
according to Campbell the trading lasted two weeks. This would
presumably end the Rendezvous at the early date of June 8. "We
remained in Cache Valley two weeks, long enough to complete the traffic
with the trappers." [Campbell narrative] p. 145, [this sounds like the
trading occurred in Cache Valley]. Yet, the change of partnership
occurred on July 18, Morgan, *William Ashley*, p. 150. Also, Daniel Potts's
letter was dated July 16, 1826. With about a month and a half in northern
Utah, Ashley and his men could have held the initial trading in Cache
Valley and then descended to Great Salt Lake. The celebrating and other
typical Rendezvous antics may have happened intermittently and in
varying spots during the entire period. Beckwourth indicates frivolity
when the goods were opened. Daniel Potts tells of some fancy eating,
political toasts, and gun salutes on the 4th of July. *Potts Letter*, 1826.
Perhaps there was another celebration on July 18 when the change in
partnership was signed and when Ashley prepared to leave. Beckwourth
indicates this on pp. 73-74. These three occurrences of mountain joviality
all happened in different areas of northern Utah.

The absent parties began to arrive, one after another, at the rendezvous. Shortly after, General Ashley . . . came in, accompanied with three hundred pack mules, well laden with goods and all things necessary for the mountaineers and the Indian trade.[207]

Jim was always the best chronicler of lighter moments in the mountains, he continues his narrative of the fun:

It may well be supposed that the arrival of such a vast amount of luxuries from the East did not pass off without a general celebration. Mirth, songs, dancing, shouting, trading, running, jumping, singing, racing, target-shooting, yearns, frolic, with all sorts of extravagances that white men or Indians could invent, were freely indulged in. The unpacking of the medicine water contributed not a little to the heightening of our festivities.[208]

From the closing sentence we learn that Ashley had not repeated the oversight of the year before when he forgot to bring medicine water. From this year on, "spirits," became increasingly more important at the trade fairs. Straight grain alcohol was purchased in St. Louis, packed into the mountains in small kegs, and repeatedly diluted with water as the trappers and Indians became more drunk. Molasses, hot pepper, and tobacco might be added to give it flavor and satisfy consumers who had been used to a more distinctive liquor. Depending upon the drinker, the concoction either mellowed or enlivened

---

[207] Bonner, *James Beckwourth*, p. 70.
[208] *Ibid.*

men at the Rendezvous. There is no doubt that it encouraged trade and enhanced profits. At $30.00 a gallon the trappers still bought it.[209]

After about two weeks of trading the party moved toward Great Salt Lake–which terminated the expedition westward.[210] Once he had packed his newly-traded furs to St. Louis Ashley would be a wealthy man. He preferred life in the city and could now afford to leave the risks of the mountains to others. Consequently, while traveling down Bear River he was forming a plan to sell out.

Trading was over by mid June but a Rendezvous was much more than trading. They celebrated Independence Day about three weeks later, likely on Bear River, and may have proceeded to Great Salt Lake. Daniel reported that,

> We celebrated the 4th of July, by firing three rounds of small arms, and partook of a most excellent dinner, after which a number of political toasts were drunk.[211]

Ashley, by audacious effort and a turn in his luck, had succeeded in extricating himself from the debt of four seasons with the fur proceeds of 1825.[212] This year he loaded out 123 packs of beaver and made his fortune.[213]

But he was the Lieutenant Governor of Missouri and

---

[209] Cushing Ells gives $30.00 per gallon as the price in 1837. That would be about a month's work for a laborer in the settlements.

[210] *Missouri Herald and St Louis Advertiser*, November, 1826.

[211] *Daniel Potts Letter to Robert Potts,* 1826.

[212] The furs obtained from the British when Johnson Gardner by "hook and crook" persuaded John Grey and the Iroquois to desert were a major windfall to Ashley. Greys River, and Greys Lake are place names stemming from John Grey who led the defection. Morgan writes that Ashley took out near $50,000 in fur in 1825. *Jedediah Smith*. P. 172.

[213] Morgan, *Jedediah Smith*, p. 412.

preferred politics to tramping around the Rocky Mountains. By selling now he could keep a finger in the business with less risk. He rightly assumed that he could make a profit on the fur trade and remain in St. Louis. With his famous credit and newly gained wealth he could be the *middle man* and supply goods to the trappers. Moreover, he would get a handsome price for the mountain trading business–the annual Rendezvous trade.

So while Daniel was gathering his notes and composing a remarkable detailed letter to be carried back with the furs, Ashley and three subordinates–Jedediah Smith, David Jackson, and William Sublette–were working out a deal. Smith had been a partner with Ashley since the previous summer.[214] An agreement including the two new men was struck somewhere on Bear River.[215]

The main points were that the new partners would become the "traders" at the Rendezvous, and would buy their goods from Ashley. Until they had paid off his note, the General intended to keep a steady hand in the profits of the trade. They would send an express to St. Louis by March 1, of 1827 with an

---

[214] The best history of Jedediah Smith is Dale Morgan, *Jedediah Smith and the Opening of the West*, [Lincoln Neb., 1953]. Morgan is an authority on this period of the fur trade. William Sublette's biographer is John Sunder, *Bill Sublette, Mountain Man*.[Norman Oklahoma, 1959]. David Jackson is a shadow. His name still stands on the beautiful valley east of the Tetons in Wyoming. And his brigade always seemed to bring in the most fur. He kept the partnership profitable while Jed Smith was running all around the West. But what is known of Jackson is mostly scratched out from the history of others who were thought to be with him. Recently Vivian L. Talbot gathered all the available Jackson information in a fine publication, *David E. Jackson, Field Captain of the Rocky Mountain Fur Trade*, [Jackson, Wyoming, Jackson Hole Historical Society and Museum, 1996].
[215] Campbell Narrative, reprinted in Morgan, *William Ashley*, p. 145.

order for goods.[216] Part of the Rendezvous entourage may have been following the leaders and witnessed the agreement.

Beckwourth, the ever questionable historian, reports the closing moments that Ashley spent among his trappers:

> General Ashley, having disposed of all his goods and completed his final arrangements, departed for St. Louis, taking with him nearly two hundred packs of beaver. Previous to his departure, he summoned all the men into his presence, and addressed them, as nearly as I can recollect, in the following words: Mountaineers and friends! When I first came to the mountains, I came a poor man, You by your indefatigable exertions, toils, and privations, have procured me an independent fortune. With ordinary prudence in the management of what I have accumulated, I shall never want for anything. For this, my friends, I feel myself under great obligations to you . . . .I wish you to accept my thanks: the gratitude that I express to you springs from my heart, and will ever retain a lively hold of my feelings.[217]

This tale by Jim may be what the mulatto *thought* Ashley should say in thanking the men who made him wealthy. Ashley wasn't known for giving speeches. Beckwourth adds that Ashley, "left the camp amid deafening cheers from the whole crowd."

Daniel Potts, though interested in the above proceedings, concentrated on writing an especially long and informative letter–in time to return with the caravan. Not having written his brother since 1822, the letter was a capsule history of the Rocky

---

[216] The trade goods with agreed upon prices are listed in Morgan, *Ibid.*, pp. 150-152.

[217] Bonner, *James Beckwourth,* pp. 73-74.

Mountain fur trade from 1822 to 1826 and arguably, it summarizes the fur trade better than any other single document from the period. It is dated *Rocky Mountains, July 16, 1826.*[218]

It is plausible that John Weber left the mountains with Ashley. From the beginning this noble sea captain has failed to emerge as an avid Mountain Man, so by this date he may have quit the trade. It is also possible that he became disillusioned when Ashley sold out to the younger upstarts in the business. The fact that from this time Potts appears to be in parties led by William Sublette may indicate that his old leader had soured on the trade and quit the business. Leadership was undecided right up to the last days of the Rendezvous. This may be the reason that Daniel had trouble making the party he desired with Jedediah Smith.[219]

John Weber has ever been a phantom on the mountain scene, and tradition has him leaving a year earlier than is supposed here. Whatever the case, the family declared that he "was beaten out of what was then a fortune by dishonest partners. He never made or saved much wealth afterwards and died poor." Actually, if the traditions are correct, he didn't die a natural death but he was killed–unfortunately by his own hand. "Life became a burden to him and he . . . deliberately committed suicide in 1859 by cutting his throat, bleeding to death in a few minutes."[220]

---

[218] *Potts's Letter to Robert Potts,* July 16, 1826." See Appendix B.

[219] *Potts's Letter, to Robert Potts, Sweet Lake, 1827,* See Appendix B.

[220] This account of Weber comes from a newspaper published about 1906 in the Jackson [Iowa] *Sentinel,* or the *Bellevue Leader.* It was apparently written by Captain Weber's son, William. It was reprinted in Camp, "The D. T. P. Letters," pp. 24-25, and in James W. Ellis, *History of Jackson County, Iowa,* [Chicago, 1910], Vol. I, pp. 370-371. This quotation is from Morgan, *Jedediah Smith,* p. 189.

The only other account of Weber was printed in the *Salt Lake Tribune,*

July 4, 1897, p. 31. It is reprinted below:

J. C. Hughey of Bellevue Ia., takes an interest in The Tribune's *Fifty Years Ago Today*, sketches, and sends the following interesting bit of history :

In the spring of 1852, I became acquainted with Capt. John H. Weber, one of the first white men to look upon Salt Lake. I had the privilege of many conversations with him, as we lived in the same boarding house. From his story I learned that in the spring of 1822 a company was formed at St. Louis consisting of Messrs. Ashley, Weber and Henry, known as the American Fur Company. Mr. Ashley furnished the outfit, consisting of two keel boats loaded with privisions, firearms, tents, traps and such other articles as were considered necessary for the successful prosecution of such an expedition in trapping and bartering with the Indians. The propelling force consisted of about fifty men, mostly Canadians.

In six months from the time of starting they arrived at the mouth of the Yellowstone river, where they made a "cache" of things not to be taken with them. The boats returned to St. Louis, while Capt. Weber and his partner, each with thirteen men, entered upon their work as trappers and traders with the Indians, beaver being the furs mostly sought after, and largely found in the vicinity of the Columbia river. The Captain told me more than once of his discovery of Salt Lake in 1823. He called it a great boon to them, as salt was plentiful around the border of the lake and for some time before they had used gun-powder on their meat, which was principally buffalo. He said meat was the staff of life, and but seldom ate any bread.

Capt. Weber was also the discoverer of Weber canyon and Weber river, both of which bear his name. The keel boats continued to make annual trips with supplies for the trappers and to secure the furs for the market. In the autumn of 1827 they returned to St. Louis; in 1832 he moved to Galena, Ill., then famed for its lead mines, a few years later he came to Bellevue, Ia., where he died in February, 1859.

By birth he was a Dane, for six years he sailed a Danish vessel as a skipper, before coming to America. He was a large well-formed man with an eye like an eagle and a voice like a trumpet. His son, William, lives within two miles of town, was born six months after his father left for the mountains. When I knew him he had forgotten his native language and spoke the English language freer from provincialism than most natives

Thus passes the man who by all accounts should loom larger in the history of the fur trade. The only testimony of John H. Weber's sojourn in the mountains is his name on a river draining from the Wasatch Mountains into briny Great Salt Lake.

Men remained in the mountains for a variety of reasons, not the least of which was the desire to explore strange country. Daniel Potts succumbed to this lure following the Rendezvous of 1826. Evidently expecting to be a member of Jedediah Smith's party to California, he wrote,

> We expect to start in a short time to explore the country lying S.W. of the Great Lake, where we shall probably winter. This country has never yet been visited by any white person–from thence to what place I cannot say, but expect the next letter will be dated at the mouth of Columbia. My long absence has created a desire to hear from you, as well as the rest of my people, also my associates. I have been on the very eve of returning this summer, but owing to this unexplored country, which I have a great curiosity to see, I have concluded to remain one or two years.[221]

As the parties were finally chosen, Potts was disappointed that he could not get on with Jedediah Smith and his "South West Expedition" to California. He instead engaged with a brigade going into extremely perilous country. A year later he recounts the incident:

> Shortly after writing to you last year I took my departure

---

do.

[221] *Potts's Letter to Robert Potts*, July 16, 1826.

for The Black-Foot Country much against my will, as I could not make a party for any other route.[222]

At the time, Daniel little realized that he was about to see sights more exciting than California. The incredible region of Yellowstone Park was in Blackfoot Country.

This trip would be the first known entry into Yellowstone Park and Daniel Potts is the only one who is certainly known. He told the tale. Daniel chronicled much early fur exploring, but this would be his claim to fame.

Though we touched on his Yellowstone experience in Chapter II, now we will tell the "Yellowstone discovery saga" with detail.

---

[222] *Potts's Letter to Robert Potts, July 8, 1827.*

"BLACKFOOT COUNTRY" AND YELLOWSTONE PARK

ROCKY MOUNTAINS, 1826

To skin hunters, "Blackfoot Country" was the northern section of the Rocky Mountains. It included much of present Idaho, Wyoming and Montana and extended into Canada. The tribe of warriors who inhabited this region were the scourge of the mountains and specialized in dealing out death to their enemies. No other Indian tribe of the period carried on such a hostile campaign to exterminate the white trappers. An unfortunate incident on the Lewis and Clark Expedition started the ill feeling. While scouting the Marias River Lewis and three of his men chanced upon a band of young braves. First they parleyed and shared the pipe, but later when Joseph Field carelessly set his rifle down, an Indian grabbed it and ran. When the smoke cleared two Indians were dead or badly wounded.

A greater reason for Blackfoot anger was Americans trading rifles and ammunition to their enemies. The Blackfeet monopoly on firearms from the British would be upset. So they were hostile to the Americans and anger and killing on both sides kept the feud lively.[223] By 1826, when Daniel Potts was compelled to trap the Northern Rockies, he feared unpleasant encounters with these natives, and was not disappointed in his expectations.

Leaving the Rendezvous, they struck out for Snake River.

---

[223] In 1806, Meriweather Lewis, while reconnoitering the Marias River, killed two Piegan or Blackfeet. Reuben Gold Thwaites, *The Original Journals of the Lewis and Clark Expedition, 1804-1806* [New York: Antiquarian Press Ltd., 1959], Vol. V., p. 223. The tribe responded by going south in 1807 for revenge. From *David Thomson, The Man Who Measured Canada,* National Geographic [May, 1996]. p. 128.

He says the company "took a Northerly direction about fifty miles . . . and at the forks of Henry's & Lewis's forks . . . we was Dayly harassed by the Black-feet:.."[224]

Since Daniel's narrative for the earlier and later parts of the season are sweeping in the extreme, it is necessary to rely on the rascal Jim Beckwourth for information. Beckwourth's narrative is a patchwork chronicle, with him freely mixing his events through the years, but once unscrambled it is a valuable source. Jim declares that the party followed the Snake River up to its forks and then made a halt on Lewis's Fork where a base camp was established. From here the trappers were to be dispersed later in the season.[225] In the meantime, according to Beckwourth, a sensational meeting with the natives occurred. He claims credit for starting it. On one of his solitary forays, Beckwourth chanced onto an Indian intensely occupied grooming himself. Since the native was a Blackfoot, Jim shot him and brought the head back to camp as a trophy.[226] [For the average trapper, the scalp would have been more than sufficient.] The direct result of this atrocity was a large scale assault on the Americans by the Blackfeet.

> The next morning our camp was infested by two thousand five hundred warriors of the Black Foot tribe. We now had something on our hands which demanded attention. [What a wonderful understatement.] We were encamped in the bend of the river–in the "horse-shoe." Our lodges were pitched at the entrance, or narrowest part of the shoe, while our animals were driven back into the bend . . . .The Indians made a furious charge. We immediately placed the

---

[224] *Potts's Letter To Robert Potts, Sweet Lake,* July 8, 1827.
[225] Bonner, *James Beckwourth,* p. 126.. This sequence from Beckwourth may apply to the summer of 1826. Laying aside Jim's exaggerations, it squares with the known events of the period.
[226] *Ibid.*

women and children in the rear, sending them down the
bend, where they were safe unless we were defeated.[227]

With the help of the courageous Beckwourth, the whites
defeated these Blackfeet, killing, according to Jim, one hundred
and sixty-seven of them. The casualties among the trappers
were also "very severe; sixteen killed, mostly half-breeds." The
Indians got the worst of it in Beckwourth's stories. After the
battle Jim remembered that:

> As usual, there was a scalp-dance . . . in which I really
> feared that the fair sex would dance themselves to death .
> . . .After all, it was a victory rather dearly purchased.[228]

A wonderful value of Beckwourth's stories is the flavor.
Though his dates are off and he makes himself the hero, he gets
the fun details.[229]

The company was perhaps under the direction of Sublette
and Jackson, but the men likely divided up. Then they fanned
out, searched the various streams for beaver, and explored.[230]

---

[227] *Ibid.*, pp. 126-127. To Beckwourth's credit as a historian, there is a
"horseshoe bend" in Snake River near the Forks.

[228] *Ibid.*

[229] *Ibid.*, Since his book was dictated years after the events, it is
remarkable that Beckwourth's stories are as accurate as they are.

[230] It is conjectural that Sublette led the party of which Daniel was a
member on the basis that Yellowstone Lake was known for a time as
"Sublette's Lake." This information appears on the Burr and Wilkes
Maps. See Morgan and Wheat, *Jedediah Smith Maps*, [maps in pocket].
No actual map of Jedediah Smith's has been found, but these were
obviously derived from one by him. Frank H. Bradley of the Hayden
Survey makes reference to one of Smith's maps showing Yellowstone
Lake: "The first map which, so far as is known, represents the lake with
anything like its true form is a manuscript by Jedediah S. Smith, who
hunted through these mountains from California to the British
Possessions, during the years from 1821 to 1830. The original was
purchased in Oregon by the War Department, but is supposed to be in the

Ascending the various waterways, the parties worked their way north and east from Snake River. They were headed into strange and unknown country[231]

The Birthplace of Rivers

They followed the rivers for a number of good reasons, most relating to travel. First, animals and Indians had made deep trails up and down the main Rivers and it was easier to follow the beaten path rather than blaze a new trail. Also, they needed water for men and horses. And finally, *that is where the beaver were.* If not on the main river these furry, long-toothed rodents would be chewing down trees and building dams on smaller, joining streams. So rivers were the key.

---

hands of Mr. George Gibbs of New Haven, Connecticut." F. V. Hayden, *Sixth Annual Report of the Geological Survey of the Territories Embracing Portions of Montana, Idaho, Wyoming, and Utah, 1872* [Washington: Government Printing Office, 1873], p. 233.
[231] *Potts's Letter to Robert Potts 1827.*

From the forks of Snake River the men proceeded up

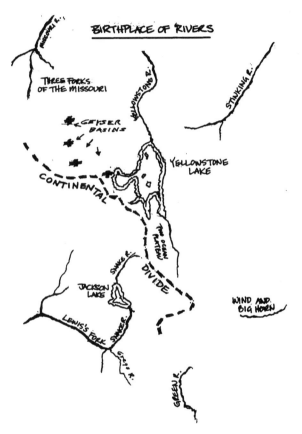

Henry's Fork. After going about thirty miles to present Ashton, they bent off to the right and crossed the magnificent Teton Range, [Potts's "large rugged mountain"]. Here they once again struck Snake River on Lewis's Fork near the Continental Divide. Potts correctly noted that the Snake River headed "on the top of the great chain of Rocky Mountains which separates the water of the Atlantic from the Pacific."

At this point in his narrative Daniel wrote an amazing

summary of western river origins.

> At or near this place heads the Luchkadee or Calliforn
> [Green River], . . . Stinking Fork [Shoshoni], Yellowstone,
> South Forks of the Missouri, and Henry's Fork. All these
> head at an angular point . . . .[232]

Potts had his geography right. This knowledge had eluded
cartographers for centuries. He correctly observed that the great
river systems of the West all headed near each other on the
Continental Divide. These rivers were the Green, the Shoshoni,
the Yellowstone, the Wind, both forks of the Snake, and the
Three Forks of the Missouri. From their Rocky Mountain
beginnings, these nine streams go in all directions. It is
remarkable that Potts understood their flow and destinations
this early.[233] Since they were seeking beaver, which were always
near water, it was natural that he would soon learn the *mountain*
streams. But Potts knew more; he understood where these rivers
drained into the ocean. He likely had been pumping the
Canadian and Mexican trappers.

In his next sentence, Daniel noted *more* unusual
geography–the thermal hot springs near Yellowstone Lake.

Scalding Hot and Icy Cold Water–
On the Mountain Top

In what seems topsy turvy geography, Daniel Potts wrote
that the Yellowstone River was headed by a large fresh water
lake "*on the very top of the mountain.*" Lakes are supposed to
be in valleys. But Potts's "mountain" was the Continental
Divide, and he is right. He noted the lake was icy cold and "as

---

[232] *Ibid.*
[233] *Ibid.* For Potts's river origin statement see p. 11. For Potts's river origin statement see p. 11.

clear as Crystal." He loved it.

Millions of later visitors would share his admiration for this place. With its frigid lakes, tumbling rivers, spectacular waterfalls, and incredible thermal activity, the area of Yellowstone Park is arguably the most spectacular scenery in North America. But before Daniel Potts set his pen to describe the place it was unknown; valid history of man in Yellowstone begins when Daniel Potts saw the region in 1826.

But we promised to tell the full story about this place and its early visitors. Before Potts, the Indians were there, notably the Sheepeaters. Though their names are unknown we know some fascinating particulars about them.

Sheep Eater Indians

Guesses regarding the earliest men to see the fascinations of Yellowstone come only from physical evidence they left. And there was some. Rude shelters, made of poles propped up tepee style remained long after the white-men came. Though most natives avoided this area, a branch of the Shoshone, the Sheep Eaters, built these shelters and lived in the Park–at least in the summer.

Without horses they were vulnerable and poor, but the Sheep Eaters compensated with a remarkable survival tactic; they used the strange and steamy Yellowstone area to *hide* from their warlike neighbors. It was a refuge for them because other tribes took pains to avoid Yellowstone.

Assuming it was the abode of evil Spirits, they were afraid of it. In fact, able Indian guides were so unacquainted with Yellowstone they became lost there. It was said the Nez Perces were forced to impress a white man to guide them through during their incredible fight and flight from the U.S. Army in 1877.

SHEEP EATER FAMILY encamped near the head of Medicine Lodge
Creek, Idaho. From a photograph by W. H. Jackson, 1871.
Courtesy Bureau of American Ethnology

Sheep Eater Family

Sheep Eater meant just that. Branches of the Shoshoni were known by what they ate. There were Root Eaters, Salmon Eaters, Sheep Eaters, and very oddly, dust or Earth Eaters.[234] Unlike their neighbors, the Shoshoni didn't practice war. Known as the Sentinels of the Rockies, and lacking the horse and gun, they lived in small bands, and depended upon what was at hand for food and defense.

---

[234]According to their historian, branches of the Shoshoni linguistic group were designated by the food they ate. There were the Root, Squirrel, Sunflower Seed, Salmon, Sheep, Pine Nut, and oddly, the Dust or Earth Eaters. Trenholm and Carley, *The Shoshonis Sentinels of the Rockies,* [University of Oklahoma Press,1964], p 4.

Mountain sheep were plentiful in high alpine meadows. Their ability to effortlessly bound up steep ledges made them less fearful, so the Sheep Eaters were able to creep close enough to bag them. They used the whole animal for food and covering. Remarkably even the massive full curled horn was put to a special use.

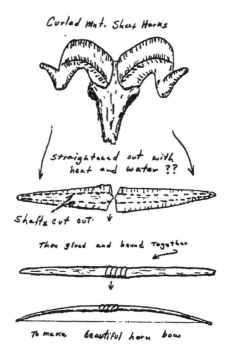

Curled Mnt. Sheep Horns

Straightened out with heat and water ??

Shafts cut out.

Then glued and bound Together

To make beautiful horn bow

The Sheep Eater Bow
Made From Antlers

They were poor, but not ignorant. From the horns they fashioned a rare and beautiful weapon. In some way not fully understood, the Sheep Eaters straightened out these curved, hard antlers then cut out bone shaves, and finally glued them together to make a bow for shooting arrows. In 1835, the trapper Osborne Russel met Sheep Eater Indians in Yellowstone and admired their weapons. He wrote that their "bows were beautifully wrought from Sheep, Buffaloe, and Elk horns secured with Deer and Elk sinews and ornamented with porcupine." An antler bow was stronger than wood. So besides hiding in the Park, the Sheep Eaters had fine bows made in a secret way for hunting and defense.[235]

Perhaps their secret was to soak the antlers in scalding geyser water until they were pliable enough to unroll. However they did it, the finished bow was remarkable and their technology was unknown to more wealthy tribes.

Besides their rude shelters the Sheep Earters left well worn trails. Chittenden, in his history of the area written in 1895, says that old trails were found by the early explorers "generally on the lines since occupied by tourist routes." These natural paths were followed when the horseless Sheep Eater walked from the Park to their wintering ground on Wind River. So from prehistoric times Indians occasionally traveled through the Park and a few lived there.

They told tales about the region which were a patchwork of truth and bubbling myth. And for their listeners, it was hard to tell how much to believe. Bits and pieces of truth and myth slowly became known to the whites. The name, "Yellowstone" may stem from the stupendous yellow-toned walls of the canyon which drains Yellowstone Lake and cradles two thundering water falls. From the Indians of the Upper Missouri, early French-Canadian trappers learned of a "Roche Juane"

---

[235] Russell, *Journal of a Trapper*, p.26. The scalding hot pools in Yellowstone were likely used to soften the bone horns until they could be uncurled.

River, the native equivalent of this meaning Yellow Rock River.[236] Yellow is the dominant color of the canyon, but every hue is displayed. In 1871, the first, and arguably the best, artist to paint this canyon was Thomas Moran. And he said that "its beautiful tints were beyond the reach of human art." Moran was awe struck by the canyon as are visitors one hundred years later. Before we continue with Daniel Potts's visit to Yellowstone Park, a review of the earlier history of that region, and a recounting of other whites who might have proceeded him there is in order.

Lewis and Clark and Other Early Travelers

When Lewis and Clark made their famous expedition along the Upper Missouri, they failed to learn anything unusual concerning the "Roche Juane" River other than the existence of falls on it. Even this information was concluded to be incorrect.[237] The leaders of this expedition gained most of their knowledge of lands south of their trail from Indians and traders.

---

[236] Hyrum Chittenden, *The Yellowstone National Park* [Cincinnati: Stewart and Kidd, Company, 1915], p. 1. Also Dee Linford, "Wyoming Stream Names," *Annals of Wyoming*, Vol. XV [July, 1943], p. 269. "The most important trail" in the Park was known as the Great Bannock Trail. It extended from Henry's Lake across the Gallatin Range to Mammoth Hot Springs . . . thence to Blacktail Deer plateau to the ford above Tower Falls; and thence up the Lamar Valley, forking at Soda Butte, and reaching the Bighorn Valley by way of Clark's Fork and the Shoshone River. It was an ancient and much traveled trail and had become "a deep furrow in the grassy slopes, and it is still distinctly visible in places, though unused for a quarter of a century." p. 10 [1905 edition]. Regarding the name "Yellowstone," another viewpoint of why the river was so-named are the yellow sandstone cliffs on the lower portion of the river. In either case the river is well named.

[237] Thwaites, *Original Journals*, p. 320.

While wintering with the Mandans Captain Clark sketched two maps of the Yellowstone River based on these sources.[238]

In the fall of 1805 one trader, who had also been among the Mandans the previous winter, made a "journey of discovery" high on the "Roche Juane" River. Francois Antoine Laracque accompanied by Indian guides surveyed the Tongue, Powder, and Big Horn Rivers before descending to the Yellowstone near present Billings, Montana.[239] He reported a legend of a "montiou or devil" on the Big Horn, "who lives in the [water] fall and goes out of it to devour every person or beast which approaches very near."[240]

Other tantalizing rumors drifted down the Missouri that unusual stuff was at the head of the Yellowstone River. One such tale came to the attention of James Wilkinson, Governor of Louisiana Territory. On October 22, 1805 he described an Indian map to President Thomas Jefferson. He said it was,

> a Savage delineation on a Buffalo Pelt, of the Missouri & its South Western Branches, including the Rivers plate & Lycorne or Pierre jaune: [Yellowstone] This Rude Sketch without Scale or Compass "et remplie de Fantaisies redicules" is not destitute of Interests, as it exposes the location of several important Objects, & may point the way to useful enquiry–among other things a little incredible, *a volcano is distinctly described on Yellow Stone River.*[241]

---

[238] Ibid. Vol I, p. 244. Maps in *Atlas*, Vol 8, No. 12 and 13.

[239] John W. Hakola, ed., *Frontier Omnibus* [Missoula, Montana: State University Press, 1963], p. 21.

[240] Ibid, p. 20.

[241] Clarence E. Carter, ed., *Territorial Papers of the United States* [Washington, 1934], Vol. XIII, *Territory of Louisiana–Missouri, 1803-1806* [1948], pp. 199, 243. See also Merrill Mattes, "Behind the Legend of Colter's Hell," *Mississippi Valley Historical Review* [September, 1949], p. 262.

Wilkinson had already decided to investigate the rumor, for in a letter to the Secretary of War, September 8, 1805, he wrote:

> I have equipt a Perogue out of my Small private means, not with any view to Self interest, to ascend the Missouri and the River Piere Juane, or Yellow Stone, called by the natives, Unicorn River, the same by which Capt. Lewis I find since expects to return and which my informants tell me *is filled with wonders*.[242]

History suggests that Wilkinson was a man of ambitious schemes. It is doubtful that the expedition was outfitted "not with any view to self interest," but no more is known of this episode. We wonder what happened to the map and if the perogue reached its destination. The next explorer in the region, and the one who received lasting, and probably, misdirected fame for his discoveries, was John Colter.

What About John Colter? Did He Go To Hell?

The answer to the above question is mostly no. Unless hell is what you call the sulfurous hot springs area on the Stinking River. He did go there. But it isn't likely he went to Yellowstone which some early travelers likened to the fires of hell.

You might ask, why is it an issue in this book? After all, John Colter has been credited as the first white man in Yellowstone for more than a century. Why not let him have it? In answer, history is always being rewritten—as soon as new sources surface to cast more light on the subject. And besides, Colter never said he went there. That's worth something.

---

[242] Ibid. My italics.

Trapper tradition says there actually was a place called "Colter's Hell." And fur trade writers have said the "legend of Colter's Hell" was common talk around the campfires of early hunters. As the legend goes, John Colter was supposed to have wandered into an area where "the smell of brimstone" and hidden fires from smoking pits lurked to engulf the unwary traveler. It was a hazy, vaporous, place where hot water and noxious sulphur steam bubbled out of the ground.

Actually, there is truth to this legend, "Colters Hell,"*was a real place*. It is located on the Stinking River near modern Cody Wyoming. The river's name came from smelly sulfur gas puffing out near modern Cody Wyoming. Colter went there. However, there is more to the story. Non-trapping historians misunderstood and made a *switch*.

When the volcanic activity in present Yellowstone Park became known, *it seemed to match* Colter's legends–so some historians wrongly assumed Yellowstone Park was "Colter's Hell." Laymen picked up the idea and from that time forward –for almost fifty years–John Colter was associated with Yellowstone. The Park fit the legend, made a good story, and there were thousands of people coming to Yellowstone each summer for Park Rangers to tell the story to. This tale was copied and quoted from one writer to another. And historical monuments repeated it–there is a bronze plaque bolted to the Teton County Courthouse, in Idaho, and a bronze monument in the Jackson, Wyoming town park, both declaring Colter to be the earliest white visitor in the region. So the "John Colter in Yellowstone" idea now *has a life of its own,* even though extant records and common sense causes serious students of history to dispute it.

Following is a summary of *non* legendary history about Colter and Yellowstone.

"Colter's Hell" Is Not Yellowstone

The romantic notion that John Colter stumbled onto Yellowstone doesn't square with his contemporaries. As first hand sources accumulated, it became apparent that earlier writers had confused one hot spot for another. Some later historians tried to set the record straight. In fact, Burton Harris, John Colter's biographer of 1952, wrote that the making of Colter's Hell synonymous with Yellowstone Park was "*a modern invention.*"

Harris wrote that the location of Colters Hell is *not* near Yellowstone Lake, but instead is on the "Shoshone " or Stinking River, the actual spot located about half way between Cody Wyoming and where the river emerges from the mountain.[243] The appellation, "Stinking River" derives from the offensive sulfur smell coming from these hot springs near the river.[244]

---

[243] Burton Harris, *John Colter*, p., 88. Harris correctly locates "Colters Hell" separate from Yellowstone but he still maintained that Colter was the first white man in Yellowstone Park. The location for " Colters Hell" on the Stinking River is now clearly substantiated by early explorers such as Joe Meek, and the Catholic missionary Father De Smit. Washington Irving, who wrote early on the subject also got it right. The tide is slowly turning regarding Colter being first in Yellowstone. For example, the noted fur trade historian Dale Morgan wrote that: [Daniel] "Potts records the first known visit by white men to Yellowstone Lake." Morgan, *Willaim Ashley*, p.162.

[244] See "Stinking Water River," on The Ferris map of 1836 in Gowens, *The Fur Trade History of Yellowstone Park.*, op.cit., Map 13. Residents of Cody petitioned the Wyoming legislature that the name "Stinking " be changed. It is now the Shoshone River. The residence of Mud Lake, Idaho could spruce up their image doing the same.

This doesn't take anything away from Colter. Reliable history shows him to be the prototype of later Mountain Men. He was a capable hunter who followed Lewis and Clark all the way to the Pacific Ocean. However, on the return trip, on August 5, 1806 near the Mandan villages and before completing his term of service, Colter requested a discharge in order to join Joseph Dickson and Forest Hancock on a trapping foray.[245]These two were from Illinois and planned to hunt on streams of the upper Missouri. Colter's request was granted by the Captains on the basis that no one else of the corps would ask to leave.

A year later Colter turned up alone where the Platte spills into the Missouri.[246] Here, he met the ambitious Manuel Lisa, who was pushing his company of men up the Missouri. By this date Colter was an experienced veteran of Upper Missouri trade and travel. Lisa recognized his value as a scout and bent his energetic persuasive powers to enlist him. Colter joined.

Before he would return, his continuous absence from the settlements would be six years. Lisa had already enlisted two others of the Lewis and Clark men, Peter Wiser and George Droullard. And by 1809 Lisa had signed up even more men with Lewis and Clark connections. Reuben Lewis, the younger brother to Meriwether, became a partner as did William Clark himself. Reuben would accompany Lisa to the mountains and besides seeking furs would be able to keep his brother Meriwether, who was now the governor of Missouri, posted on new developments and discoveries.

Ascending the Missouri and then the Yellowstone to the

---

[245] Thwaites, *Original Journals*, p. 341.
[246] Stallo Vinton, *John Colter, The Discoverer of Yellowstone Park* [New York: Edward Eberstadt, 1926], p. 43.

mouth of the Big Horn River, they established a post. This cantonment was named Fort Raymond, after Lisa's son. It occupied a position very near the one built by Andrew Henry in 1823. Actually, Andrew Henry was with Lisa in 1809, and may have helped build Fort Raymond. And like most frontier forts, its name was more formidable than the place itself. Usually these early posts consisted of only a cabin or two, were temporary and soon vanished.

The river was navigable to this point, but Lisa realized that further travel into the mountains would best be done on horseback or afoot.[247]

Lisa Sends Men Out To Trade

It was November, and to assure that friendly Indians knew that a new trading post was on the Big Horn, Lisa dispatched men to invite them in. The first to go was Edward Rose. After packing some trade goods and the customary gifts Rose left with a small party.

All accounts of Rose describe him as a savage, sinister-looking fellow of mixed blood who with extraordinary strength and acts of bravado thrived on the ragged edges of civilization. The Crow would call him "five scalps," because he once stormed a fortified band of Minnetarees alone, killed five of them, and drove the rest out of hiding. Another reason the Crow held him in high respect was that he often came bearing gifts–paid for by his trader. And he dispensed them liberally.

---

[247] Harris, *John Colter*, p.72. Eighteen years later, in 1824, the first "mountain catch" of furs gathered by Daniel Potts and his friends did this trip in reverse. It was packed to a navigable place then sent on down the Yellowstone River by boat.

Because he understood some native tongue and would throw himself onto desperate missions, Rose would play the roll of spokesman between the Indians and whites for some twenty years. In this case, Lisa likely sent him to a Crow village in the Yellowstone Valley, [not near the Park].

Soon, another man, George Drouillard, likely with a few companions, was dispatched by Lisa. Drouillard, like Colter, was a veteran of the Lewis and Clark trek. Not much is known about Drouillard's excursion, but he likely went up the Yellowstone to Clark's Fork, then south over the mountains to the Stinking Fork [the Shoshone], then down to it's junction with the Big Horn, and back to Fort Raymon by way of Pryors River.

Meriwether's brother, Reuben Lewis, wrote Meriwether about another veteran of the Lewis and Clark "Journey of Discovery"who was sent out by Lisa.

His name was Peter Wiser. He took Jean Baptiste Champlain and headed west to the Three Forks of the Missouri where they turned south following the Madison up to its sources. From there they crossed over the Divide and down to the rich fur country in Snake River basin.

With both Peter Wyzer and Champlain as sources, Reuben wrote a remarkable letter to his brother Meriwether. In it he declared that the route to the upper branches of the Columbia by way of the Madison "was short and without mountains." Also, "the beaver is as abundant as in our part of the country." Reuben also wrote that, he would endeavor to get Mr. Shamplain to make a sketch of the area. Here is Reuben's letter:[248]

---

[248] Fred Gowans, *A Fur Trade History of Yellowstone Park: Notes Documents, Maps* [Orem, Utah, 1989]. p. 105. This letter by Reuben to

3 forks of the Missouri Apr 21 1810

The return of your oald acqaintance Coalter, gives me opportunity of addressing you a few lines . . . [John Colter was returning to St Louis and delivered this letter.] Mr Shamplaain tells me that the Martin abound in the mountains dividing the waters of the Spanish River as it is called or what is supposed to be the Rio Del Nort, from the waters of some of the Southern branches of the Collumbia on a River falling into the gulf of calaifornia which he thinks most probable.[249] Beaver abound in the same country but it lies so high that it is allmost perpetual snow. The upper branches of the Collumbia are full of beaver and the rout by the middle fork or Madisons River is short without mountains it is about 5 or 6 days Travel to an illigable place for a fort on that river where the Beaver [from the account of Peter wyzer] is as abundant as in our part of this Country, Buffalow and game of every kind in great abundance . . . I . . . shall indeavor to get Mr. Shamplain to give me a sketch of the South and S E of this plalce which I think may be very much relied on as he is a young Man of observation & forward it by the first boat . . . .

This letter is crucial regarding the Colter/Yellowstone myth. It is significant that *after Colter's supposed trek south*, Reuben Lewis, who was on the scene, considered Peter Wizer and Jean Baptiste Champlain to be the authorities on lands south of the Three Forks where Yellowstone Park lies. In this letter to Meriwether Reuben doesn't suggest that his brother should question Colter—even though Meriwether will see Colter

---

his brother Meriwether accurately describes the route via Madison. Highway 287 follows this natural route from Three Forks today. We wonder if the sketch by "Shamplain"was sent and will surface somewhere.
[249] This could be Green River or Bear River.

face to face when he delivers this letter. If Colter had knowledge of the region in question, Meriwether could get his views by a personal interview which would be much more authoritative than a map from "Shamplaine." But Colter, unlike, Wiser and Champlain, apparently didn't know about lands west of the Continental Divide. He simply seems to be the mail carrier.

However, back in 1807, in addition to Rose, Drouillard, Peter Wiser and Shamplaine, Lisa also sent Colter. If, as reported, Lisa sent him out *walking*, by then they must have been short of horses.[250]Colter's journey to the Crows, supposedly made alone but likely with others, is the basis for his alleged discovery of the Yellowstone Park area. The only account of the hike is by Henry Brackenridge, who obtained his information from Manuel Lisa. The latter presumably got it from Colter. This makes the report *third hand*. Leaving his readers to guess what direction Colter traveled, Brackenridge wrote:

> He Lisa continued his voyage to the Yellowstone River where he built a trading fort. He shortly after dispatched Coulter, the hunter before mentioned, to bring some of the Indian nations to trade. This man, with a pack of thirty pounds weight, his gun and some ammunition, went upwards of five hundred miles to the Crow nation; gave them information, and proceeded from them to several other tribes. On his return, a party of Indians in whose company he happened to be was attacked, and he was lamed by a severe wound in the leg; notwithstanding which, he returned to the establishment, entirely alone and without assistance, several hundred miles.[251]

---

[250] Brackenridge's narration has Colter walking.
[251] Henry M. Brackenridge, *Views of Louisiana, Together With a Journal of a Voyage up the Missouri River in 1811* [Pittsburgh: Cramer, Spear

This third-hand account is the whole story. It doesn't say where Colter went or what he saw. And there isn't a corroboration from Colter or his family that backs it up. Brackenridge was a popular writer and would have been delighted to garnish his report of Colter's travels with tales of hot bubbling mud pots, scalding blue pools and water bursting from the earth. That Brackenridge is silent is indicative that he had no such story to report.

Evidence that Colter made a trip for Lisa is on the William Clark map of 1814.[252] As superintendent of Indian affairs in St.

---

and Eichbaum, 1915], pp. 90-92. See Chittenden, *Yellowstone Park,* p. 38. According to Chittenden, an article in the *Louisiana Gazette,* of St Louis, Feb. 28, 1811 by Brackenridge states: "Mr. Lisa informs me that about sixty miles from his fort [on the Big Horn], there is a volcano that actually emits flames." From this we see that Brackenridge reported anything unusual. It is possible that Lisa's informants assumed that steam was actually smoke from a fire. Another author, John Bradbury, wanted to know where the skeleton of a fish 40' long on the Missouri had been found. General Clark told Bradbury that Colter could point it out. However, Colter "could not give" him the information he sought. John Bradbury, *Travels in the Interior of America.* [London, Sherwood, Neely and Jones, 1819]., pp. 25-28. The weakness of the "Colter visited Yellowstone" idea is that there are no details coming from Colter to his friends or family about it. Even a quiet man wouldn't keep that experience a secret.

[252]Gowens, *The Fur Trade History of Yellowstone Park.*, Ibid., Maps number 9 and 10. In 1809 after his return from the mountains, George Drouillard stopped at William Clark's office in St. Louis. Clark penciled a general idea of Drouillard's travels after he departed Lisa's Fort Reunion in 1807-8. Drouillard perhaps also gave him information regarding Colter's travels to the crow near the Stinking River, Wyoming. The following year after returning from the mountains Colter likely visited Clark. Maybe at that time Clark noted his "route" on his ever changing map. The map was cleaned up and published in 1814. However, it isn't the same as the original. And Colter never saw the finished map. He

Louis, Clark tried to keep abreast of new western discoveries. He gathered fresh information from returning fur traders and added it to an ever-changing manuscript map. Notations from this manuscript map were transferred to an official engraved map in 1814. On the 1814 map in an area between the Yellowstone and Big Horn rivers there is a dotted line labeled "Colter's route 1807." With this notation and the third-hand statement from Brackenridge as their basis, some historians speculate that:

> Colter ascended the Bighorn, followed it up to the Shoshone River near present Cody, went south along the foot of the Absoroka Mountains, up Wind River to Union Pass, into Jackson's Hole, thence probably across Teton Pass into Pierre's Hole, thence north via Connant Pass to the west shore of Yellowstone Lake and northeast to the crossing of the Yellowstone near Tower Falls, thence up the Lamar River and Soda Butte Creek, back across the Absarokas, and then south to the Shoshone River and back to Lisa's Fort by way of Clark's Fork and Pryor's Fork.[253]

Making this itinerary and the Clark Map fit actual geography is difficult. Here are some reasons why.

Puzzling Out " Colter's Route" on the Clark Map

The above itinerary has Colter hiking to modern Cody Wyoming, then south to Wind River and over Union Pass to Jackson Hole, thence over Teton Pass, and finally looping back

---

married a girl named Sally and became a farmer but died of jaundice in Nov1813. Harris, p. 162.

[253] Merrill J. Mattes, *Colter's Hell and Jackson's Hole: The Fur Trappers'*. This itinerary derives from a composite of theories of several writers.

through Yellowstone Park to his post on the Big Horn River. This scenario depends on the assumption that Lake Eustis and Lake Biddle [or Riddle, depending on the edition] are respectively Yellowstone Lake and Jackson Lake.

Much has been written about these two fugitive lakes and their place on the Clark map, but their true meaning is still conjectural.[254] In 1814, when the map was printed, major landmarks south of the Missouri were assumptive. It is likely that the most accurate version of the Clark map was his manuscript of 1809. However, it only goes as far as the south fork of the Shoshone, so the area beyond that, as shown on the published versions, is speculative. Following are some problems with "Colter's Route" and the map:

> 1. Making Lake Biddle into Jackson Lake[255] puts it *on the wrong side of the Continental Divide.* On Clark's map, Lake Biddle drains into Wind River, Yellowstone, the Missouri and finally the Atlantic Ocean. Actually, Jackson Lake drains south into Snake River, from there to the Columbia, and finally into the Pacific Ocean. If, as his supporters claim, Colter forded Snake River in the winter, it would have been a bone chilling experience. If Snake River didn't flow so fast it would freeze up. Its temperature

---

[254] *Exploration of the Yellowstone and Grand Teton Park Region* [Yellowstone, Wyoming: Yellowstone Library and Museum Association and the Grand Teton Natural History Association in Cooperation With National Park Service], pp. 14-15.

[255] The Lake "Biddle" or Riddle" designation hints an enigma. The Hayden Survey Report of 1872 suggested this. After naming a small lake on the Continental Divide "Lake Riddle," the report says: "Lake Riddle is a fugitive name, which has been located at several [sites], but nowhere permanently. It is supposed to have been used originally to designate the mythical lake among the mountains, whence, according to the hunters; water flowed to both oceans." Hayden, *Geological Survey of the Territories*, p. 250.

is often that cold. It would be a memorable experience and it isn't likely he would have forgotten which way the river was running.[256]

Some historians suggest lake Biddle/Riddle is not Jackson Lake but instead Brooks Lake, near the top of Togwattee Pass and draining into Wind River. This notion at least reflects the map.

2. And assuming Jackson Lake is lake Biddle, another problem is the Clark map shows prominent mountains hugging the *east* instead of *west* side of this lake. The stupendous Teton mountains rise abruptly and almost vertical from the west side of Jackson Lake. If one were compelled to pass through Jackson Hole and climb Teton Pass in the winter, [as Colter is supposed to have done], it isn't likely he would have confused which side of Jackson Lake the Tetons stood.[257]

---

[256] Where the Indian and buffalo trail crossed Snake River on its way to Teton pass it flows almost exactly from north to south. The river from "Lake Biddle" [supposedly this same Snake River], of the Clark map flows almost *straight east and to the wrong watershed*. This is a major hurdle. Gowens, *The Fur Trade History of Yellowstone Park, Ibid.*, Maps number 9 and 10. In 1809 after his return from the mountains, George Drouillard stopped at William Clark's office in St. Louis. Clark drew a rough map of Droillard's travels west from Lisa's Fort in 1807-08 and included Colter's travels to the Crow camp near Cody, Wyoming. The following year Colter visited Clark when he returned from the mountains. Perhaps at that time Clark extended Colter's route on his ever-changing map. A polished edition of this map was published in 1814, however there are considerable discrepancies between it and the source map. And Colter never saw this map as he had died before it was published. See, Paul Lawerence, *John Colter- Journey of Discovery A New Look At an Old Mystery* [Jackson, Wyoming Unita Press, c 1978], p. 12. regarding the map issue.

[257] Incidentally, Brooks lake, east of the Continental Divide, has prominent, craggy mountains to its east–like on Clark's map. And it does drain into Wind River similar to Clark's lake Biddle.

3. Then, there are the Tetons themselves. From some spots these mountains can be seen for a hundred miles or more. They are spectacular landmarks. For this reason, the Astorians in 1811, and again Donald Mackenzie in 1819, called them the "Pilot Nobs."[258] No mountains in the West could be mistaken for them. But oddly, they are not recorded on the Clark map. If Colter crossed the Continental Divide into Jackson Hole, a breathtaking view of the Tetons would be his for several days. He likely would have reported these prominent peaks to Manual Lisa and William Clark. And Clark would have noted them on his map. But he didn't.

4. Moving north, if Clark's "Lake Eustis " is Yellowstone Lake, somehow Colter missed the thermal activity on its shores because the map doesn't show any. If he was in the region, it is unlikely that Colter would have failed to notice thermal features which in size and variety are unsurpassed in the world. And it isn't likely the hot springs near Cody which came to be "Colters Hell" would impress him *more* than Yellowstone and thus appear on the map instead.

In the absence of first hand sources it is difficult to determine what is meant by "Colter's Route" on the 1814 Clark map. One careful student of this cartography has declared that *no single site below the Big Horn region can be positively identified.*[259] But giving the map makers their due, in 1814,

---

[258] Stuart's Journal, pp. 108-111.

[259] J. Neilson Barry, personal correspondence with W.C. Lawrence [Jackson Hole Museum and Teton County Historical Society, archives]. See also, Barry's correspondence with Merrill C. Beal, [Idaho State University, Eli M. Oboler Library, Special Collections Department, archives]. See his series of brief articles, J. Neilson Barry, "Modern Map Showing John Colter's Map In Clarks' Map 1814," *Wyoming Annals*, X [1938], pp. 100-101; "Tracing from Map 1814 English Edition," *Ibid.*, pp. 102-103; "The Yellowstone River as Placed by Degrees," *Ibid.*, pp.

landmarks south of the Missouri were only speculated from hazy reports of wondering fur hunters–then translated and sketched by people who were far away from the mountains. Given their lack of first hand information and reliable reports, the discrepancies between Clark's manuscript map and the version that was finally engraved are not surprising. Some hands that created the engraved map were four times removed from the scene. So the map used to put Colter in Yellowstone is cut from thin history.

Sticks and Stones

Two physical items are part of the Colter legend. The first is a chunk of wood. It is reported that in 1889, Philip Ashton Rollins and Tazwell Woody [Teddy Roosevelt's hunting guide] found carved on a large tree on Coulter Creek, a deep indented blaze, which after being cleared of sap and loose bark was found to consist of a cross, thus "X," and under it, the initials 'J C'[260]

This tree was later cut down by the Park authorities in 1889

104-105; "John Colter's Map of 1814," *Ibid.*, pp. 106-109. See also J.Neilson Barry, " Autobiography," *ibid.*, X[1938], pp. 117-118. W.C. or "Slim" Lawerence who lived on Jackson Lake, gathered a remarkable collection of artifacts from the Jackson Hole area, and established a museum in the town of Jackson. He speculated with the author that "Lake Biddle or Riddle" was Brooks Lake which is located near the top of Togwattee Pass and drains into Wind River. Spectacular peaks are located easterly of Brooks lake [as shown on the map]. Crow Indians hosted Potts and his fellows there the winter of 1824. Since it was the Crow that Colter was supposed to be seeking,, perhaps he found them in this natural wintering area in 1807. Here again we are spinning tales out of thin history–typical of most of the Colter legend.

[260] Lawarence, *John Colter, Journey of Discovery*, p. 14.

or 1890, but unfortunately, the piece with the blaze and marks was lost. Since no date was carved, and the log is not available to examine, the age of the marks is speculative. However, Coulter Creek was named for John Merle Coulter of the 1872 Hayden Survey, not our John Colter of 1807. Merle Coulter was reportedly fishing on the creek when surprised by a large black bear. He jumped into the creek and it was later named for him. The "J C"could have been carved by him or others of the party.[261] But this is speculation, the initials bore no date, and the tree is gone. The second physical item in the Colter lore, is a stone.

As the story goes, in 1931 a carved rhyolite stone in the shape of a head was unearthed in Teton Basin [Pierres Hole]. On one side of the stone was scratched "John Colter," and on the other, "1808."Opinions have varied widely regarding the stone, from "a great conversation piece,"[262] to "the most cherished item in the Fur Trade Museum."[263] Proving anything for certain about the stone is a challenge, and there is evidence

---

[261] *Ibid.*

[262] Mattes, *Colter's Hell and Jackson's Hole*, pp. 15-16.

[263] If this item was made from wood, there are techniques to determine its age. Being stone, it is doubtful that it can be authenticated. Circumstances suggest it was perpetrated by Aubrey Lyons on Superintendent Sam Woodring of Grand Teton National Park, see Paul Lawrence, *John Colter: Journey of Discovery, A New Look At an Old Mystery* [Jackson, Wyoming"Unita Press, 1978], pp. 13-14: This account of a hoax regarding the Colter Stone is based on a conversation with W.C. Lawrence, [no relation to Paul Lawrence], of Moran, Wyoming, who knew both Lyons and Woodring personally. In brief, Superintendent Woodring wanted a museum for Teton Park and needed museum articles to exhibit. Aubrey Lyons wanted a horse concession [a monopoly] in the Park. So Lyons chiseled the "Colter Stone," out of soft rock and placed it where it would be "found" by a neighbor. He then traded the neighbor a pair of boots for the stone, and offered it to Woodring as an exhibit for his museum. He got the horse concession.

it may have been carved as a fraud or a joke. Also, dulling a skinning knife by carving on stone is not a well known pastime of mountain men.[264]

So, what do you think? Did John Colter Go To Hell? Seriously, the question is, did Colter go to Yellowstone? Able Historians, including Colter's Biographer, Burton Harris, agree that the fabled "Colter's Hell" is a thermal area on the Shoshone River and not Yellowstone Park.[265] If Colter trailed from Fort Raymond up the Shoshone River to modern Cody, then south to Dubois and over the Continental Divide, through Jackson Hole and over the Teton Range, then back to his Fort Raymond by way of Yellowstone Park, alone and in the winter, it would have been hell.

But I Think not. That it is not a logical trail–especially not of a lone man traveling in the winter, [traveling alone in the

---

[264] Lawerence, John Colter, Journey of Discovery, p. 13. J. Neilson Barry speculated that it was carved as a joke by the Hayden Party of 1872 who traversed the area of the "find," see "The Six Carved Stones," a paper embedded in a letter from J. Neilson Barry to W.C. Lawrence, Jackson Hole Museum and Historical Archives.

[265] Mattes, *Colter's Hell and Jackson's Hole,* 19-24. See also note 205. Hiram M. Chittenden, the esteemed engineer and historian, wrote in the original edition of his book in 1895 that Colter's Hell was a thermal zone within Yellowstone Park. *Yellowstone National Park* [p. 19]. Later buffs repeated the idea. A bronze statue honoring Colter as the discoverer of the Park was erected in the Jackson Wyoming town park. The statue also lists war veterans, and it was financed by Homer Richards, who's son was killed in WWII. Another bronze plaque honoring Colter is mounted in Riggs, Idaho. These efforts were done before the actual site of Colter's Hell was researched and published. Colter's biographer, Harris, though he still maintains that Colter went to the Park, correctly asserts that "Colters Hell" is on the Shoshone River and *is not in Yellowstone Park.*

History is like gossip, if you tell it often enough, and cast it in bronze, it gains a life of its own irrespective of the original facts.

winter isn't logical]. Colter was prudent and not a fool. And he would have more likely found the Crow Indians and some Shoshone too on the east rather than the west side of the Continental Divide. They likely banked their winter fires in Big Horn Basin or further south in "the valley of the warm winds" near Dubois, Wyoming where Daniel Potts and his friends found them during the winter of 1823.

Indians, elk, and buffalo were wise enough to avoid Jackson Hole, Teton Pass and Teton Basin in the winter. It is likely that John Colter was wise enough to do the same. He was an able mountain man–six years in the wilderness proved that. *But he was also wary and prudent.* Witness Thomas James's report of Colter's departure from the mountains in 1810.

> ... when [James] Cheek was killed and Colter had another narrow escape, he came into the Fort, and said he had promised his Maker to leave the country, and "now" said he, throwing down his hat on the ground, " if God will only forgive me this time and let me off I will leave the country day after to-morrow and be d—d if I ever come into it again," ... [266]

Then, Colter immediately built a canoe, loaded up two passengers and the mail, and shoved out into the river. He paddled steadily and arrived in St. Louis in a short thirty days.

In summary: faulty cartography, questionable physical evidence, and pure legend have blurred the path of John Colter through present-day southwest Montana and northwest Wyoming. In a nut shell, it was too long ago and there are no first hand or primary sources, so it isn't likely his trail will ever be known. It's makes a nice story, but good judgement bets that

---

[266] Thomas James, *Three Years Among The Indians And Mexicans*, pp. 65-66.

Colter didn't cross the Continental Divide, Jackson's Hole, Snake River and Teton Pass in the winter to find Indians who wouldn't be there. Yet the legend of Colter and Yellowstone has a life of its own that will likely continue in spite of sound history.

"Colter's Hell" isn't Yellowstone. Even early non-historians, like Washington Irving, wasn't confused about that.[267] The man was likely dispatched by Lisa to invite Indian trade, as was Edward Rose, Droullard, Wiser and Shamplain. But none of them brought back stories of the spectacular stuff in Yellowstone. Very signifi cantly, none of the sources suggesting Colter was in Yellowstone can be cer- tainly traced to Colter himself. He never claimed to have made such a journey and never wrote anything about it.

Hazen Hawkes finds Henry–Hoback stones
Courtesy Bonneville Museum and Margaret Hawkes Lindsley

---

[267] The most-quoted descriptions of Colter's Hell were not those of eyewitnesses, but rather of writers like Washington Irving. See his version of Bonneville's journals. pp. 170,[there are many editions of Irving's works so page numbers may vary]. However, Irving didn't confuse Colters Hell with Yellowstone. He places it on the Stinking River where it belongs. So did Joe Meek, see, Stanley Vestal, *Joe Meek, The Merry Mountain Man* , [Lincoln, Bison Printing, 1963], p. 96.

John Hoback and the Overland Astorians

Three men who's names are always linked together came to the mountains with Manuel Lisa in 1807. They were John Hoback, Jacob Rezner, and John Robinson. By 1810 these three were at the Three Forks of the Missouri and about ready to follow Andrew Henry, a new partner in the company, on a trapping foray to the south. The balance of the Missouri Fur Company men, including Colter, had drifted down river to St Louis.

Henry wasn't charging blindly into the unknown; two other company men, Peter Wiser and "Shamplain," had told him that the waters of the upper Columbia were rich with martin and beaver. They also directed him to go by way of the Madison River where the route was short and easy.[268] So he likely followed their directions and headed up the Madison then over the low Divide and down into beaver-rich headwaters of the Snake River. His route is suggested by two features that have ever since borne the name Henry's Lake and Henry's Fork of Snake River.

Once in the valley they swung to the east and got their first view of the magnificent Teton Range. They headed in that direction and made camp in a protected canyon meadow now called Connant Creek. Perhaps they arrived too early for trapping for they spent considerable effort chiseling their names on stones. On one big rock they carved "CAMP HENRY 1810." The rock is so large that it lies unmoved in the meadow where settlers found it. Another has the names of Henry,

---

[268] Fred Gowens, *A Fur Trade History of Yellowstone Park:* [Orem, Utah*]*, p. 105.

Hoback, and several others. Remnants of dugouts [cave or cellar dwellings] in the nearby bank were remembered by early pioneers in the area.[269]

But the winter was severe. So the party moved down to Henry's Fork of Snake River and built cabins. This site became "Fort Henry." The spot was about five miles downstream from St. Anthony and seven miles north of Rexburg, Idaho. The site was dug up in recent times and a rifle barrel, an axe, a medallion, a chain, and three carved stones emerged. The stones read: "Gov. Camp 1811–H. Wells," "Al the cook but nothing to cook," and "Ft. Henry 1811 by Cap Hunt,"[270] [This last stone was carved by the Overland Astorians who arrived a year after Henry].

The following spring they divided again; Henry led most of them north and east by way of the Three Forks region while Hoback and his two companions climbed Teton Pass, crossed Jackson's Hole, then went up Togwatee Pass and headed east. As these three were trudging toward the settlements, they met

---

[269] Personal interview with Hazen Hawkes, the discoverer of stones at "Camp Henry." See Margaret Hawkes Lindsley, *Major Andrew Henry in Idaho* [n.p. [c1985]], especially "Discovery of 'Camp Henry'," pp. 22-24. These are information filled and a pleasure to read. The trappers who's names were scratched on the stone were: John Hoback, a Kentucky trapper; P. Mcbride, Pet or Pat Mcbride, from Missouri, last heard "headed for the Spanish settlements;" Jackson, Bel or Belt Jackson, an older relative to Davie Jackson, [Jackson's Hole named for him] ; L. Cather, Leonard Cather, Scotch Irish descendent of Jasper Casper who immigrated from "The Kingdom of Ireland" to Virginia in 1735. The Cather Family Tree records that he moved from Kentucky to Missouri when a young man then "went to the mountains, lost track of." These descriptions are from the Bonniville County Museum in Idaho Falls Idaho, where the stone is displayed.

[270] Merrill D. Beal and Merle W. Wells, *History of Idaho* [New York: Lewis Historical Publishing Co., 1959], pp. 92-94.

the so-called Overland Astorians led by Wilson Price Hunt near the Niobrara River. [This is the "Cap Hunt" referred to above on the stone.] They were headed for Oregon to establish a fur post at the mouth of the Columbia River. It was May 26, 1811. Remarkably, the Astorians persuaded Hoback and his friends to cancel their journey to civilization, turn around, and return to the mountains as guides.[271]

Several weeks later, Hoback led them along the stream that would be named for him, then down its steep canyon where it joined Snake River.[272] The Snake was large and swift. But hoping to change from horses to boats, Hunt sent three men down the canyon to check it out. Then his thoughts turned "to another subject of importance,"

> He had now arrived at the headwaters of the Columbia, which were among the main points embraced by the enterprise of Mr. Astor. These upper streams were reputed to abound in beaver, and had as yet been unmolested by the white trapper.
>
> Here then it was proper to begin to cast loose those leashes of hardy trappers that are detached from trading parties in the very heart of the wilderness. The men detached in the present instance were Alexander Carson, Louis St. Michel, Pierre Detaye, and Pierre Delaunay . . . .[They] were to trap upon the upper part of Mad River, and upon the neighboring streams of the mountains.[273]

The men sent to check out Snake River reported wild and foaming rapids in the canyon. They called it "Mad" River and

---

[271] Irving, *Astoria*, chapter 18
[272] Merrill J. Mattes, Jackson Hole, *Crossroads of the Western Fur Trade 1807-1840*, [Jackson, Wyoming: Jackson Hole Museum and Teton County Historical Society, 1994 "Center Books, 1"], pp.20-25.
[273] Irving, *Astoria*, chapter 31.

wrote off any thoughts of floating down it. The balance of the party continued along the Indian trail through Jackson's Hole and crossed the river near where Wyoming Route 22 spans the stream today, [1999]. The Tetons stood out as magnificent landmarks and thus were called the "pilot knobs."

Hoback and company guided them west up the steep Indian trail over Teton Pass then down into Pierre's Hole and on to the abandoned cabins of Henry's post. Here the guides broke off to trap. They were Hoback, Rezner, Robinson and also two companions named Cass and Joseph Miller.[274]

The Hoback party likely hunted south to Bear River. Nothing more is known of the four left in Jackson Hole.[275] And nothing indicates they knew of Yellowstone.

Early British Brigades

The next whites to get near Yellowstone came from a different quarter. After six years of reprieve from trappers, in the spring of 1819, the Snake Country played host to a band of British and M'etis trappers.[276] The War of 1812 had crushed American interests at Astoria and discouraged western exploration on many fronts so the British moved in to exploit the Pacific Northwest.

The leader of the first Snake Country Expedition was

---

[274] *Ibid.*

[275] *Stuart's Journal*, p.8. Stuart wrote that the Hoback party made their hunt to the south of Fort Henry.

[276] Alexander Ross, *The Fur Hunters of the Far West*, edited by Kenneth Spaulding [Norman: University of Oklahoma Press, 1956]. Ross was a Scottsman by birth, who before working for the British was an employee of the American, John Jacob Astor.

Donald Mackenzie; his adventures were recorded by Alexander Ross.

> [W]e advanced, suffering occasionally from alarms for twenty-five days, and then found ourselves in a rich field of beaver, in the country lying between the great south branch [Snake River] and the Spanish waters [Green River] . . . .
>
> The Rocky Mountains skirting this country on the east soon deviate from their stupendous heights into sloping ridges, which divide the country into a thousand luxurious vales . . . . .[277]

They saw the Tetons . . .

> The most remarkable heights in any part of the great backbone of America are three elevated insular mountains, or peaks. They are seen at the distance of one hundred and fifty miles and the hunters very aptly designate them the Pilot Knobs.[278]

Perhaps some Astorians were with Ross who had earlier called the Tetons: " Pilot Knobs."

Ross also described natural pure salt, maybe on Salt River in Star Valley where brine springs flow 85 per cent salt. It dries 4 inches deep on the flats as white as snow. Then, without locating them, Ross described natural hot springs,

> Boiling fountains, having different degrees of temperature, are very numerous, one of two were so very hot as to boil

---

[277] *Ibid.* , pp. 135.
[278] *Ibid.*, p.177. Ross's " Pilot Knobs," are the Tetons, and his "Trois Tetons."are the Three Buttes in Idaho.The Tetons were unmistakable and unforgettable. The French-Canadian name 'Three Paps," Tetons or teats was also distinctive, graphic, and unforgettable, especially to lonesome fur trappers. [Did I say that right?]

meat. In other parts among the rocks hot and cold springs might alternately be seen within a hundred yards of each other, differing in their temperatures.[279]

After the North West Company was succeeded by Hudson Bay Company–or as Ross might call it, Hudson's Bay Fur–he as leader led an unmanageable band of mixed blood trappers to the sources of the Jefferson River.

While there, he described a hot spring like "those so often mentioned in former expeditions."[280] This might suggest an entry into Yellowstone Park, but the description is without location, and too bland for the incredible geysers and hot springs in Yellowstone. There are hot springs throughout the Rocky Mountains.[281] Excluding Yellowstone, there are fifty separate hot springs in Wyoming alone. Charting the British trappers through Snake River Country is difficult because they referred to very few known geographic features.

More Sticks

One physical link has been held up suggesting the British were in the Yellowstone region. At the head of the falls on Yellowstone River, Park Superintendent Norris is credited with finding an inscription on a tree that read: J.O.R. August 19,

---

[279] *Ibid.*, p. 177

[280] *Ibid.*, p. 237.

[281] Compare Ross with Williams Ferris and the "Boiling Kettles," in *Rocky Mountains*, p. 35. Some major hot springs are Lava and Heise in Idaho. In Wyoming there are fifty separate thermal features or groups of springs including Thermopolis, the "world's largest," These do not include springs in Yellowstone Park , Roy Breckenridge and Bern Hinkley, *Thermal Springs of Wyoming, The Geological Survey of Wyoming,*,[Laramie, W;yoming ,1978]. See Introduction p.1.

1819. Perhaps one of Mackenzie's men paused here to leave his mark on nature. Unfortunately, the tree was cut down and the marked section lost.[283] The initials J.O.R. have not been matched to an individual or trio in the party. So we have no tree, no name, no primary source–not even enough stuff for a good story. Even if the tree still existed, additional evidence is needed to prove it authentic. For example, there stands a tree in Northern Idaho with "D. Boone 1776" carved on it. Some wag was likely having fun with a pocket knife for it isn't likely that Daniel Boone was roaming west as far as Idaho in 1776.[284]

To sum it up, if accurate history is the object, a simple rule should prevail–*use first hand sources.* In courts of law are safeguards to avoid hearsay, namely, that evidence come from the witness himself. Likewise, in history, the most accurate story is from an eye witness. Intermediaries scramble the facts and garble the tale. The notion of Colter or any one besides Indians in Yellowstone before 1826 is woven by intermediaries from faulty cartogography, doubtful artifacts and pure legend.

It remained for Daniel Potts to give a first hand report of the largest thermal area in the world.

---

[283] Chittenden, *Yellowstone Park*, p. 35.

[284] Louise Rutledge, D. Boone 1776, *A Western Bicentennial Mystery.* [Idaho Falls, Idaho, 1975]. They *were* getting closer to Yellowstone--from the mouth of the Big Horn Lisa dispatched Rose, Drulloard, Colter, Wiser, and "Shamplaine." And by an easy route still used today the last two got closer to Yellowstone than Colter. But his own good judgement bets that Colter didn't make a five hundred mile hike alone in the winter over two major mountain passes and Snake River to find Crow Indians that wouldn't be there. But what the heck, it's a good story.

DANIEL TROTTER POTTS,
FIRST TO DESCRIBE YELLOWSTONE

We left Daniel Potts back in chapter seven, when he and a party of American trappers headed north from the Rendezvous of 1826 toward Blackfoot country and Yellowstone. Then we reviewed other possible explorers to this region. Let's return to Potts's story.

Daniel and his band trailed out of the Great Basin and down into Snake River Valley. They followed the river up to the forks where Henry's Fork came in from the north and joined the larger Louis's Fork. This valley was the largest in the Rocky Mountains. It was flat and the only trees were hugging meandering river channels. Looking east over a sea of sagebrush Daniel could see the marvelous Tetons.

Blackfeet dogged them every day. Beckwourth described a battle so fierce that after the victory their squaws nearly danced themselves to death with relief and joy. Leaving the battlefield they went up Henry's Fork then veered right on a trail going over the Teton Range. It was likely the same route as present Grassy Lake Road. After descending to Lewis's Fork, they turned left and followed this stream to its origins on the Continental Divide. It was all new country.

The First Description . . .

While keeping one eye out for marauding Blackfeet Daniel was engrossed in new scenery. He continued to the head of Snake River then over the Divide and was surprised to see a large body of fresh water. It was the splendid Yellowstone Lake. And then on its south shores he saw peculiar steaming hot springs. Daniel Potts's best moment as a chronicler of exploration was made when he penned a description of these singular hot springs and the magnificent Yellowstone Lake. He was first to describe this icy cold lake and thermal features that in size and variety are unsurpassed on the globe.[284] Certainly, generations of Native Americans proceeded him--but their names and thoughts are unknown.

Later, with pen and paper in hand , Daniel shaped vivid descriptions of Yellowstone including a dramatic "escape" from an exploding geyser. There were strange, smoking, exploding things in Yellowstone, the like as never had been seen. Potts began with the big picture,

> [The] Yellow-stone [River] has a large fresh water Lake near its head on the very top of the Mountain which is about one hundrid by fourty miles in diameter,and as clear as Crystal[285]

Fish Can Swim Over the Mountain

This early observation by Daniel Potts about Yellowstone Lake is remarkable. Though draining into the Missouri River, Yellowstone Lake "is almost on the very top of the mountain." It nearly straddles the Continental Divide. In fact, at this place some streams seem undecided about which ocean to feed, and remarkably, a fish can swim over the Divide. The observant Osborne Russel, who crossed this Divide several years later than Potts, wrote,

> about midway of the prarie stands a high snowy peak from whence issues a Stream of water which after entering the plain it divides equally one half running West and the other

---

[284] Breckenridge and Hinkley, *Thermal Springs of Wyoming*, p.67.
[285] *Potts Letter to Robert Potts*, 1827.

East thus bidding adieu to each other one bound for the Pacific and the other for the Atlantic ocean. *Here a trout of 12 inches in length may cross the mountains in safety.*[286]

Russel observed that a fish bent on crossing the Divide would first swim up Snake River, then to Two Ocean Pass which is a marshy meadow where the waters of North Two Ocean Creek and South Two Ocean Creek divide and flow to

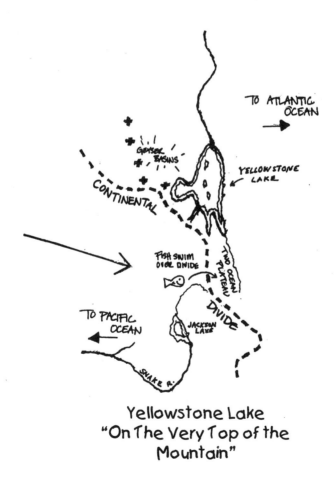

Yellowstone Lake
"On The Very Top of the
Mountain"

---

[286] Russel, *Journal of a Trapper*, p. 43.

opposite oceans. The fish would then swim through the marsh and down to Yellowstone Lake. The Native Cutthroat Trout in Yellowstone Lake doubtless took this route since they are less prevalent on Atlantic streams and couldn't possibly have swam up the two roaring vertical Yellowstone falls.[287] But Daniel didn't know about the mountain climbing fish. His interest immediately centered on beautiful Yellowstone Lake and the spectacular steaming geysers. He took special note and later wrote this first description of these thermal springs.

> on the South borders of this Lake is a number of hot and boiling springs some of water and others of most beautiful fine clay and resembles that of a must [mush] pot and throws its particles to the immense height of from twenty to thirty feet in height. The Clay is white and of a Pink [West Thumb Paint Pots] and water appear fathomless [Abyss Pool–the Park's deepest] as it appears to be entirely hollow under neath. There is also a number of places where the pure sulphur is sent forth in abundance one of our men Visited one of those wilst taking his recreation ther at an instant the earth began a tremendious trembling and he with dificulty made his escape when an explosion took place resembling that of Thunder. During our stay in that quarter I heard it every day.[288]

---

[287] Remarkably, Cutthroat trout in Yellowstone Lake likely migrated over the Continental Divide from Snake River and the Pacific slope. The two vertical falls in Yellowstone Canyon totally block fish from swimming up river from the Atlantic drainage.

[288] *Potts Letter to Robert Potts, Sweet Lake*, July 8, 1827. Yellowstone Lake was for a time designated "Sublette's' Lake," as the Burr and Wilkes maps show. See Gowens, *The Fur Trade History of Yellowstone Park*, op.cit. , maps 16 and 19. This indicates Sublette likely led the party–perhaps with his partner David Jackson. Tradition says Sublette named Jackson's Hole for his partner who liked to trap there. Jackson also got his name on the beautiful lake that mirrors the Tetons.

This is the West Thumb Geyser Basin: not as large as Old Faithful Basin, yet more scenic because of its lakeside location. This geothermal area has it all–hot springs, steaming blue pools, fumaroles, and mud pots. It has spectacular Twin Geysers, a double vented geyser blowing water up to 120 feet and the Abyss Pool which is the deepest pool in the Park. There is also Black Pool and the notable Fishing Cone where you could swing a freshly caught fish from the lake to the Cone and parbroil it. Another feature is Lakeshore Geyser with a spectacular location in the edge of Yellowstone Lake. But perhaps the most popular West Thumb thermal is the Paint Pots. They are very similar to the Fountain Paint Pots of the Lower Geyser Basin. Daniel wrote its earliest description.

His short, graphic description of Yellowstone Lake and the surrounding thermal activity makes Daniel Potts the first known visitor to the nation's largest national park. An area near West Thumb on Yellowstone Lake was named the "Potts Hot Spring Basin" in his honor. [289]

Daniel's brigade searched every stream for furs. They ranged over extensive territory trapping and also trying to puzzle out the geography of the Rockies. So likely most of the wonders of the park were discovered during the fall of 1926. And though Potts only described hot springs on the south side of the lake, he likely saw many more. It was summer, easy traveling, and only seventeen miles from Yellowstone Lake to the spectacular pools and geysers at Upper Geyser Basin. Here

---

[289] Other men [certainly the Indians], may have proceeded Potts to the Park area, but he wrote the first non-disputed eye-witness account of this wonderland. Potts diameter for Yellowstone Lake is excessive. The wandering shoreline which blocks a view of the total lake might account for some error. Perhaps it *seemed* that long when trekking around the lake in thin soled moccasins.

was the unmatchable Old Faithful and nearly one fourth of all the geysers in the world. Against blue sky and dark green timber white steam and foaming spray were visible for miles. Hissing, boiling, puffing and spraying water could hardly be missed.

They likely spread out and followed the animal and Indian trails. Since these trails are essentially located the same as today's roads, they saw features the modern tourist sees. Daniel's letter shows extensive knowledge of the region.

Notably, he knew the lake was the source of Yellowstone River. Either Iroquois defectors knew the connection and told Potts or else Daniel traveled through the Park, continued north, and learned it himself. That some men did go farther north is indicated by Robert Campbell, a new recruit who may have clerked for the company. He said they–"ascended the Snake river and tributaries near the Three Tetons and *hunted along to the forks of the Missouri, following the Gallatin,* and trapped along across the head waters of the Columbia." So its likely that some of the party followed the placid Yellowstone River a few miles downstream from the Lake and saw its spectacular plunge over two falls into a dazzling yellow canyon.[290]

The Secret Was Out

Stories about Yellowstone quickly passed from one mountaineer to another and all were curious to see it. However

---

[290] Potts wrote that the river draining Yellowstone Lake was the La Roque Juan or Yellowstone River. So himself or others of the group would have had to trace it through its Grand Canyon. Recall that Potts demonstrated extensive knowledge of various rivers near the Continental Divide.

not everyone went there. In these early years trappers moved like military—in small armed camps. It was wise to go in parties large enough to challenge the Blackfoot. But they were highly rewarded. Joe Meek went and got his story out.

Joe Meek

Three years after Potts and his companions were in Yellowstone Bill Subette headed another party there. Among them was young Joe Meek. With a reputation for good stories and fun he is known as " The Merry Mountain Man.[291] While traveling through Yellowstone Meek got separated from his band and lost. On the morning of the fifth day of fruitless wandering, Joe climbed a small mountain and was startled to see the whole country beyond was smoking with gases issuing from small craters, each of which was emitting a sharp, whistling sound . . . "Interspersed among these on the level plain were larger craters, some of them from four to six miles across. "Out of these craters issued "blue flames and molten brimstone."[292]

Thermal activity must have lessened in the Park since Joe saw his "blue flame and molten brimstone," or else Joe is stretching the truth a bit. This report is sensational. He was known for telling a good story. But it *was* truly spectacular. His tale likely grew out of an experience at one of the geyser basins.

Still later, Ferris and Russel, who visited Yellowstone in the 1830's described the area more credibly.

---

[291] Vestal, *Joe Meek, the Merry Mountain Man*, [Caxton, 1952].
[292] Chittenden, p. 37.

Warren Ferris

As a nineteen year old stripling Warren Ferris came to the mountains with the American Fur Company in 1830. Three years later he was in Yellowstone. His description, with an eye to publication and with added detail, is similar to Potts' s. And it ends similarly with a "narrow escape."

Ferris writes,

[C]louds of vapor seemed like a dense fog to overhang the springs, from which frequent reports or explosions of different loudness, constantly assailed our ears.

From the surface of a rocky plain or table, burst forth columns of water, of various dimensions, projected high in the air, accompanied by loud explosions, and sulphurous vapors, which were highly disagreeable to the smell.

The largest of these wonderful fountains, projects a column of boiling water several feet in diameter, to the height of more than one hundred and fifty feet–in my opinion.

. . . these explosions and discharges occur at intervals of about two hours. After having witnessed three of them, I ventured near enough to put my hand into the water of its basin, but withdrew it instantly, for the heat of the water in this immense cauldron, was altogether too great for comfort, and the agitation of the water, the disagreeable effluvium continually exuding, and the hollow unearthly rumbling under the rock on which I stood, so ill accorded with my notions of personal safety, that I retreated back precipitately to a respectful distance. The Indians who were with me, were quite appalled, and could not by any means be induced to approach them. They seemed astonished at my presumption in advancing up to the large one, and when I safely returned, congratulated me on my narrow escape . . . in some instances. the volumes were projected obliquely upwards, [Riverside Geyser?], and fell into the neighboring fountains or on the rock or prairie. But their ascent was generally perpendicular, falling in and about their own basins . . . these wonderful productions of nature, are situated near the centre of a small valley, surrounded by pine covered hills . . . .[293]

Osborne Russell

With the exception of Warren Ferris, the trapper Osborne Russell may arguably have written the best day-to-day account of a trappers life in the Far West. Similar to Ferris, Russel kept a journal. He came to the mountains in 1834 as a member of Nathanial Wyeth's expedition. By that date, tales about Yellowstone were widely known among mountain men. Osborne Russell was led there in 1839 by a friend who had been there the year previous. Russell wrote,

the first spring we visited was about 10 feet in diameter which threw up mud with a noise similar to boiling soap close about this were numerous [others] similar to it throwing up the hot mud and water 5 or 6 feet high about 30 or 40 paces from these along the side of a small ridge the hot steam rushed forth from holes in the ground with a hissing noise which could be heard a mile distant. On a near approach we could hear the water bubbling under ground some distance from the surface. The sound of our footsteps over this place was like thumping over a hollow vessel of emense size . . . in many places were peaks from 2 to 6 feet high formed of lime Stone, deposited by the

---

[293] Ferris, *Rocky Mountains*, pp. 205-206. According to J. Cecil Alter [who annotated this Ferris diary], this description of the Upper Geyser Basin was often reprinted but without author credit.

boiling water, which appeared of snowy whiteness. The water when cold is perfectly sweet except having a fresh limestone taste. After surveying these natural wonders for sometime my comrade conducted me to what he called the "hour spring' at this spring the first thing that attracts the attention is a hole about 15 inches in diameter in which the water is boiling slowly about 4 inches below the surface at length it begins to boil and bubble violently and the water commences raising and shooting upwards until the column arises to the hight of sixty feet from wence it falls to the ground in drops on a circle of about 30 feet in diameter being perfetly cold when it strikes the ground It continues shooting up in this manner five or 6 minutes and then sinks back to its former state of Slowly boiling for an hour and then shoots forth as before My Comrade Said he had watched the motions of this Spring for one whole day and part of the night the year previous and found no irregularity whatever in its movements . . . .[294]

Is this statement from Russell the earliest eye witness account Old Faithful?

Father De Smit–Colter's Hell isn't Yellowstone

De Smit went west to bring salvation to the Indians. As a Catholic priest, he was educated, and as a man, he was respected by the trappers. In a letter from this noted missionary dated at the University of St. Louis, January 20, 1852 he penned an early description that correctly locates "Colter's Hell" separate from Yellowstone. After describing Colters Hell

---

[294] Russell, *Journal of a Trapper*, [Lincoln, 1955], p. 98. Russell trekked through the park numerous times. See in his index: "Yellowstone National Park."

on the Shoshone River, he then described more "extraordinary
" thermal areas which reached more than one "hundred miles,"
near the source of the Yellowstone River.[295]

De Smit First Locates Colters Hell:

Near the sources of the River Puante [Shoshone],which
empties into the Big Horn . . . is a place called "Colters
Hell–from a beaver hunter of that name. The sulphurous
gasses which escape in great volumes from the burning soil
infect the atmosphere for several miles and render the earth
so barren that even the wild wormwood can not grow on
it.[296]

Then He Locates Yellowstone

However, I think that the most extraordinary spot in this
respect, and perhaps the most marvelous of all the northern
half of this continent, is in the very heart of the Rocky
Mountains [the Continental Divide] between the 43rd and
45th degrees of latitude, and the 109th and 111th degrees
of longitude . . . between the sources of the Madison and
the Yellowstone. It reaches more than a hundred miles.
Bituminous sulphurous and boiling springs are very
numerous in it. The hot springs contain a large quantity of
calcareous matter, and form hills more or less elevated . .
. the earth is thrown up very high, and the influence of the
elements causes it to take the most varied and most
fantastic shapes. Gas, vapor and smoke are continually
escaping by a thousand openings from the base to the
summit of the volcanic pile; the noise at times resembles

---

[295] Chittenden, pp. 44-45.
[296] *Ibid.*

the steam let off by a boat. *Strong subterranean explosions occurs like those in "Colters Hell."* The hunters and the Indians speak of it with superstitious fear, and consider it the abode of evil spirits, that is to say, a kind of hell. Indians seldom approach it without offering some sacrifice, or, at least without presenting the calumet of peace to the turbulent spirits, that they may be propitious.

Near the Gardiner River, a tributary of the Yellowstone, and in the vicinity of the region I have just been describing, there is a mountain of sulphur."[297]

Jim Bridger's Story

As one of the youngest men with Ashley and Henry, Bridger came to the mountains in 1823. He was at times a camp-mate of Daniel Potts. James Bridger remained in the mountains for some thirty years. This sixteen year old grew up and became renowned as a teller of tall tales. However, some of his tall tales later proved to be true. Since Bridger couldn't write, his story is told by another. This excerpt about Yellowstone, taken from Gunnison's History of the Mormons, [1852] is such an example.

"He [Bridger] gives a picture, most romantic and enticing of the head waters of the Yellowstone. A lake, sixty miles long, cold and pellucid, lies embosomed among the high precipitous mountains. On the west side is a sloping plain, several miles wide, with clumps of trees and groves of pine. The ground resounds with the tread of horses. Geysers spout up seventy feet high, with a terrific, hissing noise, at regular intervals. Waterfalls are sparkling, leaping and thundering down the precipices, and collect in the pool

---

[297] Chittenden, pp. 44,45. My italics.

below. The river issues from this lake, and for fifteen miles roars through the perpendicular canyon [Grand Canyon of the Yellowstone] at the outlet. In this section are the 'Great Springs,' [Mammoth Hot Springs], so hot that meat is readily cooked in them, and as they descend on the successive terraces, afford at length delightful baths. On the other side is an acid spring, which gushes out in a river torrent; and below is a cave, [Cinnabar Mountain] which supplies 'vermillion' for the savages in abundance." [298]

This review of early Yellowstone impressions spans 45 years. Now we return to 1826 and Daniel Potts.

Potts Returns From Blackfoot Country

In 1826 a newcomer arrived in the mountains who, like Potts, could scribble about the times. He was Robert Campbell, and went to Blackfoot Country with Daniel. Summarizing the fall hunt, he wrote that his party,

> ascended the Snake river and tributaries near the Three Tetons and hunted along to the forks of the Missouri, following the Gallatin, and trapped along across the head waters of the Columbia.[299]

Campbell could have filled in historical gaps this season but this sketch of the route back to Utah is almost as frugal as Potts's. He and Daniel may not have been together since he didn't mention Yellowstone. He only wrote: "From this place

---

[298] Quoted from Chittenden, P. J. W. Gunnison came West with the U.S. Topographical Engineers in 1849 to survey the Great Basin.

[299] Campbell's quote is from "Robert Campbell Dictation" in the Missouri Historical Society manuscript collection, Morgan, *West of William Ashley*, p. 161. It is odd that Campbell didn't write anything about Yellowstone. Perhaps he didn't see the area.

by a circuitous rout to the North west we returned."[300]

Potts skipped the details of his return, preferring to recount an exciting encounter with a Blackfoot hunting party. Their horses saved them.

> [T]wo others and myself pushed on in the advance for the purpose of accumulating a few more Bever and in the act of passing through a narrow confine in the Mountain we were met plumb in face by a large party of Black-feet Indians who not knowing our number fled into the mountain in confusion and we to a small grove of willows here we made every prepparation for battle after which finding our enemy as much allarmed as ourselves we mounted our Horses which where heavyly loaded we took the back retreat. The Indian raised a tremendious Yell and showered down from the Mountain top who had almost cut off our retreat we here put whip to our Horses and they pursued us in close quarters until we reached the plains when we left them behind on this trip one man was closely fired on by a party of Black-feet several others where closely pursued.[301]

When Americans met the Blackfeet there was either a life and death fight, or headlong retreat–no slack was expected from either side and none was given.

---

[300] *Potts Letter to Robert Potts, Sweet Lake,* July 8, 1827.
[301] *Ibid.*

WINTER TRAVELS AND A SUMMER FAIR

1827, UTAH

Immediately after arriving at winter quarters and counting up the furs William Sublette hastened to get an order for trade goods out to Ashley before the deadline was up. The firm of Smith, Jackson and Sublette had approached the coming Rendezvous with caution. They didn't want to order more goods than the season's furs would justify, so they agreed to get word to Ashley by March 1, 1827. The Trapping catch was good–especially Jackson's–now they needed to tell Ashley in time. An *express* to St. Louis was the only way.

It was winter, conditions didn't favor travel by horseback so two tough and reliable walkers were needed–some of the ground would be traveled on snowshoes. Sublette picked himself and Moses "Black" Harris. Harris–like James Beckwourth had Afro-American parentage. And he stood out among trappers for more reasons than his dark skin. He was a traveler by horse or afoot and made several long journeys as an express. He went with Jedediah Smith in the spring of 1826; with Sublette this winter of 1827-28. And five years later in 1833, he was on an express with Benjamin Harrison. Sometimes, both to keep warm and avoid Indians, he walked by night and slept by day. He was capable of extreme and excruciating violence on one hand. But, there was also the side captured in James Clyman's poem "which though not intended as an epitaph might have been appropriate for one:"

> Here lies the bones of old Black Harris
> Who often traveled beyond the far west
> And for the freedom of equal rights
> He crossed the snowy mountain heights
> Was a free and easy kind of soul
> Especially with a belly full.[302]

---

[302] *James Clyman, Frontiersman,* Camp, ed. p.64.

The journey began on January 1, 1827 and may have brought out the worst side of Harris; a full belly was rare. Traveling on foot and out of food, they were finally compelled to kill and eat their pack dog who succumbed only after a wild and frantic struggle. After intense suffering from the elements the pair reached St. Louis on March 4, 1827. Ashley consented to honor his contract in spite of their being four days tardy.[303]

Daniel Potts's Expedition to the Sevier Country

Meanwhile the men in the mountains were wintering in Cache Valley holed-up in teepes and dugouts on Cub River. For more horse feed , a better chance at shooting game, or just plain independence, part of them camped on Logan River. But this winter remained warmer than usual and Potts got wonder-lust. He and some companions headed out to explore south and west of Great Salt Lake–the region he had wanted to visit the previous trapping season.

They didn't know much about middle Utah. Jedediah Smith had passed through it on his way to California but Smith hadn't returned from his "South West Expedition," so his assessment of the land and beaver wasn't known. A year and a half previous to that, Ashley had initiated a not-so-successful voyage of exploration down the Green River and nearly drowned.[304]Scant and misleading information of the region existed from the Dominquez-Escalante expedition who went north from Taos in 1776–a journey that resulted in a map whose focal point was a large lake called "Laguna de Los

---

[303] Further detail and bibliographic references in Sunder, *Bill Sublette*, pp. 71-73. Ashley was likely relieved to see them. It was in his best interest to retain these ambitious men as buyers of his goods.
[304] Dale, *The Ashley-Smith Explorations*, pp. 137-151.

Timpanogos,[305] now Utah Lake. The name Timpanogos derived from the Indians in Utah Valley–and is now the name of a magnificent mountain east of the lake. These Spanish padres admired this pretty valley and its streams. With an eye to their mission they supposed Provo River sufficient to irrigate a large pueblo of Spanish subjects.

But the fathers missed a claim of first discovery by not following the Jordan River north to Great Salt Lake.

Having already made the decision to turn back, information from the Indians was enough to suit them.

> the other lake with which [Utah Lake] communicates, according to what they told us, covers many leagues, and its waters are noxious and extremely salty, for the Timpanios assure us that a person who moistens any part of his body with the water of the lake immediately feels much itching in the part that is wet.[306]

The Spanish map showed a large river issuing from Lake Timpanogos then flowing across the western desert to the Pacific Ocean. Somewhat parallel to this unnamed river was another named Rio de S. Buenaventura. It flowed south through the lake "Laguna de Miera," then southwest to the Pacific Ocean near modern day Monterey, California. American cartographers had used this Spanish map then added embellishments of their own. Not until John C. Fremont explored and named the Great Basin was this ocean drainage for the Basin finally removed from maps.

The Great Basin is a vast stretch of the West encompassing all of Nevada and parts of Oregon, Idaho and California.

---

[305] Herbert Bolton, *Pageant in the Wilderness* [Salt Lake City: Utah Historical Society, 1950], see map.
[306] *Ibid*, p. 186

Instead of flowing to the oceans, here the streams flow inland to the lowest parts of the basin then evaporate leaving nothing but minerals–principally salt.

But in 1827 Fremont hadn't yet made his discovery of the Great Basin. So Daniel Potts and his colleagues were trying to find good beaver country and puzzle out the geography for themselves. They left Cache Valley in February and headed south to Utah Lake. Potts may have been the leader. He writes:

> Shortly after our arrival last fall in winter quarters, we made preparations to explore the country lying south west of the Great Salt Lake. Having but little or no winter weather, six of us took our departure about the middle of February, and proceeded by forced marches into the country by way of the Utaw Lake –which lies about 80 miles south of the Sweet Water Lake, is thirty miles long and ten broad. It is plentifully supplied with fish, which form the principal subsistence of the Utaw tribe of Indians. We passed through a large swamp of bullrushes, and resembling muskrat houses. These we soon discovered to be wigwams, in which the Indians remained during the stay of the ice. As there is not a tree within three miles, their principal fuel is bullrushes.[307]

Potts was delighted with the natural grandeur:

> This is a most beautiful country. It is intersected by a number of transparent streams. The grass is at this time from six to twelve inches in height, and in full bloom. The snow that falls, seldom remains more than a week. It assists the grass in its growth, and appears adapted to the climate.[308]

Daniel and his band were traveling with the Utah Lake on

---

[307] *Potts Letter to Dr. Lukens, Sweet Water Lake,* July 8, 1827.
[308] ibid.

their right and the stupendous Wasatch Front mountains rising nearly vertical on their left. Though it was a warm winter, he was fascinated that the foliage of the Rockies was adapted to such a short growing season. Grass was growing and flowers blooming only a few feet from melting snow. He wrote the truth. Years later in 1872, the Hayden Survey reported "flowers peeping through the snow" on the Lower Saddle of Grand Teton–11,600 feet high!

Leaving Utah Valley, the party traveled "due south about thirty miles to a small river running S.E. to S.W." They were apparently following present State Route 91 through Juab Valley to the Sevier River. Potts' name for the stream,"Rabbit River,"on account of the great number of large black tail rabbits or hares found in its vicinity,"[309] didn't stick.

Proceeding down the Rabbit-Sevier River about fifty miles south of Utah Lake, they came upon an unnamed body of water now called Sevier Lake. Reminiscent of James Bridger's approach to Great Salt Lake, Potts investigated further. He didn't know there was a Great Basin, but he could see that this lake had no outlet, and soon discovered it was salty also. From the Indians he learned that in almost any degree of the compass the country was inhospitable.

> We descended this river about fifty miles to where it discharges into a salt lake, the size of which I was not able to ascertain, owing to the marshes which surround it, and which are impassable for man and beast. This lake is bounded on the south and west by low Cedar Mountains, which separate it from the plains of the Great Salt Lake. On the south and east also, it is bounded by great plains. The Indians informed us that the country lying southwest, was impassable for the horses owing to the earth being full of

---

[309] They struck the river about the vicinity of the Sevier Bridge Reservoir.

holes. As well as we could understand from their description, it is an ancient volcanic region[310]

The Indians had it right; the area was once volcanic. Both Potts and Jedediah Smith, who had passed this way two summers earlier, described these local Indians in terms so similar they must have visited the same group.[311] According to both, the natives were very poor, even "miserable," they wore clothing of sewed rabbit skins and ate roots and grass. With tongue in cheek, Daniel declared this food *wasn't habit forming*. So much of their time was spent in search of food that these Pi-Ute Indians had very little energy to develop a culture or acquire creature comforts. Potts writes:

> This river is inhabited by a numerous tribe of miserable Indians. Their clothing consists of a breech-cloth of goat or deer skin, and a robe of rabbit skins, cut in strips, sewed together after the manner of rag carpets, with the bark of milk weed twisted into twine for the chain. These wretched creatures go out barefoot in the coldest days of winter. Their diet consists of roots, grass seeds, and grass, so you may judge they are not gross in their eating habit. They call themselves Pie-Utaws, and I suppose are derived from the same stock [as the Utaw Indians].[312]

Though the handiwork of this tribe was scanty, Jed Smith, when he came through later that summer, was impressed with their marble pipes and flint knives. He obtained an example of each but unfortunately they were broken before he got them to

---

[310] *Potts Letter to Dr. Lukens, Sweet Water Lake*, July 8, 1827.

[311] Letter from Jedediah S. Smith to General William Clark, Little Lake of Bear River, July 12, 1827 [full annotated copy in Morgan, *Jedediah Smith*, pp. 334-337].

[312] Potts's Letter to Dr. Lukens, Sweet Water Lake, July 8, 1827.

William Clark at the Indian Office in St. Louis.[313]

Traveling generally eastward, Potts struck the Sevier River again and ascended it to its source. At the southernmost end of their journey they climbed out of the Great Basin and dropped down onto the Green River drainage. Then some uninvited Indians showed up.

> Here the natives paid us a visit and stole one of our horses. Two nights afterwards they stole another, and shot their arrows into four horses two of which belonged to myself. We then started on our return. The Indians followed us, and were in the act of approaching our horses in open daylight, whilst feeding, when the horses took fright and ran to the camp. It was this that first alarmed us. We sallied forth and fired on the Indians, but they made their escape across the river.[314]

Other than a good and helpful squaw, the most costly asset a trapper owned was horses. Potts makes no mention of an Indian wife, but he did lament his bad luck with horses–their importance and value can be judged by his final summary:

> On this trip I have lost one Horse by accident and the last spring two by the Utaws who killed them for the purpose [of] eating one of which was a favourite Buffaloe Horse this loss cannot be computed at less than four hundred and fifty Dollars by this you may conclude [it] keeps my nose close to the grind stone. [315]

---

[313] Morgan, *Jedediah Smith*, pp. 334-337. Jedediah Smith covered more ground than any mountain man. He went to California twice, returning respectively first by way of Oregon and secondly through the Nevada desert. It is unfortunate that his untimely death thwarted the book he planned to write.

[314] *Potts's Letter to Dr. Lukens, Sweet Water Lake*, July 8, 1827.

[315] *Potts Letter to Robert Potts*, 1827

With his horses killed, it swept away much of the season's profits. He was still fortunate. Many a trapper lost hide and hair not attached to his horses. Even the wary, mountain-smart, Jedediah Smith lost his horses, his men twice, and eventually his hair.[316]

As Daniel's party headed back north they called upon the Utah Indians. Potts notes their number, and ends with what must be a wry comment:

> We then paid a visit to the Utaws, who are almost as numerous as the Buffaloe on the prarie, *and an exception to all human kind, for their honesty.*[317]

In the previous paragraph Daniel wrote that the Utah Indians shot arrows into two of his horses, then followed them and tried to steal their horses in broad daylight–some honesty!

The Rendezvous of 1827

The mountain fair of 1827 got off with a boom.[318] Ashley had sent a piece of artillery, a four pounder, with the supply caravan under Brufee and Scott. Two mules pulled this cannon which made the first wheel tracks over South Pass. It was reportedly brought to intimidate the Indians, but shots fired at

---

[316] Jedediah Smith survived three Indian massacres but not the fourth, in 1831, while on a trading venture bound for Santa Fe his party ran out of water. The men spread out in various directions, with Jedidiah and Fitzpatrick going south. Traveling by himself, Jedediah was apparently killed by a Comanche war party. Mexicans who traded with the Indians brought his pistols and rifle into Sante Fe. Morgan, *Jedediah Smith*, pp. 329-330.

[317] Potts Letter to Dr. Lukens, Sweet Water Lake, July 8, 1827. My italics.

[318] Gowens, *Rocky, Mountain Rendezvous*, pp. 33-38.

the Rendezvous emboldened the trappers, impressed the Indians and enlivened the party .[319]

The site was on Sweet or today's *Bear* Lake, near present Lake Town and business got under way in mid-June. The Bear Lake region had always been a favorite haunt of Potts, and he wrote its first description in 1826:

> [In] The first valley as you approach from the head of the river, is a small sweet lake, about 120 miles in circumference, with beautiful clear water, and when the wind blows has a splendid appearance.[320]

These were not the words of a disinterested observer, but rather of one at home and at peace with the place. Bear Lake continues to charm. It is an ever changing turquoise caused by the sun reflecting off sands of limestone suspended in the water. Its name distinguishes its "sweet" or drinkable waters from the briny water of Salt lake.

Before Potts and his party arrived at the Rendezvous of 1827 the camp was attacked by a band of Blackfeet who seem to be south of their normal stomping grounds. Daniel chronicled the fracas,

> A few Days previous to my arrival at this place a party of about 120 Blackfeet approached the Camp and killed a Snake and his squaw the alarm was immediately given and the Snakes Utaws and Whites sallied forth for Battle the enemy fled to the Mountain to a small concavity thickly groon with small timber surrounded by open ground In this engagement the squaws where busily engaged in throwing up batterys an draging off the dead there was only six

---

[319] Morgan, *Jedediah Smith*, p. 225.
[320] *Potts Letter to Robert Potts*, Rocky Mountains, July 16, 1826. Again, "Sweet" lake is in contrast to the sour and salty "Salt Lake."

whites engaged in this battle who immediately advanced within Pistol shot and you may be assured that almost every shot counted one The loss of the Snakes was three killed and that of the Utaws was none though who gained great applause for their bravery the loss of the enemy is not known six where found dead on the ground besides a great number where carried off on Horses.[321]

While Beckwourth chose to stage this battle a year earlier, similarities indicate his and Potts's are the same brawl. It took place five miles from the base camp and, according to Beckwourth, the skirmish was an inter-tribal mountain war:

There were over three hundred trappers mounted in a few moments, who, with Captain Sublet at their head, charged instantly on the enemy. The Snake warriors were also on hand, thirsting to take vengeance on the Black Feet.[322]

After a six-hour battle, the assailants "began to want nourishment" and went back to their camp for food. The Snake Indians were told to "rub them out" while the others were gone to lunch, but these natives were also hungry and almost beat the whites back to camp. During the interim, the Blackfeet escaped. Later, however, considerable booty was taken from the battlefield. He continues,

The fruits of our victory were one hundred and seventy-three scalps, with numerous quivers of arrows, war-clubs, battle-axes, and lances. We also killed a number of their horses, which doubtless was the reason of their leaving so many of their dead on the field of battle. The trappers had seven or eight wounded, but none killed. Our allies lost eleven in battle, besides five slain before: but none of those

---

[321] *Potts Letter to Robert Potts, Sweet Lake*, July 8, 1827.
[322] *The Life and Adventure of Thomas Beckwourth*, p. 109.

killed in battle were scalped.[323]

Mountainiers at the Rendezvous of 1827 were happily surprised when a scraggly ghost showed up from the western deserts. It was the extraordinary traveler Jedediah Smith. Emaciated and exhausted but ever game, Smith and two companions had barely survived crossing the hot, bone dry, summer desert from California.

They hadn't seen or heard of him for a year and most had given their booshway up for dead. The restless Smith had gone deep into the Southwest to the Mohave villages where half the party was massacred. His timing was bad. The Mohave were smarting from a defeat by Ewing Young and were out for revenge. Smith collected his remaining nine men, had them gather up what supplies they thought they could carry, and struck off west across the desert. They eventually ended up at San Gabriel Mission on the coast.

Leaving his men and furs in California, he and a few companions made the first white crossing of the Sierra Nevadas then suffered and thirsted their way back across a scorching Nevada desert. Without knowing the trails or water holes they ate their horses and plodded and puzzled their way from one place of water to the next. Jedediah and two men barely survived before arriving emaciated at the Rendezvous on Bear Lake.

But the hardened Smith remained only ten days before heading back to California for his furs and men.[324] Jedediah Smith was an effective leader, a driving businessman and the foremost American explorer of the early West. He evidently told Mexican authorities about the Rendezvous on Bear Lake,

[323] *Ibid.*, p.110 .
[324] Morgan, *Jedediah Smith*, pp. 193-215.

for this interesting account was sent by the Mexican Secretary of State to the American Minister, Joel Poinsett, in 1828:

> [F]our days' journey beyond the lake of Timpanogos, there is a fort situated in another lake, with a hundred men under the command of a general of the United States of North Anerica, having with them five wagons and three pieces of artillery . . . . [T] hey arrived at the said fort in May, and left it on the 1st of August of the year last past, with a hundred horses loaded with otter skins . . . . [T] he said general caused a peace to be made between the barbarous nations of the Yutas Timpanagos and the Camanches Sozones, [Shoshone] . . . [T] he Americans will have returned to the fort by the month of December.[325]

In spite of errors, the Secretary got most of it right. And the Mexican report was an improvement over a similar one the year previous. In it the American trappers were alleged to have been *fishing*.

Potts was dissatisfied with the dwindling odds of making his fortune in the fur trade. Upon finding themselves with a complete monopoly, Smith, Jackson and Sublette had raised the price of trade goods. By this date, Daniel no longer was obligated to the company and was seeking to sell his furs in a better market than the Rendezvous. In a letter to Dr. Lukens he stated, "There is a poor prospect of making much here, owing to the evil disposition of the Indians, and the exorbitant price of goods. Then he listed some prices of Smith, Jackson and Sublette.

His list is produced below along with Ashley's prices of 1825 for comparison. Beads, blankets and scarlet cloth took a real jump.

---

[325] Quoted from the full text in translation by Morgan, *Jedediah Smith*, p. 229.

Trade Goods	Potts, 1827[326]	Ashley, 1825[327]
Powder	$2.50 per lb.	$1.50
Lead	1.50	$1.50
Coffee	2.00	$1.50
Sugar	2.00	$3.00
Tobacco	2.00	$1.50
Vermilion	6.00	$5.00
Beads	5.00 [high!]	$1.75
Pepper	6.00	
Blankets–three point[328]	15.00 [high!]	$9.00
Cotton Stripe, per yard	2.50	
Calico do		[2.50]
Scarlet Cloth [coarse]	10.00[high!]	$6.00
Blue Cloth [coarse]do	8.00	$5.00
Ribband, per yard	0.75	$0.50
Brass nails, per dozen	0.50	

Horses cost from 150 dollars to 300, and some as high as 500.

Potts's list is often quoted by fur trade historians because of the rarity of such records. The notable exception is Ashley's account book for the Rendezvous of 1825. A comparison of the two indicates a general price hike by the new company. Potts

---

[326] *Potts's Letter to Dr. Lukens, Sweet Water Lake,* July 8, 1927.

[327] Morgan, *The West of William Ashley,* pp. 118-127. It is difficult to ascertain from this record book how much Ashley charged Weber's contingent for goods since none of these men were listed. Ashley's prices varied with the status of the trapper: engaged, free, or whatever. Some of the men were hired on a yearly salary, while others were completely independent.

[328] "A three point" blanket sold for three beaver skins, a "four point," was thicker and sold for four. Hudson Bay blankets were made with black slashes or marks on the edge to indicate their points or value. They still are–though trading beaver for them has long past!

was disillusioned about making much money selling his fur to the traders. The real money in this business was not in hunting or trapping the icy streams, but rather in exchanging trade goods for furs–in buying and selling–or trapping the trappers.

Men of vision like Ashley, Smith, and Sublette had learned this earlier and for their risk and foresight made big money. They set prices and were the only traders at the Rendezvous. To make his fortune, Daniel Potts would have to look elsewhere. So in 1827 he was determined to put forth one more major effort to capitalize a venture of his own.

FORTUNE FROWNED–
PRESERVATION SMILED

1827, [UTAH AND IDAHO]

Daniel Potts was the Chronicler of the early fur trade, and when he failed to write, fur trade history suffered. His writings regarding the fall and winter of 1827 are scanty, so that time is somewhat of a mystery. However, in a brief letter to his brother Robert written from St. Louis in 1828, he passed over the period with a tantalizing statement:

> [M]y adventures and escapes for the last year in the mountains *far exceeds* all the remainder part of my stay in the mountains as I had risked everything to make or die in the attempt in this fortune frouned, though preservation smiled.[329]

Potts and his friends were determined to get a stake this season in spite of high prices and wild Indians. And this "make or die" attitude resulted in some of them getting killed. For this last violent effort Daniel said they went *west*. The following meager hint is all he wrote regarding the location of their hunt.

> To-morrow I start for the west, and shall not return under a year, when I expect to start for St. Louis.[330]

Sublette reveals a glimpse of this misty period in a letter to Ashley. He wrote that in 1828 the firm of Smith, Jackson and Sublette,

> had about one hundred men employed upon the territory claimed by the United States, West of the Rocky Mountains, who were divided into three or four parties, and operated in different directions.[331]

---

[329] *Potts's Letter to to Robert Potts*, St. Louis, October 13, 1828.

[330] *Potts's Letter to Dr. Lukens, Sweet Water Lake*, July 8, 1827.

[331] Letter of William H. Ashley to Thomas H. Benton, St. Louis, January 20, 1829, copied in Morgan, *West of William Ashley*, pp. 186-188.

Apparently Potts and a band went west into present Idaho. They planned to winter out of Utah for the first time since 1824. However, plans in the mountains were often bent by fierce Indians, foul weather and bad luck. This year, Daniel's party had trouble with all three.

He was with a party of forty free trappers. Perhaps all of them had started out with a desperate "do or die" attitude. On September 28, Peter Skeen Ogden ran into them on the banks of the Weiser River and thought they were headed for the Owyhee.[332] Some of them remained with Ogden for a while trapping and trading with Hudson Bay Fur Company. However, Mother Nature gave indications of a grim winter; by early September the snow had fallen to knee-deep levels. And by the end of November the men couldn't fight it any longer so they gave up and headed towards the warmer valleys in Utah.[333]

On their way to Salt Lake four detached trappers mysteriously disappeared–Ephraim Logan, Jacob O'Hara, William Bell and James Scott. Ashley got this news from Sublette,

> Logan, O'Hara, Bell, and Scott, the four men missing, were with 15 or 20 other men, on their way from the river Columbia to the Grand Salt Lake. The four in question diverged from a direct route to their place of destination, for the purpose of exploring some small rivers, intending

---

[332] "Peter Skene Ogden Journal 1827-1828, ed. T.C. Elliot," *Oregon Historical Society Quarterly*, XI [1910], p. 362. Quoted from Morgan, *Jedediah Smith*, p. 292. The Weiser River was named for Peter Weiser, one of Lewis and Clark's men. Later, in 1807, he was sent out by Manwell Lisa to invite Indians to trade. It was he and "Shamplaine" who discovered the easy route from the Three Forks to Snake River Valley. They likely got closer to Yellowstone Park area than the man given credit for it–John Colter.

[333] Ibid., p. 365

to again join their companions in the course of two or three days; but since they left the party, now about twelve months, nothing directly or indirectly has been heard of them. They no doubt were killed, but by whom we know not.[334]

Upon reaching their old haunts on Bear River Potts and his band were surprised to find the weather was terrible there also. Numerous mountain men say the winter of 1827-1828 was the most severe that anyone could remember.[335] The fierce winds and ever falling snow also kept Jackson and Sublette from entering the mountains with trade goods .[336]

So Potts's vow to "make or die" by risking everything this season went unfulfilled on both counts–though his "adventures and escapes" exceeded all the previous years. Indians and foul weather ruined hopes for a rich hunt. Daniel reported the bad weather and casualty count to his brother Robert,

> the Indians on one part and the hard winter on the other has been my sad ruin, and [I] have lost not less than one thousand dollars, the first snow fell on the third of September when it snowed for three days without intermission, the snow remained on the ground upwards of knee deep and I think must have felt fully waist deep this had not the least effect on any kind of vegetation as it appears adapted to the climate the winter remained gentle untill the first of December when the power [of] vengence was poured out on us the N.E. winds and more particularly the South accompanied with a continued snow until the

---

[334] Letter of William H. Ashley to Thomas H. Benton, January 20, 1829 [see Morgan, *The West of William Ashley*, pp. 186-188]. There is now a "Logan" Utah in Cache Valley, the traditional wintering spot for American trappers.

[335] *Potts' Letter to Robert Potts, St. Louis*, October 13, 1828.

[336] *Peter Skene Ogden Journal* 1827-1828, p. 374.

first of march when it somewhat abated the snow remained upwards of four feet on the level the sweet lake was bridged over on the 8 of may for twenty days in succession the great spirit the sun refused to visit us the like has [never] been known by the oldest livers which I suppose is not less than one hundred or upwards the horses which the winter did not destroy the early visits of the Black feet swept away with from twelve to fifteen scalps of our hunters.[337]

Though many of the horses died of starvation some were killed for food. Ogden seemed to have a direct line into the American camp and he reported that,

the Americans are starving on Bear River according to report, no buffalo in that quarter, they are reduced to eat horses and dogs.[338]

These months holed up in cramped shelters eating horse meat were aggravating. Potts was determined to catch every beaver possible and ventured out during breaks in the winter. But his early efforts failed entirely: the bitter weather continued into summer.

It was cold. Sweet lake was bridged over with ice on the eighth of May for twenty days in succession; unheard of before or since. Normally flowers would bloom in May. Daniel wrote that such winter had never been known by the oldest mountaineers or Indians. It delayed the spring hunt and set the Rendezvous date almost a month later than the previous year.[339]

---

[337] *Potts's Letter to Robert Potts, St. Louis,* October 13, 1828.

[338] Peter Skene Ogden Journal 1827-1828, p. 371.

[339] It was a terrible winter; Bear Lake being froze over in April or May is unheard of. Regarding the Rendezvous termination date, Potts said that it took him "about seventy days" to reach "the bounds of civilization." The letter to his brother was dated October 13, 1828, "about a week" after he arrived, [October 6]. So the Rendezvous broke up in the latter part of

When the streams finally cleared Potts worked his traps for the last time. Since summer was fast approaching and he wanted to go back to St Louis with the fur caravan, he couldn't get too far from the place of embarkation. He doubtless stayed near his old stomping grounds around Sweet Lake and Bear River. And having spent six years in the mountains with his scalp firmly attached, he avoided unnecessary peril. Trapping the Snake Country was dangerous. To illustrate the risk, note this from Peter Skeen Ogden's journal,

> . . . There remains now only one man living of all the Snake [Country] men of 1820, and rather extraordinary all have been killed, with the exception of two, who died a natural death, and are scattered over the Snake Country, indeed for a country so lately discovered it is almost incredible the numbers that have fallen in it.[340]

Potts wanted to get back alive. He was determined to resist the temptation he had succumbed to before–that powerful urge to remain in the mountains he had come to love. But, before his departure Potts reported one more wild melee with the Blackfeet.

Robert Campbell, having spent the winter and spring among the Flatheads to the north, was bringing the season's catch to the Rendezvous. Beckwourth may have been with

---

July, 1828. Gowans, *Rocky Mountain Rendezvous*, p. 42, has the Rendezvous beginning in "the first part of July."

[340] Entry for Jan. 1, 1829. *Ogden's Snake Country Journals, 1828-29.* Ogden was well posted on the Americans and may be including their losses also. After all, many of the American trappers–like John Grey and "Old Pierre–had first come to Snake Country with British parties. "Old Pierre" Tontavantogen was killed at the head of the Jefferson in 1827 and John Grey is said to have been killed by a neighbors wife in 1845.

him.[341] The party halted within a short day's march of the main camp. Early in the morning as the cook was packing horses, he was jumped and killed by Blackfeet Indians. Campbell immediately mustered his band of about thirty men to a willow spring for hiding and defense. They battled for three or four hours–until the whites ran low on ammunition. To save his party, Campbell mounted a fast horse and along with "a little Spaniard" rode through the enemy lines where " the balls flew like hail," and dashed to the Rendezvous for relief.[342] Daniel may have been an eye witness as the two men on lathered horses came racing into camp. He wrote,

> A party of about one hundred Black feet mounted attacted thrty odd of our hunters with their familys this engagement lasted for upwards of three hours when a couple of our men mounted two of their swiftest horses [and] dashed through the ranks of the horrid tribe where the balls flew like hail and arrived with express at our camp in less than one hour a distance of more than sixteen miles in this we had one man killed & two wounded one child lost. that of the enemy six or eight killed and wounded.[343]

The relief party was unnecessary. A Flathead Indian who spoke Blackfoot yelled out that reinforcements were on their way. Seeing the two desperate men race wildly through their ranks toward the Rendezvous for help, the Indians took the hint and broke off the fight. They decided, as the rhyme goes, to "fight then run away and live to fight another day." But they got away with $5000 worth of fur, forty horses, and some merchandise.[344]

---

[341] The Life and Adventures, pp. 104 -105. Here Beckwourth makes himself the hero and takes credit for Campbell's bravery.
[342] Morgan, *West of William Ashley*, p. 314
[343] *Potts' letter to Robert Potts, St. Louis,* October 13, 1828.
[344] Morgan, *William Ashley* pp. 186-187.

Daniel Leaves the Mountains

Supplies for the Rendezvous of 1828 came earlier than usual; Sublette and Jackson had got the pack train into the mountains the previous fall. Since many of the men had already done their trading, some of the excitement was missing at the summer fair. And, there were two more reasons–there was no summer mail–and the whiskey didn't likely last through the winter.[345]

Nevertheless, the trappers were delighted to see their friends again. The games and jollifications were as prevalent as usual. Many of them couldn't read letters anyway.

It was Daniel Potts's last mountain Rendezvous so he stripped himself of mountain gear; he sold, bartered or gave away what he no longer needed. His traps and tools were worth much more in the mountains than they would be in St. Louis. Then he bade farewell to companions who had shared with him the adventure of exploring the Rocky Mountains.

---

[345] Daniel Potts's usual letters did not arrive with the summer caravan but were still in St. Louis. *Potts' Letter to Robert Potts*, St. Louis, October 13, 1828.

With seventy packs of beaver, the caravan headed by William Sublette got away about August 1, 1828. Winding over the mountains and through the upper Green River Valley Potts saw one last time the incomparable Rocky Mountains his pen

His Appearance Was Bad and
His Speech Was Worse

had captured in letters. They followed the route pioneered by Ashley, descending the Platte to the Missouri, and reached St. Louis in little more than sixty days.

Within the Bounds of Civilization

After years in the wilds Daniel was fascinated and uncomfortable in St.Louis. The sights, food and clothes were new. But he didn't fit.

He *had been* a man of some gentility and education; he

came from a family that had known wealth and distinction. But after six years in rough company his appearance was bad and his speech worse.

The cloth-clad society of St. Louis seemed to converse in a different tongue. It vexed Potts considerably,

> Since my arrival, for the want of language, I am scarcely able to converse with any men of talents which occasioned verry disagreeable feelings.[346]

The language of the mountains was a mix of, French, English, Spanish and Indian–liberally seasoned with profanity. Concise and colorful, it served well around the campfire. And if complemented with suitable signs the Indians understood. But, this kind of talk didn't go over with the genteel folk of St. Louis at all.[347] Daniel was embarrassed

But in spite of culture shock, Potts was relieved to be safe. In the mountains danger was always close at hand; a grizzly bear or an angry Indian might jump from behind any rock or out of any patch of trees. Potts earlier observed that "a man in this country is not safe neither day nor night and I hardly ever expect to get back."[348]

The vigorous outdoor life had been good for him. His weight was one hundred eighty nine pounds and he was in excellent health. Of the mountains he had earlier written: "this country is the most healthy [place] in the world I think." An all meat diet seemed to do the trappers well.

---

[346] *Daniel Potts to Robert Potts*, St. Louis, October 13, 1828.

[347] For a delightful representation of the speech, mannerisms and everyday life of mountaineers, see George Frederick Ruxton, *Life in the Far West, edited by LeRoy Hafen* [Norman: University of Oklahoma Press, 1951].

[348] *Potts' Letter to Thomas Cochlen, Rocky Mountains*, July 1824.

Even the ladies enjoyed it. In fact, the missionary wife, Narcissa Whitman, first of two white women to cross the Continental Divide, wrote,

> I never saw anything like buffalo meat to satisfy hunger. We do not want anything else with it. I have eaten three meals of it and it relishes well.[349]

Immediately after arriving in St. Louis, Daniel contacted Ashley in hopes of getting a letter from home in Pennsylvania. Mountain bound mail was sent to Ashley in St. Louis then relayed by him to the trappers. A letter had been sent, but unfortunately, it was mislaid. Daniel's desire to know of his family and friends went unsatisfied. The last word he had from them was a letter at the Sweet Lake Rendezvous of 1827.

So he wrote them. This letter, dated October 13, 1828, is the source for what happened to him after 1827. Though it was full of tantalizing hints, it lacked the flavor, vigor and detail of his mountain letters. Out there he was in the thick of adventure and eager to share it. He tried to describe on paper the danger and charm of the Rocky Mountains. But now, back in St. Louis his attention was absorbed with the life he hadn't seen for six years. The storytelling could wait.[350]

Daniel was fascinated by the changes since 1822. But he had changed too, and now it was time to re-adapt. He stripped off his leather garb and enjoyed the feel of cloth. He also took in the town. With its many sources of merriment and merry-making, there was much to do in St. Louis. But he didn't squander his money. He came from a long line of entrepreneurs and instinctively knew that half the art of acquiring wealth was learning how to save it.

---

[349] Gowens, *Rocky Mountain Rendezvous*, p. 167.
[350] *Potts Letter to Robert Potts*, 1828.

Within little more than a week after he arrived in St. Louis he settled his account with the traders and received $ 650.00. Adding this to previous earnings he wrote his brother, "I have a small capital which I flatter myself with is pretty good business." His older brother Robert was a storekeeper in Philadelphia–naturally Daniel wanted to share his success.[351]

It was also natural to think about his next venture. There was opportunity in Texas where stray cattle were free for the taking. For several decades industrious frontiersmen had conducted "filibustering" expeditions into the Spanish territory, collecting both cattle and horses that had escaped from the ranches in Mexico and driving them north to the United States. Now steamboats made it easier. His sources told him that good profit could be made by rounding up stray animals and shipping them by boat to the markets of New Orleans.[352] He plunged into this scheme himself.

Daniel Potts Disappears

Less than two weeks after Daniel's arrival in St. Louis he boarded one of the new-fangeld, puffing, hissing, steam boats and headed down the river for New Orleans. But just before he left, he received a happy surprise; Ashley had discovered two letters for him that were mislaid–one from his brother Robert. He hadn't yet posted his own letter, so he added some lines.

---

[351] For comparison it is useful to make a conversion of Potts's earnings. With his $650.00 from 1828 added to what he had earned previous years he could have saved about $2000.00–this figure has him making an average of $400./year. That would compare to around $80,000. in 1999 money. But he didn't make the riches anticipated. Remember in his letter of 1824 he hoped to make $1200./each season..

[352] See Appendix B, *A Biography of Daniel Potts.*

Since writing this letter I have received your and Weirs letters which alters the case amazingly those letters were mislaid. Tomorrow I embark.[353]

Direct your letters to New Orleans where I shall remain until New Years whereas it is necessary for you to write in haste. previous to leaving that place I shall inform you where I go and my business.

That's Daniel's last known message.

However, family tradition relates that Potts wrote from Texas to his brother that he was buying and shipping cattle to New Orleans. It sounded good to Robert and he sent several thousand dollars to get in on the deal. He placed the money to Daniel's credit with merchants in New Orleans.[354]

G.T.T.

In Mississippi frontier days, there was a saying applied to a *missing* person. The saying was "G.T.T," and meant "Gone To Texas." After writing a last letter to brother Robert, Daniel Potts was G.T.T. And our last reference has him outside his natural element. This explorer and chronicler of the fur trade had *gone to sea*. If true, it wasn't a wise choice.

Potts family tradition has it that Daniel drowned while on a cattle-shipping voyage between Texas and New Orleans.[355]

---

[353] We wonder what "case" was so amazingly altered for Daniel Potts. The letters contained unexpected information.

[354] That was a lot of money. If "several" means $3000. Converted to 1999dollars it would be equal to upwards of $180,000. dollars. The venture must have sounded very good indeed to Robert.

[355] The Potts Family, [Cannonsburg, Penn.1901].

Something went wrong because Daniel had faithfully written his family through six years in the West. It wasn't like him to break off. The substantial investment sent by his brother was never drawn and Daniel Trotter Potts was never heard from again.[356]

And So,

Without plan or intent, Daniel Trotter Potts became an eye witness and chronicler of the times when white hunters first explored the Rocky Mountains. He wrote the earliest known description of many western features, including Yellowstone Park. His letters were familial, written without thought of publication or personal gain. They are accepted by historians as highly reliable. He avoided the temptation to enlarge upon his own figure and embellish his adventures with wild animals and Indians. The truth was lively enough. In a time when most of his colleagues were unable or not inclined to write, Potts recorded what he saw and fleshed out the story of this exciting time in Western History.

Better stated, Daniel Potts's letters are a window into the margins of prehistory; they afford a glimpse at the adventure and excitement when white men first invaded the domain of the Rocky Mountain Indians.

We feel the elation of this man as he discovered new lands. His letters flow with a touch of poetry in memorable phrases like: "the majestic and stupendous mountains and transparent streams," the "fathomless hot pools, crystal lakes," and beautiful valleys, "adorned with many flowers,"and "truly

---

[356] Ibid.

sublime mountains which reflect the brilliance of the diamond in its various colors."

AFTERMATH–FROM 1828 TO 1900

THE CHANGING ROCKY MOUNTAINS

Before 1823 knowledge of the Rocky Mountains was spotty, unreliable or simply unknown. Maps of lands south of the upper Missouri River [cutting across middle Montana] were filled with mythical terrain or empty space. The trappers changed that. They virtually tramped up every river and climbed every mountain pass. They were eye witnesses on the ragged edge of prehistory and made a lot of history themselves. A few trappers–like Daniel Potts, wrote first descriptions of western events so history was finally recorded.

Trappers were trailblazers for the buffalo runners, miners, and farmers that followed. And with each new wave of westerners, eye witness reports multiplied, maps became more reliable, and the trails were more easily followed. News of passable trails over the Rocky Mountains–and open land with mineral wealth–caused one wave of frontiersman after another to surge westward seeking their particular dream. Animals and Indians were swept aside.

Two developments that forever changed the Rocky Mountains were the coming of pioneers and the end of the buffalo.

Wagon Wheels and Women West

The first wheels to cross the Continental Divide cradled a cannon to the Rendezvous of 1827. Ten years later twenty loaded carts drawn by mules were urged over South Pass and rolled down to the Green River Rendezvous. The Protestant missionaries, Dr. Marcus Whitman, Henry Spaulding and remarkably, their wives, accompanied this caravan to the Rendezvous. Their aim was to preach Christianity to the

Indians. Their wives were the first white ladies in the mountains. And at the Rendezvous these white women were a remarkable novelty and an unforgettable sight to trappers and their Indian squaws. Osborne Russell writes they "were gazed upon with wonder and astonishment." Pausing only a few days, the missionaries were led by Hudson Bay men westward to "Oregon"–at that time a vast territory that included Washington, Oregon, Idaho, Montana, and most of Wyoming. They had arrived at the Rendezvous with two wagons. Leaving the heavier one there, they converted the other one to a cart at Fort Hall and made the first wheel marks between there and Fort Boise.

So it was missionaries bent on bringing the gospel to the Indians who also brought the first white women west. And these ladies fascinated the Indians more than anything the missionaries had to say. [357]

Oregon territory was colossal. It included much of the Northwest. When the secret was out that a roadway through the Rockies had been found, men eagerly headed west to exploit it. One enthusiastic promoter was Hall Jackson Kelley. Inspired by Kelley, the businessman Nathanial Wyeth gathered men and supplies to establish a colony. And remarkably, his route became the "Oregon Trail." Ironically, he knew little about the route as he started out and his party gladly hooked on to William Sublette's trade caravan going to the famed Rendezvous of 1832 in Pierre's Hole. With about 1000 Indians and whites gathered in this beautiful mountain valley it was the largest Rendezvous ever. Afterward, William's brother, Milton Sublette, led Wyeth's party on to Oregon.

Interest grew. In 1840, thirty carts and six wagons went to

---

[357] Russell, *Journal of a Trapper*, p. 41.

the Green River Rendezvous. Tagging along for protection was the Catholic Father Pierre De Smet and three Protestant missionaries with their wives. After the Rendezvous they continued to Oregon with wagons under the guidance of Robert Newell. The "merry mountain man" Joe Meek drove one wagon and Caleb Wilkins another. Meek could see that the good times in the fur trade were over. Changing hat styles, over-trapping and competition had ruined the business. Besides, times had changed. Now that forts had been established and wagons were rolling west there was no need for the popular Rendezvous to supply trappers. Newell, Meek and Wilkins made a trace for emigrants–for in 1843 about 1000 men women and children with 5000 oxen and cattle took 120 wagons to Oregon. And in 1845 the migration had grown to something like 3000 which almost doubled Oregon's population.

Despite the vast open land, emigrants were a shock wave to the Indian way of life. They scared game from the trails, tempted Indians with their sugar and whiskey and shot wild animals just for the fun of it. Both sides were thieves, the Indians stole horses and supplies and the whites violently retaliated. Both feared and misunderstood the other–and for good reason. They knew that times were changing and that it was either whites or Indians that would rule the West–not both. Settlers were struggling to establish themselves and farm a patch of land; conversely, Indians were being robbed of the same land.

But the most immediate bind for Indians was dwindling animals. This made living the old ways a challenge and threatened their very survival.

It was a continuation of what had been happening since Columbus–land hungry people from the iron age over running cultures still in the stone age. That these cultures were making inefficient use of vast lands made them an attractive target for land hungry whites with guns.

Soon after the last fur Rendezvous countless wagon trains were winding west on Indian and trapper trails. Each wave of emigrants had their own object and their own dreams. Without doubt the most systematic and orderly pioneers were the Mormons.

The Mormons

They were organized. And religious persecution in Ohio, Missouri and Illinois forged them into a unified people. In 1843–four years before it happened–their prophet, Joseph Smith, predicted they would go to the Rocky Mountains and build cities and temples. And though he wanted to lead them west it was not to be. In June of 1844 he was killed by a mob in Carthage Missouri. [358]

Brigham Young succeeded Joseph Smith and likely had more suitable skills to lead the Mormons west; Young was organized, flexible, and firm, and kept an eye on the big picture. Perhaps he kept an eye on everything. It is said that Young "slept with one eye open and one foot out of bed." Without loss of stride he picked up Joseph's mantle and made plans to move the whole church west and away from persecution. In his diary on December 31, 1845 Brigham wrote,

---

[358] In 1843, while drinking a drought of ice-water Joseph Smith said: "brethren, this water tastes much like the crystal streams that are running in the Rocky Mountains which some of you will partake of . There is Anson [Call], he shall go and assist in building cities from one end of the country to the other . . . many of you will be gathered to that land assisting in building cities and temples. " Anson Call, *The Journal of Anson Call*, [Afton Wyoming, Ethan and Christine Call] pp. 22,23.

... examined maps with reference to selecting a location [to settle] west of the Rocky Mountains, and reading various works written by travelers to those regions.[359]

He studied maps of John C. Fremont who got his start from trappers. Armed with this first hand experience the Mormons decided not to go to Oregon and California but instead to settle near Salt Lake in the Rocky Mountains–*a place they thought no one else wanted*–where they could live and worship in peace. Within three years this poor but united group had moved west, diverted mountain streams to irrigate the dry ground and planted crops in Utah valleys. They cleared land and built towns in a wilderness that Daniel Potts and a host of other trappers had explored only twenty years before.

Trappers and Indians set many place-names that the settlers continued using. Cache Valley, Weber and Provo Rivers, Bear River, Ogden,'s Hole, Utah Lake, Soda Springs, Yellowstone River, Great Salt Lake, Snake River and Salt River Valley were all named by trappers or Indians.

By 1880 the Mormons had settled most of the valleys known as "Snake Country" to trappers.

Apart from taking their land, they were kind to the Indians. Young believed that "it was cheaper to feed the Indians than to fight them. " He also tried to teach Indians new ways and to farm the land. They didn't take to it much. It was hard for most Indians to accept the loss of their nomadic life.

---

[359] *The Journal of Brigham Young*, [Provo, 1980]. P.119.

New Pioneers and Old Trappers

Some mountain men from the "glory days" of fur trapping were still there to meet the pioneers. They hung on even though beaver were scarce and the price had gone to pieces. And a few were changing with the times serving the westering emigrants with guide service, advice, and trade. Jim Bridger chose a pleasant grassy meadow on Black's Fork, built a rude cabin and became a trader–to the pioneers. Some of his first customers were Mormons in 1847. After crossing South Pass Brigham Young and his vanguard company camped with Moses Black Harris, [another old trapper now doing guide service] on the Dry Sandy. He shared unwelcome news. Brigham wrote, "Moses Harris, a mountaineer, camped with us . . . he said the country around Salt Lake was barren and sandy, destitute of timber and vegetation except wild sage."[360]

On June 28, the company met Jim Bridger who had been away from civilization for more than 20 years. He also cast a dim light on Brigham's plans to settle near Salt Lake. Remember this is the same man who abandoned the bear-mauled Hugh Glass to supposed death in 1823 and later discovered Great Salt Lake.

> Met Cap. James Bridger who said he was ashamed of Fremont's map of this country. Bridger considered it imprudent to bring a large population into the Great Basin until it was ascertained that grain could be raised; he said he would give one thousand dollars for a bushel of corn raised in the Basin.[361]

---

[360] *The Journal of Brigham Young*, [Provo, 1980] p.220.
[361] *Ibid.*, Bridger was suggesting a spendy gamble–$1,000 was at least a year's wage. Possibly, he was sowing fear because he didn't want a large settlement in Salt Lake Valley competing with his post.

Bridger had watched prices and demand for beaver fall from the Rendezvous Days, [the last Rendezvous was in 1840], and with a partner Louis Vasquez[362] had built a post in southwestern Wyoming to serve wagon pioneers. He couldn't read or write, but he was savvy, and understood the coming wagon trains would need to resupply. And they would have real money! His plans are ascertained from a letter he had dictated to Pierre Choteau and Co. Who he hoped to engage as a supplier.

> I have established a small store, with a blacksmith shop and a supply of iron, [Bridger had been a blacksmith for Ashley twenty years earlier] in the road of the emigrants on Black's Fork of Green River which promises fairly. They in coming out are generally well supplied with money, but by the time they get here they are in need of all kinds of supplies. Horses, Provisions, Smithwork, etc. brings ready cash from them; and should I receive the goods hereby ordered will do a considerable business with them! ... The fort is a beautiful location on Black's Fork of Green River, receiving fine, fresh water from the snow on Untah range the streams are alive with mountain trout ... [363]

Bridger's location for a store catering to pioneer trade was wisely chosen. It was well watered on wide bottoms with fertile soil–a welcome rest stop for emigrants and their jaded animals. However the post itself was shoddy. The traveler Joel Palmer observed,

> this fort is owned by Bridger & Basquez [Vasquez]. It is built of poles and dogwood mud. It is a shabby concern.

---

[362] Louis Vasquez was of aristocratic Spanish heritage, and in contrast to Bridger, was well educated. He, like Bridger had been in the mountains for many years.

[363] Grenville, Dodge, *Biographical Sketch of James Bridger*, [New York, Unz & Co. 1905] pp. 5,6.

There are about twenty five lodges of Indians or rather white trapper lodges occupied by Indian wives. They have a good supply of robes, dressed deer, elk and antelope skins, coats, pants, moccasins and other Indian fixins which they trade low for flower, sugar, etc. they have a herd of cattle, twenty or thirty goats and some sheep.[364]

So in 20 years the mountain trade had gone from beaver fur to buckskin. Fort Bridger was a welcome trailside store that featured mountain men and their Indian families as tourist attractions. Thousands of people went by land. They streamed west with horses, buggies, wagons and afoot–sometimes abreast to avoid their own dust and sometimes in long snake like streams–over trails marked by trappers.

The Gold Miners

It was inevitable that newly discovered lands would have riches to exploit. In 1848, only one year after the Mormons came to Utah, gold was discovered in California–and it could be gathered from stream beds with a shovel and a pan! When word of the discovery reached the East in September, men abruptly dropped the plow or whatever they were doing, left their family and headed west to get rich. Within a month sixty crowded ships, many of them in disrepair, were headed out to go around the horn to California. Since the trip was dangerous and expensive, thousands of men went by land. They streamed west with their best horses, wagons, and buggies–over trails blazed by trappers and built by pioneers.

Remarkably, the gold hunters and Mormons were a

---

[364] Joel Palmer, *Journal of Travels to the Mouth of the Columbia River*, [Cincinnati, James, 1847] p.35.

blessing to each other. Before the miners got to Utah they were trail weary and their horses worn out. So they rested, replenished food stores and traded their tired but quality animals for fresh ones. It worked well for both. Also, eager to get to the gold diggings quickly, they lightened their loads. Beds, stoves, food stuff, and furniture were thrown from the wagons. The Mormon settlers, more than a thousand miles from a supply store, had need for these and backtracked the trail on "pickup missions," hauling wagon loads of useful cargo back to their new but poor and threadbare habitations. Indians, seeing furniture and food disposed by gold seekers were in wonderment about these people who seemed to have so much they threw it away. There seemed to be more and more armed white men but less buffalo. It wasn't good.

What Happened to All the Buffalo?

Buffalo was the staple food of Indians and mountaineers. The whole Indian way of life was wrapped in buffalo. They slept under buffalo robes, wore buffalo coats and made tepees and moccasins from their hides. Living through cold mountain winters was inconceivable without one or two thick buffalo robes to crawl under. Besides being useful they were plentiful, no one knows for sure but there were perhaps 20,000,000 head! They roamed the plains in numberless herds and occupied every valley in the Rocky Mountains–even the high places. Their deep trails went from South Pass to the Great Basin, Snake River Valley, Pierres Hole, Jackson Hole and even Yellowstone Park. The buffalo had been there for centuries. But that was about to change.

By the 1830s it was obvious to Indians and observant trappers that buffalo were getting harder to find. They were less and less seen in mountain valleys–by 1840 hardly at all. White trappers had caused it. In bad starving times trappers ate anything, wild thistle, singed dog skins, even antelope eyeballs and in times of thirst were known to drink their own urine.[365] They were thankful for any meat. On the other hand, when buffalo were numerous the whites were deliberately wasteful. They shot them just for sport. They commonly killed animals weighing almost a ton for only the hump rib and tongue. Recall Daniel Potts killing a buffalo for sport back in 1823? He wasn't alone, white men killing buffalo and letting them rot was a common story. In contrast, the Indians had use for all parts of the animal and wasted little. For generations they were able to take what they needed without threatening the herds.

After the trappers, emigrants took up killing buffalo. They were fascinated by large animals and shot them down for target practice. With this steady harassment, the buffalo thinned out and retreated from mountain valleys and pioneer roads to the open plains. However the real threat to buffalo was yet to came. Enter the professional hunters.

There was money in it. By the 1870s the fur trade was past and gold and silver had played out from California to Montana. But the West still had a vast resource to exploit–the buffalo. Robes were worth $3.00 each and by 1869 a railroad across the continent was complete. It provided a way to haul the hides back East. Unlike trapping beaver, just a few men could kill and skin hundreds in a day. And that's what they did. But the railroad made it feasible to haul the tons of heavy hides to market.

One buffalo hunter, or "runner," was Frank Mayer. He lived to be 104 years old–born in 1850 and died in 1954. An observant and straight speaking man, he wrote a book detailing

---

[365] Stuart, *On the Oregon Trail*, p. 67.

his enthusiasm and efficiency. This was his system:.

> ... Shooting from the back of a running horse was always
> uncertain. I wanted none of it. I wanted efficiency ... some
> unknown genius of observation gave all of us runners our
> cue to killing buffalo ... if you wounded the leader, [which
> was usually an older cow] and didn't kill her outright, the
> rest of the herd whether it was three or thirty, would gather
> around her and stupidly "mill"–which means poke her with
> their horns, strike her with their hooves, and just lose their
> heads when they smelled her blood ...
>
> And all you had to do as a runner, was pick them off one
> by one until you wiped out the entire herd. Then you went
> to another herd and repeated the process.[366]

Buffalo hunters, like beaver trappers, miners and many
other budding entrepreneurs counted their chickens before they
hatched. Mayer writes,

> when I went into business, I sat down and figured that I
> was indeed one of fortunes children. Just think! There were
> 20,000,000 buffalo each worth $3.00–$60,000,000. At the
> very outside cartridges cost .25 each so when I fired one I
> got my investment back twelve times over. I could kill 100
> a day, $300. gross, or counting everything, $200 net profit
> a day ... $6,000. a month–three times what was paid, it
> seems to me, the President of the United States.[367]

Mayer said it was his "German nature" that made him
efficient. But he wasn't the only one using this technique, there
must have been a lot of German buffalo runners. First, he would
get up-wind of a herd, work his way to about 300 yards or more
from them, then rest his rifle on two crossed hardwood sticks.

---

[366] Frank Mayer and Charles Roth, *The Buffalo Harvest*, [Denver, Sage
Books, 1958], p.33.
[367] *Ibid.*, p.61.

While out of sight and far enough away so the gun's report wasn't too loud, he searched for the lead cow through the long gun scope and began to work. He continues,

> I have worked hundreds of stands, as we called them, by this method, without losing a single animal I wanted.
>
> The number of animals a runner could take at a stand varied. My largest was 59. But Billy Dixon, a famous runner, once took 120 hides without moving his rest sticks. A colonel I knew on the ranges told me of counting 112 carcasses within a space of two hundred yards.[368]

They were good shots at long range.

> . . . Bob McRae once worked a stand of 54 and took 54 hides with 54 cartridges. I didn't do quite so well with my run of 59; I used 62 cartridges. I reckon these incidents will show you the kind of shooting we had to do. Most of our shots were at 300 yards or beyond. At 300 yards we had to be able to shoot all day long and score one hundred per cent results. We had to do this to come out even.
>
> I once took 269 hides with 300 cartridges. This was business. We had no time to experiment or theorize.[369]

He liked his rifle,

> Of course we had to have the right rifles, because no rifleman is ever a whit better than the rifle he's shooting . . . .
>
> . . . I think its safe to say that eighty percent of the buffalo killed were killed with either a Remington or a Sharps rifle. For their time and place, they were perfect . . . with carefully hand loaded ammunition and perfectly adjusted telescope sights, we could [kill] at any range from fifty to

---

[368] *Ibid.*, p. 5.
[369] *Ibid.*, p.37

500 yards. We could do this in the face of heavy winds, straight on, fishtail, or full cross currents. At distances above 500 yards and up to 1000 yards [more than half a mile] the .45-120-550 Sharps . . . is absolutely unsurpassed by any weapon known to man, . . . I paid exactly $237.60 for mine which in 1875 was a small fortune . . . [At $2.00 per day it was equivalent to 4 months wages.].[370]

But Mayer's earnings weren't as he projected.

Oh, those were fine dreams! But they never seem to materialize exactly. Always something coming up, some damned thing that took all the profit away. One time, because of a long rainy spell about a fourth of the hides would spoil while drying. Or I would go into a new country and find it completely shot out, as frequently happened. Now and then, in spite of my care and skill as a stalker, the buff would spook mysteriously, and all I would get for my pains was a horseback ride back to camp. And sometimes . . . well, there was always something . . . . it will astonish you [that my take] was so small, for the work I did, the skill I employed, the dreams I wasted.

The hell of it was that presently–within a year or a year and a-half after I got into the business–we hit what now is called diminishing returns. We call it scarcity of buff. It was. The more he was hunted and hounded the wilder the buffalo became, and with , say, 5,000 rifles a day leveled at him, it wasn't long until there was very little of him, or her, left to shoot. So we had to spend more and more time in the wagons exploring one range after another.[371]

Some buffalo runners could see ahead. One Sunday morning a well known runner showed up at Mayer's camp. After sharing some whisky and talk, Charley said, "Mayer, you

[370] *Ibid.*, p.85.
[371] *Ibid.*, p. 61-63.

and the other runners are a passel of dam' fools . . . don't you realize that in just a few years there won't be a dam buff left in the world?" But Mayer poo-pooed that kind of talk and declared "there are hundreds of millions of them."Charley responded, "Are you getting as many as you used to?" "Well no. But that's my fault. I'm hunting the wrong place." "Where is the right place?" Jones persisted. "Damned if I know but we are about to take off and find it tomorrow," Mayer answered. "You'll never find it . . . Unless we're careful there won't even be a specimen to keep in a zoo." said Jones.

To his credit, Charley Jones destroyed his rifle and personally gathered about seven buffalo calves to his ranch which became seed stock to restore the buffalo. Mayer admitted Jones was right and dedicated his book, *Buffalo Harvest*, to Charley. Because of saving these calves he became known as "Buffalo Jones."

In Mayer's estimation between 1871 and 1878 from twelve to twenty million buffalo were taken. Essentially *all* the buffalo were killed off.

> One by one we runners put up our buffalo rifles, sold them, gave them away, or kept them for other hunting, and left the ranges. And there settled over the range a vast quiet, punctuated at night by the snarls and howls of prairie wolves as they prowled through the carrion and found living very good. Not a living thing, aside from these wolves and coyotes stirred. The buffalo was gone.[372]

So fifty years from the time Daniel Potts left the West buffalo were no longer a facet of mountain life. And along with

---

[372] *Ibid.*, p. 89.

the buffalo, the roaming bands of Indians disappeared. [373]

Without Indians and buffalo the "empty" West was ready for new animals: Texas longhorns, cowboys, and farmers.

---

[373] Indians still traveled about on a limited basis. In the 1940s Shoshoni and Bannock Indians from Fort Hall Reservation were still setting up tepees in Star Valley, Wyoming and trading finished buckskin gloves and moccasins for hides. The authors father remembers his father threatening to trade him to the Indians for a pair of gloves!

BEAVER DICK AND WHITE MAN'S SICKNESS

Beaver Dick was a mountaineer and squaw-man who came to the mountains about 1858–at the tail end of fur gathering.

With his Shoshone wife, *Jenny*, he was raising a family in Snake River Valley Indian style. In his own words he was,

> grandson of James Leigh formerly of the 16 lancers england. I was borne on January 9th in 1831 in the city of Manchester England. Came with my sister to philodelphia u. s. a. when i was 7 years old. Went for the mexicin war at close [of] '48 attached to E Co. Ist infantry 10 months then came to rocky mountains and here i die.

His diary and letters are charming. They tell the story of the Rocky Mountains at the tail end of the mountain men and the beginning of pioneer farmers. But they also chronicle his personal tragedy.

Beaver Dick's Snake River Valley of the 1860s and 70s is much changed from what Daniel Potts saw in 1826. Potts skirmished with Blackfeet Indians, *forded* the river, then continued north and made the first known visit to Yellowstone Park. In contrast, by 1870 not to far from where Potts forded the stream, there was a *bridge* over Snake River. The valley even boasted a store, [albeit 50 miles away from Dick's Cabin]. The Shoshone and Bannock Indians, instead of traveling and hunting through the mountains as they chose, were supposed to be on a reservation near present Blackfoot. However, they often ignored the rules of their white conquerors and wondered away to hunt as they had in the past. Sometimes they needed to leave the reservation because the government failed to provide the promised food.

And there was a sprinkling of settlers in this largest valley in the Rocky Mountains. Beaver Dick Leigh chronicles the transition from trapping to farming. And he "had the pleasure" of showing new settlers where to farm. His family still relied on wild meat for food and skins for moccasins, and they steadily trapped for a source of cash. Yet he fenced land, had a garden, and cut six ton of hay.

When the U. S. Government Survey of 1872 arrived in the valley Dick made lasting friends as he guided them to the Tetons and Jackson Hole . The story of his life comes from his diary and from detailed yet unadorned letters he wrote to these friends. These letters are graphic and to the point. The survey team honored Dick and his wife by naming two lakes in future Teton Park for them. Charming Jenny Lake and Leigh Lake nest against natural moraines at the base of the Tetons in Jackson Hole. Beaver Dick seemed to be a man content with his lot and ever ready to aid pioneers trickling into the valley.

Dick had a cabin on Teton River near present Rexburg Idaho. With his five métes or half breed children they made a family of seven, and his wife was about to have another baby. As mentioned earlier, life in the high valleys was much changed since the time of Daniel Potts and the Ashley men. As early as the 1840s buffalo "were a stranger" to the mountains.[374] By 1860 Mormon emigrants had settled most of the Utah valleys and other emigrants were moving into Montana and parts of Idaho. Instead of relying on hunting for survival the new emigrants made more efficient use of the land by seeding and tilling it. They were farmers.

Indians were slow to understand and adopt the new order. They scrabbled for survival using government moneys, begging from whites and hunting for the ever more limited game. Successive discoveries of gold and silver had drawn men west to California then back east to Nevada, Colorado, South Dakota, and Montana. Wherever they went white men caused changes. Many were good, some not.

But as far as Beaver Dick was concerned one thing they brought was terrible. It was *smallpox*, the white mans disease. It decimated Indian families and whole tribes. Even Dick wasn't immune. The following quotation is from a letter he sent to Dr. Josiah Curtis, a surgeon and one of the fourteen climbers who started the ascent of Grand Teton in 1872. It is quoted to show the pathos that was part of countless Indian families. Beaver Dick tells his own sad story best.

My Dear Friend:

I sit down to give you an account of myself and my lost family. I moved up to the elbow of the Teton River on the 25 of April 1876. There I built a log cabin and fenced me a farm and raised some little vegetables, I also built a horse corral and a hay corral and put up 6 tons of hay in it. I also

---

[374] A trapper of the 1830s said this. However, there may still have been a few buffalo in Yellowstone. In winter they picked at sparse grass where geyser heat kept the snow melted much as they do today.

went and packed Tom Lavering and his partner [John Hague] and their skins out of the mountains.[375] I kept a diary up to August which I will copy and send to you some other time.

On the first day of August, Tom and my son Richard started on a trapping trip up the middle river, [likely Teton River or Warm River], while me and my wife hauled in the hay. Tom and Dick found nothing worth trapping and came back the last of August, and me and Tom went and trapped the North Fork of Snake with a boat. At my wife's request, I took her and family to camp. About the 25th of September we trapped down to a mile of my old winter cabin at the junction of the Teton River. When we got through trapping, my wife said she would like to spend the winter in our old cabin as she might want some assistance during the winter and our old place was too far up from anybody. So I moved my family and house goods to the old cabin at her request. Tom built a cabin near me. And then we went to Warrens store on Blackfoot River for supplies. On the 2nd of November I caught a bad cold and suffered from my old complaint whatever it is.

On the 11th of November we passed Humpy's camp at the Point of Rocks 2 miles from John Adams place. Humpy's wife came out and asked me for some bread. I told her I had none packed and went 6 miles to the foot of the Crater Buttes and camped. While we were eating supper by the

---

[375] From this letter we see that Snake River Valley had a sprinkling of settlers in 1876 and there was a merchant [Warrens Store] within 40 to 60 miles depending on which cabin or tent Dick was at. The Blackfoot Indian Reservation has nothing to do with the Blackfeet Indians. This reserve had been set aside for the Shoshone and Bannock.

Snake River Valley was the edge of the frontier in 1875 and on the verge of being settled. Trains of salt wagons from Salt River Valley [Star Valley] had been trailing through this valley, across Taylors Toll Bridge at Eagle Rock [Idaho Falls] and then to the gold mines in Montana.

light of the campfire, Humpy's wife and 3 year old daughter came and said Humpy had committed suicide and her and her child were starving. We gave her something to eat and blankets to sleep in. The next morning she came where we were crossing our supplies with a boat and said she wanted to go over the river to see my wife. I put her across. When we had got everything across, we went home. My wife told me that Humpy's father had died and her mother had broke out in face with little bumps.

Apparently Humpy's wife was already sick with smallpox and was using the suicide story as an excuse to get relief from Dick and Jenny.

Tom said it might be smallpox or measles, so I told my wife to give the women some provisions and tell her to go to the boat and camp, and I would put her across the river in the morning so that she could go and tell the doctor on the reservation. But when I went to the boat I could not find her. There was a Mr Aynes [Haynes] living near me and he was going to the South Fork to Texas trapper's camp for some harness he had loaned him. I told him to tell Tex [Parker] if that woman came to his place, to send her off for we suspected she had been where the smallpox was. Tex has a wife and 5 children. The woman was there already and Aynes fetched her back trying to get her to go and live with him,[376] but she came to my camp and asked what I wanted her for. I told her I did not send for her and told her to go away. She said she was heavy with child and could not walk. So I told my wife to give her our lodge and some provisions and let her camp in the bushes, my wife and children keeping away from her until she took in labor.

---

[376] Haynes would be foolish to have this lady who was suspected of smallpox stay with him. Here must be more to this story.

Then my wife packed her eatables and wood to the lodge door but did not go in.

Now, none of us knew anything of the smallpox and we supposed she was going to give birth to a child, and if there was smallpox in the camp, she was clear of it as she had been 10 or 12 days away from it. So me and Tom and Dick Junior went to the island to kill a large buck for moccasins, and camped out one night. The next day, when within 2 miles of our home, on our return, we met my wife and the rest of my family coming to meet us. I knew what was the matter as soon as I saw them. The Indian woman was dead. When we got home we went and examined the woman and could see nothing suspicious about her and came to the conclusion that she had died in child bed. I asked my wife to take the little Indian girl into the house and wash and clean it. She said not to do it. Something told her that the child would die, but at my request, she took it to the house and cleaned it up. It played with my children for four days as lively as could be, and that night it broke out all over with little red spots. We thought it was a rash from being washed and kept it in a warm house as the child had a cold at this time. At this time I had the bloody flux and was very weak from it. I had it for 5 days when it stopped on me.

The child appeared to be in no misery, so when I felt better me and Tom took the wagon and went up to my ranch at the elbow of the Teton to kill deer for winter's meat while it was fat. I killed 4 deer by noon the next day, but my gun shot too low which caused me to miss several other shots. So we came down to re sight my gun, and Tom borrowed Dick Junior's gun for this hunt as his gun snapped very often and we did not want to take time to fix it. This was on the 13th of December. We started up again on the 14th, my family all feeling and looking well, only my wife. In her state she was often so. I told Dick he could come up there 4 days from then and take a day's hunt with us. We went hunting the next morning, Tom on one side of the river and me on the other. The dogs ran some deer out and I killed one of them. While I was dressing it I looked across the creek and saw someone with Tom. They were a long way from me but something told me it was my son Richard, and that there was something wrong at home. I started for the cabin and they did the same when they saw me. Dick said his mother had a bad headache and wanted me at home. He told me that himself and William were taken with a pain in the belly and my two daughters were unwell the day we left home. He had ridden from there to here in 2 hours, 20 miles and I got on the same mare and went [back] in less time than that. When I got there it was an awful sight to see. My wife was sitting on the floor by the stove and my youngest daughter with her, both their heads tied up and suffering very much. My oldest daughter was in bed complaining with a pain in her back and belly. Her looks when she answered my question struck my heart cold. William's legs gave out and I put him to bed. Tom and me was taken the same day and last night we did not sleep much. We were burning up apparently sometimes and chilly other times. We had both lost our appetites and did not eat. When we went to hunt we thought it was cold for we have had some very cold and bad weather the last 5 weeks. I left Dick to come down with Tom and the wagon.

Well, my wife was in labor and I had a hard time all alone with my family all night, and next day about 4 oclock, my wife gave birth to a child. She had broken out all over with small red spots, but after the birth of the child, they all went back on her. I knew what the disease was as soon as I come into the house, although I had never seen it before.

My wife felt better and I put her to bed. She slept well during the latter part of the night and I had a hard time with the children all night. In the morning my wife said she wanted to get up and sit by the stove. I got her up and as I layed her on a pallet I had fixed for her, she fainted. She shook all over and made a rumbling noise. When she came to, she said to me, "What is the matter Daddy?" I told her she fainted from weakness, that was all. I was satisfied that her hours were numbered and I spoke encouragingly to her but my heart was dead within me. About noon, she asked me to give her some Harpers' Magazines and those pictures that you sent us. She wanted to look at pictures. She looked at them and talked and asked me questions about them quite lively. It was hard work for me to answer her without betraying my feelings, but I did so. The children had got quiet and some of them asleep, and I told my wife I would go out and set fire to a brush pile to signal for Tom and Dick to come home. While doing so, my legs got weak and it was all I could do to get back to the cabin. I had been back about 10 minutes when Tom drove up, [377]with Dick taken with the smallpox. Dick went out and killed a large doe deer after I left them, and he took sick that same night. Tom was the same as me. I got Dick in the house and to bed, and Tom went over to get Mr Aynes. While Tom and Aynes were sounding the ice to see if a horse could cross, my wife was struck with death. She raised up and looked me straight in the face and then she got excited and cursed Mr Aynes for bringing the Indian woman back to us. She said she was going to die and all our children would die, and maybe I would die. Doctor, this was the hardest blow I had yet. Then she laid down and smiled at me. All at once she turned over to the fire place and commenced stirring the fire. She was cold. She was laying betwixt the stove and the fireplace, but there was no fire in the stove. I laid her down again and at her request I put 2 pair of my socks and her shoes on her feet and covered her with blankets and a robe. She smiled and said she felt a little warmer. I then took my gun and shot a

---

[377] Note that Tom "drove up" in a wagon. Beaver Dick Leigh was a transitional man who saw the change from trapper-Indian times to pioneer days. He lived part time in a tent and part in a cabin, had some settlers tools, a stove and a wagon and a team of horses.

signal for Tom and Aynes. They came and I told Tom what had happened, but did not tell Aynes all.

She was laying very quiet and for about 2 hours when she asked for a drink of water. I was laying down with one of my daughters on each arm keeping them down with the fever. I told Aynes what she wanted, and he gave her a drink and 10 minutes more she was dead.

Dick turned over in bed when he heard the words and he said "God bless my poor mother!" I was talking as encouragingly as I possibly could to him, when he said, "Well, if we have to die it is all right. We might as well die now as some other time." That remark was another hard blow on me.

We wrapped my wife up in a blanket and buffalo robe and put her in the wagon bed. The next morning Mr. Aynes started to the reservation for the doctor or information how to treat the disease, and Tom went 4 miles to get John Hague. Hague came over and chopped wood and carried water to us. He said not to give any cold drinks to the children or drink any ourselves, which advice we followed until Aynes came back from the doctor. He was gone 3 days. He said the doctor said to give them all the cold water they wanted for it would not hurt them. Myself and Tom did not know what to think or do about it, But I said I did not like the idea of cold water and did not give them any. Myself or Tom. I had not slept one minutes since the time I got home from the hunt. Aynes, after taking one night's sleep, came into the house and took a change of watching with me and Tom that was getting very low down.

I can not describe my feelings or situation at this time. I knew I must have sleep and could not get it. While laying down a few minutes to rest my legs, I saw Aynes giving the children cold water and asking them often if they did not want to drink. I begged of him not to do so. I could not sleep so I got up and administered to my family again with the determination of doing all I could until I died, which I was sure I could not [last] more than 24 longer for my eyes would get full of black spots and nearly blind me, and death would have been welcome only for my children.

I saw the spots go back on William and Anne Jane, my oldest daughter and was satisfied that it was the effects of cold drinks. This night about 10 oclock I had to lay down exhausted. Night before last, I took 80 drops of laudanum inside of an hour at 2 doses but it had no effect on me. This night I felt some signs of sleep but with the sign came a heavy sweating and burning and tremors. My clothes and bedding were ringing wet in half an hour. When it left me, I told Tom and Aynes where everything was that they might want and asked them to save some of my family if it was possible, and turned over to die.

I can not write one hundredth part that passed through my mind at this time as I thought death was on me. I said, "Jenny, I will soon be with you!" and fell asleep. Tom said I had been asleep half an hour When I woke up everything was wet with perspiration. I was very weak. I laid for 10 or 15 minutes and saw William and Anne had to be taken up to ease themselves every five minutes, and Dick Junior was restless. I could not bear to see it.

I got up and went to help Tom and Aynes. I saw that the spots had gone back on Dick. My determination was to stand by and die with them. This was Christmas eve. Anne Jane died about 8 oclock. About this time every year I used to give them a candy pull, and they mentioned about the candy pulling many times while sick, especially my son John.

William died on the 25th about 10 oclock in the evening. John and elisabeth were doing well. They were ahead of the rest in the disease. The scales were out and drying up. On the night of 26th I changed watching with Aynes I let

Aynes sleep from evening until 12 oclock, as I could not sleep until 1 or 2 oclock, then only for one or two hours with sweat and tremors, when I would get up. Tom was taken with dyrreah and was too weak to get up to assist us any more.

On the 26the, Dick Junior died, betwixt 4 and 5 in the evening. Last night when I woke up the fire was out but some small coals, the lamp burned down and the door of the cabin partly open. I was freezing apparently when I woke up and saw Aynes leaning against the wall asleep. It gave me a start that I cannot describe. I woke him up, and then got up myself.

My son John had commenced to swell again by daylight and about 8 oclock on the 27the he died. On the night of the 28th I woke up cold again and found Aynes leaning against the bed fast asleep again. After sleeping 5 or 6 hours the fore part of the night, I got up as quick as my strength would let me and woke him up but it was too late; she [Elisabeth] was over all danger but this, and she caught cold and swelled up again and died on the 28th about 2 oclock in the morning. This was the hardest blow of all. I was taken with the bloody flux this night and me and Tom layed bewixt life and death for several days. Me and Tom had to beg of Hague to stay and get us wood and water every day.

Since Aynes came back, his plea was that his cattle wanted looking after when there was a 15 year old boy at home and nothing else to do but look after them. When all my family was dead and buried he was determined to go, when me and Tom was not able to do anything and Aynes arm was all swelled sore from vaccination.[378] I begged of him to take 2 of my horses and saddles and go to Major

---

[378] Haynes must have been vaccinated when he went to the Indian Reservation.

Danilson [Indian agent at Fort Hall] and carry a letter from me asking him for some blankets and clothing so that when we got well, we could change and go amongst people and not spread the disease. But Hague could not see how he could go until I offered him $2.50 [perhaps $65.00 in 1999 money] a day; then he could go. It took him 6 days to make the trip with 2 fat and as good mares that are on the Snake River. I had not slept more than 2 hours, and that was a miserable sweat and tremor sleep for the last 13 days, and I sent to Dr. Fuller on the Reserve for something to promote sleep. The flux had made me wakeful again. I did not expect to live to see Hague return, but God had spared me for some work or other. I believe I am prepared to do it whatever it is.[379]

Hague told along the road that only three of my family was dead. What his object was I cannot tell, although I wrote to Danilson by telling him that my family was all dead and buried. Well, when he got back the sixth day, me and Tom had got the dyareah checked with some Dovers powders and I was getting from one to two hours sleep in twenty four hours.

My thanks and best wishes are due to Dr. Fuller and his advice and promptness in sending me medicine which I shall not forget. I shall with God's help write you more about this Indian affair some other time and tell how the Humpy family came to get the smallpox.

Mr. Aynes said that Dr. Fulller would have come up to my assistance, but the Agent said that his and the doctor's place was on the Reserve. That we all know, but was not the Indians' place on the Reserve too, in place of laying on the public high road, begging from every passerby for

---

[379] Beaver Dick later married again. His second wife, another Shoshone, was named *Sue Tadpole*. With her he raised another family.

food, fifty two miles from the Reserve?[380]

There had been 3 persons died in the family within 10 days within one mile and a half of John Adams on the road, but no one knew what the disease was.

Adams lives on the bank of the Snake River now. Market Lake has overflowed and washed him out. I stopped at John's as I came up and took dinner, but he did not know anything only Humpy was a little sick. John caught the disease about the same time my family was dying but got over it.

On the 20th of Feb. I took a span of horses and a sled and went to the islands on the South Fork for my health for ten days. Tom accompanied me . . . I shall live and die near my family, but I shall not be able to do anything for a few months for my mind is disturbed at the sight that I see around me, and work that my family has done while they were living. The many little presents that you have sent to me and my family I shall keep in memory of you and them.

[End of letter]

---

[380] When the Oregon Trail was active with westering immigrants Indians begging along the trail were common. The immigrants killed and scared away wild game making it difficult for the natives to survive in traditional ways.

This sad letter by Beaver Dick chronicles the death of his entire family within twelve days around Christmas of 1876.

His wife Jenny – born 1847

Richard Junior – born 1864

Anne Jane – born 1866

John – born 1868

William – born 1870

Elizabeth – born 1872

New born infant, Richard helped deliver just prior to Jenny's death.

Hardtimes for the Indians
Bonneville County Museum

CONCLUSION

When Daniel Potts saw the Rocky mountains in 1825, life there was much as it had been for thousands of years. Except for horses and a few guns, the Indians were living much the same as had their fathers and grandfathers.

Within fifty years it was vastly different, and for the Indians not good. White men had brought coffee, tobacco, whisky, and disease. Elk, deer, beaver, and bear were reduced, and the buffalo were *destroyed*. Prime water holes were fenced off and owned by the new settlers. The West provided a home and a dream for many thousands of white people from Europe.

And white men brought many positive changes; agriculture replaced hunting and was much more productive. With enormous effort, pioneers diverted snow melt to irrigate the dry land. Mountain valleys were soon laced with large canals and smaller ditches. Domestic animals grazed in fenced pastures where buffalo once roamed. The new settlers planted trees and crops where before there was only sagebrush. Pioneers by choice settled on the best springs and streams. Using water and hard work the land soon produced food far in excess of local needs.

But the Indians were slow to take up farming. And when their centuries-old pattern of nomadic hunting was broken, their beliefs and culture broke down too, and their dreams were swept away. The basic truth was that land starved colonists from Europe–armed with iron tools and guns–contended with land rich stone age Indians. It wasn't a contest.

But it is fascinating to imagine how it was when white men first came to the mountains. The West was Indians, wild animals, natural curiosities, and vast space. We are fortunate to taste Daniel Potts' wonder as he walked on the edges of prehistory. Quoting him again: the mountains were "majestic and stupendous, with transparent streams, fathomless hot pools, crystal lakes, beautiful valleys adorned with many flowers, and truly sublime peaks which reflect the brilliance of the diamond in all its various colors. "

The End

APPENDIX A

ITINERARY AND CHRONOLOGY OF DANIEL POTTS: TRAPPER–EXPLORER AND CHRONICLER OF THE FUR TRADE

He wrote the earliest descriptions of Rocky Mountain features including Yellowstone Park, Great Salt Lake, Bear Lake, Thermopolis Hot Springs, the Oil Spring and Soda Springs.

An outline of his travels from Pennsylvania through the Rocky Mountains,1822-1828, taken from his own writings.

1. July, 1821. Daniel Potts departed from his home near Philadelphia, and arrived in Illinois in July. He "tarried there until the midwinter" then went to St. Louis where he "tarried till spring."

2. April 3, 1822. Potts departed St. Louis and traveled up the Missouri River on a keel boat bound for the Rocky Mountains.

3. October, 1822. He arrived at the mouth of the Yellowstone River, which he described as, "one of the most beautiful situations I ever saw."

4. Late November, 1822. Potts and thirteen others traveled up the Missouri to the Musselshell River to spend the winter. [The Musselshell runs into the Missouri from the south and is one of the feeders into present Fort Peck Lake]. In the winter, the ice on the river froze four feet deep and did not discharge itself until the 4th of April.

5. April 6, 1823. Two days after the ice dispersed they embarked for the spring hunt heading up the Missouri for the Judith River.

6. April 11, 1823. Daniel is severely crippled when *he was shot through both knees with a rifle ramrod.* They took him downstream to Henry's Post at the mouth of the Yellowstone River to recover. He spent the summer in convalescence and may have tried to grow corn–but it was too dry.

7. September 1923. Potts embarked up the Yellowstone River for the Big Horn River "in the Crow Indian Country."

8. The fall of 1823. The party traveled up the Big Horn River where Daniel Potts was impressed with what is now called, "The Worlds Largest Hot Spring," [Thermopolis, Wyoming]. Later, he wrote the first description of this spring and of Wind River. He observed that the Wind River changed its name to the Big Horn River [as it does now], after passing through a canyon.

9. Winter of 1823-24. Potts and his group wintered with the Crow Indians near present Dubois, Wyoming on Wind River. Here, because of a "rain shadow," the wind blows clouds away. And for the Rocky Mountains, the winter here uncommonly warm and dry. Indians called it "the valley of the warm winds." [The incessant wind still makes it cold for a white man.]

10. Summer of 1824. As Potts and his group headed south they discovered a natural oil spring on the Popo Agie River. Daniel Potts's description of it is likely the first.

11. Summer of 1824. Daniel's contingent takes "a tolerable route" to where the Sweetwater River heads very near South Pass on the Continental Divide.

12. Summer of 1824. They continue through South Pass over the Continental Divide, which Potts aptly describes as

"high rolling prairies," to Green River. This stream was better known to the Indians and trappers as the "Seet Kadu," or "Seedskeeder." Potts once calls it the "Calliforn," which likely refers to its ending up in the Gulf of California.

13. Summer of 1824. Potts and his band proceeded to Bear River, Bear Lake, and Soda Springs. Potts writes: "After passing from this valley, [Green River Valley], in a S. W. direction we had very good traveling over an inconsiderable ridge, [likely Blacks Fork], and fell on a considerable river, called Bear River . . . "

He wrote the earliest known description of Sweet [Bear] Lake and Soda Springs.

14. Winter of 1824-25. They wintered in Willow Valley [Cache Valley, Utah]. This valley became their chief wintering ground and the "depote" where they cached their furs.

Likely under the leadership of John Weber, Potts and his companions spent the winter of 1824-25 in Cache Valley. According to Peter Skeen Ogden's diary they wintered on a tributary of Bear River aptly named "Cub Creek." In 1826 Daniel Potts wrote perhaps the earliest, and certainly the most lyrical, description of Cache Valley in a letter to his brother Robert Potts.

15. Rendezvous of 1825, Green River.

William Ashley, in his journal, indicates that John Weber and his party of 25 to 30 men [which included Potts], attended this Rendezvous. This first "official" Rendezvous was held twenty miles from the confluence of Henry's Fork and Green River in present Wyoming. ["Firsts" are ever arguable, Andrew Henry may have had the first Rendezvous in 1824.]

16. Winter of 1825-26, Great Salt Lake.

According to the few sources available, Potts's party began the winter of 1825-26 in Cache or Willow Valley. Then, because of the harsh weather, they moved down to Salt Lake Valley and explored it. Potts's account is the only first hand narrative of his group that has come forth. In his letter of 1826 he wrote the earliest detailed description of Great Salt Lake and the rivers flowing into it. During the winter, four men of his party circumnavigated Great Salt Lake in a "skin canoe." Potts's intimate knowledge of the lake indicates he was close to this adventure.

17. The Rendezvous of 1826, in Willow or Cache Valley

Regarding Cache Valley, Potts says: " . . . this valley has been our chief place of rendezvous and wintering ground." Regarding the Rendezvous, Potts writes: "we celebrated the 4th of July, by firing three rounds of small arms, and partook of a most excellent dinner, after which a number of political toasts were drank." At this Rendezvous Ashley sold out to Jed Smith, David Jackson, and William Sublette.

18. Summer of 1826, To Snake River and the Teton Range.

"We took a Northerly direction about fifty miles, where we crossed Snake river or the South fork of [the] Columbia at the forks of Henry's and Lewis's forks . . . " [near Idaho Falls in Snake River Valley]. He soon could see the Tetons which he aptly calls a "large rugid mountain," [When Potts describes a mountain he usually means a whole range of mountains.]. The Shoshone called the range Teewinotte which meant, "many pinnacles."

19. From this fork of Snake River they go up Henry's Fork, then over the Teton Range to the headwaters of the other fork of Snake or Lewis's Fork.

Then Potts and his companions traveled up Louis's Fork of

the Snake "to its source which heads on the top of the great chain of Rocky Mountains which separates the water of the Atlantic from that of the Pacific."

20. Summer of 1826. The Continental Divide, the top of the Rockies and the birthplace of rivers.

Potts grasp of western geography–which was essentially the knowledge of river courses, is remarkable. While on the Continental Divide he observed that besides Snake River, "at or near this place, heads the Luchkadee . . . [Green River], Stinking fork [Shoshone River], the Yellow-stone, the South forks of the Missouri, [Madison, Jefferson and Galliton rivers] and Henry's Fork of the Snake," . . . . He also observed that "the Yellow-stone River has a large fresh water Lake near its head on the very top of the Mountain" . . . as clear as crystal."

Parts of Yellowstone Park are in excess of 8000 feet high and the park straddles the Continental Divide. When Potts wrote that Yellowstone Lake was on "the verry top of the Mountain," he was saying that it was almost on the top of the Continental Divide. Yet remarkably, fish swim from the waters of the Pacific, up the Snake to Two Ocean Plateau then down to Yellowstone Lake, which empties into the Atlantic. So, fish swim over the mountain!

Winter snow piles deep. As the snow melts it flows in all

directions and is the source of major river systems. Earlier, Daniel Potts encountered the Green River and it is notable that he knew it discharged into the Gulf of California. He also observed that Snake River was the South Fork of the Columbia. He hadn't followed these rivers to the ocean so he must have talked to others who had. Also, he knew that Bear River flowed first north from Sweet Lake, then after curving tightly around a mountain, it discharged south into Great Salt Lake. And by 1826 he knew that Salt Lake had no outlet. In a subsequent letter he explains how the Wasatch Front Range divides Utah Lake from the "Leichadu," [Green River]. Prior to 1840, a map of the West was essentially a map of river courses. And by 1826, two years after he arrived, Potts had a general grasp of the rivers.

21. Summer of 1826. Daniel Potts is the first eyewitness of Yellowstone Park. At the following Rendezvous [1827] he wrote: "On the South borders of this Lake [Yellowstone Lake] is a number of hot and boiling springs some of water and others of a most beautiful fine clay and resembles that of a mush pot and throws its particles to the immense height of from twenty to thirty feet . . . the clay is white and of a Pink . . . and [the] water appears fathomless as it appears to be entirely hollow underneath." Then Potts described a surprising geyser.

22. Winter of 1826 Potts explores Utah Lake then south to Sevier Lake.

He writes: "Shortly after our arrival last fall in winter quarters, we made preparations to explore the country lying south west of the Great Salt Lake." On this trip Potts named his discoveries. Perhaps he was the leader.

23. The Rendezvous of 1827, at the south end of Sweet Lake. With the caravan returning to St Louis with the furs, Potts sent east the earliest description of the Yellowstone Park region.

As soon as Smith, Jackson, and Sublette had taken over William Ashley's business they raised the price of trade goods. Daniel realized that "there is a poor prospect of making much here owing to the evil disposition of the Indians and the exorbitant prices of goods." He then wrote a valuable list of mountain prices.

24. 1827-28, Wieser River [Idaho]

The fall hunt was attempted on the Wieser River in present western Idaho. However, the winter of 1827 was extremely hard. It started snowing September third and continued getting worse, so they returned to Cache Valley. However, the winter was harsh there also. Daniel says "Bear Lake was bridged over with ice from May 8th for twenty days," ! It was very cold and most unusual.

25. Rendezvous of 1828, Sweet Lake.

This is Daniel's last mountain Rendezvous. He described how the Blackfeet attacked Campbell's party sixteen miles from the Rendezvous site.

26. 1828, Return to St Louis.

With Sublette, Daniel returned to civilization. For six years he had experienced the excitement of discovery in the early West and had written about it. And despite his perils, in 1828 he was in the best of health and only missing some toes he froze off in Wyoming.

27. 1828, He Goes to New Orleans.

Potts plans to gather cattle in Texas and Mexico and sell them in New Orleans.

28. Daniel Potts Disappears.

APPENDIX B

DANIEL TROTTER POTTS LETTERS, 1824

LETTER OF DANIEL T. POTTS TO T. [THOMAS] COCHLEN

Cheltenham 2n Mo 19th 1825

Dear Sister

We having heard there was a letter at Edeth Coclens [probably Cochlen] from brother Daniel J M cald to see wether it was correct finding it was so I sent up for it; and knowing it would be a satisfaction to you to hear the particulars altho the account of him is not very pleasant the following is a copy of it

Rocky Mountains July 7th 1824

Dear and respected friend

I take this as the only opportunity to write to you and beg to be excusd for my bad spelling and writing, I have more news than I am able to communicate whereas I will give you the most important. —After leaving you I arrived in Illanois in July the same year and tarried there until mid winter and from thence to Masuri where I tarried until spring from there I embarked for the Rocky Mountains and the Columbia for the purpose of hunting and trapping and trading with the Indians in a company of about on hundried men We hoisted our sails on the third day of April 1822 at Saint Lewis and arived at Cederfort about the middle of July when we where reduced to the sad necessity of eating aneything we could cetch as our provision where exausted and no game to be had, being advanced five hundred miles above the fronteers, we were glad to get a Dog to eat and

I have seen some geather the skins of Dogs up through the Camp sing and roast them and eat heartyly this so discouraged me that I was determined to turn tail up stream and bear my cours down in campany with eight others and by the way lost from the others without gun aminition provition or even cloths to my back of [unknown word] account being four hundred miles from aney white people or even knowing where to find Indians' now my dear friend how must I have felt young Birds, frogs, and Snakes where exceptable food with me and not means of fire I in the course of a few days fortunately fell in with a party of Indians who treated me with great humanity and tarried with them four days and then fell in with a trader who conducted me within 350 miles of the fronteers he being able to give me but little aid I tarried but three days when I started with provition consisting of only 3/4 of a pound of Buffaloe suet [suet is animal fat] and arrived at the fronteers in six days were by eating too much and starvation I was taken with a severe spell of sickness which all but took my life, I here met with a second Boat and ascended the Masuri the second time and arived at the mouth of Mussel Shell, on the latter end of November where I wintered with thirteen others here was a remarkable escape of my scalp as two larg parteys of Indians winterd within twenty miles of us and our better enimys the black feet this place is in latitude 48. the River frose to the emmence thickness of four feet and did not brake up until the fourth of April and we embarked in Canoes on the 6th and on the 11th I was severely wounded by a wiping stick being shot through both knees which brought me to the ground this disabled me for the springs hunt and allmost for ever - this spring two partys here met with a greait defeat one by the loss of four men the other seven about the same time a third boat was ascending the river and was attackted by Rickarays Indians and was allso defeated withe the loss of 15 killed and 16 wounded; - Indians only one or two - this so imbroild our blood

that we unanimously volunteerd our service to reinforce and
give them battle which we did with the aid of three hundred
Regulars and one thousand Soux Indians and defeated them
without the loss of one man, in this engagement about seventy
Rickarays lost their lives and evackuatid their vilage out of all
the company only thirty odd returnd and those where fired on
by the Mandans and Groosvants in the dead hour of the night
and kilid two and wounded two more of our men two guns
where fired from our men and kiled one Indian and they
retreated, one man was allso tore nearly all to peases by a White
Bear and was left by the way without any gun who afterwards
recovird; from thence we moved our cours for the mouth of the
little horn and by the way I was closely pursuid by a party of
Indians on Horsback whom I took to be Black feet and
narrowly made my escape by hiding in a little brush and they
came [so] close that I could see the very whites of their eyes
which was within five yard. —from thence I started with 7 men
others [should be 7 other men] a trapping accros the Rocky
Mountains at the commencement of winter we startd for the
Columbia Mountain to winter with the Crow Indians who are
our only friends in this country here I got straid away from my
company and fell in with Indians who were not Crows and
traveld thirty miles from one hour by sun in the evening until
midnight accros the mountain through Snow up to my middle
which frose my feet severely so that I lost two toes etire and
two others in part from this I did not recover until late in the
spring nevertheless I made this spring with the addition of ten
days last fall three hundred and fifty Dollars and the ensewing
fall and spring I expect to make about twelve hundred Dollars
if nothing happens more than I know of. —the mountains are
now covered with Snow many feet deep in places and
vedgitation within ten feet of it in full bloom. —We now are
about to embark for the Columbia waters where I expect to
remain for two years at least. A man in this Countrey is not safe

neither day nor night, and hardley ever expect to return [*return is partly crossed out*] get back. –this Countrey is the most healthey in the world I believe: –A variety of hot springs, boiling Sulpher, and Oil springs, allso salts, salt Peter, and Volcanoes; petrifaction is astonishing; such as men, animels, fish, wood, and sea shells, those into the best kind of flint, those are to be found on the highest mountains. –I have celebrated the fourth of July by the pursuit of a Bull Buffaloe two being on Horsback ran him about three miles came up along side pourd in two broad sides he took the river and it not being foardable he sunk to the bottome and the pursuit ended when I have been hunting I have often thought of you and some others of my friends how you would glory in the sport. –White Bear, Buffaloe, Elk, Deer, Alilope, and Mountain Sheep are our principle game: –I shall now bid farewell and desire you to remember my best respects to all my enquiring friends particular J. Taylor J. McCalla. C Morris. –and J. Mather inform them I am in good health and spirits I remain with high respect your most particular fiend Vo

Daniel T. Potts

Thomas Cochlen - NB the original letter was directed to T. Cochlen

LETTER OF DANIEL T. POTTS TO ROBERT POTTS, 1826

Philadelphia, Pennsylvania

Rocky Mountains, July 16, 1826

DEAR AND RESPECTED BROTHER,

After I left Philadelphia, I was taken with a severe spell of rheumatism which continued with me for about two months. I arrived in Illinois on the 1st of July in the same year, where I remained until March following when I took my departure for Missouri, from thence immediately entered on an expedition of Henry and Ashly, bound for the Rocky Mountain and Columbia River. In this enterprise I consider it unnecessary to give you all the particulars appertaining to my travels. I left St. Louis on April 3d, 1822, under command of Andrew Henry with a boat and one hundred men and arrived at Council Bluffs on May 1st; from thence we ascended the river to Cedar Fort, about five hundred miles. Here our provisions being exhausted, and no prospect of game near at hand, I concluded to make the best of my way back in company with eight others, and unfortunately was separated from them. By being too accesaary [?] in this misfortune, I was left in the Prarie without arms or any means of making fire, and half starved to death. Now taking into consideration my situation, about three hundred and fifty miles from my frontier Post, this would make the most cruel heart sympathise for me. The same day I met with three Indians, whom I hailed, and on my advancing they prepared for action by presenting their arms, though I approached them without hesitation, and gave them my hand. They conducted me to their village, where I was treated with the greatest humanity imaginable. There I remained four days, during which time they had many religious ceremonies to tedious to insert, after which I met with some traders who conducted me as far down as the Village–this being two hundred miles from the Post. I departed alone as before, with only about 1/4 lb. suet, and in six days reached the Post where I met with Gen. Ashley, on a second expedition, with whom I entered for the second time, and arrived at the mouth of Yellow Stone about the middle of October. This is one of the most beautiful situations I ever saw; from this I immediately embarked for the mouth of Muscle

Shell, in company with twenty one others and shortly after our arrival, eight men returned to the former place. Here the game being very scarce, the prospect was very discouraging, though after a short time the Buffaloes flocked in in great abundance; likewise the Mountain Goats; the like I have never seen since. Twenty six of the latter were slain in the compass of 100 yards square, in the space of two hours. During the winter the Buffaloes came into our camp; one of which I was induced to charge upon by our company without fire arms, at first with a tomahawk only. After approaching very close, the Bull prepared for action with the most dismal looks, and sprang at me. When within one leap of me, I let fly the tomahawk, which caused him to retreat. After returning to our cabin, I was induced to make the second attempt, armed with tomahawk, knife and spear, accompanied by five or six others armed. After traveling a short distance, we discovered the Beast, and in a concealed manner I approached him within fifty yards, when the [he] discovered me, and made a rapid retreat, though, there being much falling timber, I soon overtook him—finding there was no escape he made battle. On the first onset, I put out one eye with the spear; the second failed in the other eye; on the third I pierced him to the heart, and immediately despatched him. The winter set in early, and the ice on the river froze to the immense thickness of four feet and the snow of an ordinary depth. The river did not discharge itself until the 4th of April; on the 5th we were visited by a party of Indians, and on the 6th we embarked in canoes for the river Judith.

In about one day's travel we discovered where a party of Indians had wintered who were our enemies, but fortunately had not discovered us. On the 11th, I was severely wounded through both knees by an accidental discharge of a rigle [rifle] ; whereby I was obliged to be conducted to our establishment at the mouth of Yellow Stone; here I remained until September. We were favored by the arrival of Major Henry from the

Ariccarees who departed from this place with a small brigade for the relief of Gen. Ashley, who was defeated by that nation, with the loss of sixteen killed and fourteen wounded, out of forty men. After Major Henry jointed them and the troops from Council Bluffs, under command of Col. Levengworth, they gave them battle; the loss of our enemy was from sixty to seventy. The number of the wounded not known, as they evacuated their village in the night. On our part there was only two wounded, but on his return he was fired upon by night by a party of Mannans wherein two was killed and as many wounded. Only two of our guns were fired which dispatched an Indian and they retreated. Shortly after his arrival we embarked for the brig [Big] Horn on the Yellow Stone in the Crow Indian country, here I made a small hunt for Beaver. From this place we crossed the first range of Rocky Mountain into a large and beautiful valley adorned with many flowers and interspersed with many useful herbs. At the upper end of this valley on the Horn is the most beautiful scene of nature I have ever seen. It is a large boiling spring at the foot of a small burnt mountain about two rods in diameter and depth not ascertained, discharging sufficient water for an overshot mill, and spreading itself to a considerable width forming a great number of basons of various shapes and sizes, of incrustation of sediment, running in this manner for the space of 200 feet, there falling over a precipice of about 30 feet perpendicular into the head of the horn or confluence of Wind River. From thence across the 2d range of mountains to Wind River Valley. In crossing this mountain I unfortunately froze my feet and was unable to travel from the loss of two toes. Here I am obliged to remark the humanity of the natives towards me, who conducted me to their village, into the lodge of their Chief, who regularly twice a day divested himself of all his clothing except his breech clout, and dressed my wounds, until I left them. Wind River is a beautiful transparent stream, with hard gravel bottom about 70 or 80 yards wide, rising in the main range of Rocky Mountains, running E N.E., finally north through a picteresque small mountain bearing the name of the stream: after it discharges through this mountain it loses its name. The valleys near the head of this river and its tributary streams are tolerably timbered with cotton wood, willow & c. The grass and herbage are good and plenty, of all the varieties common to this country. In this valley the snow rarely falls more than three to four inches deep and never remains more than three or four days, although it is surrounded by stupendous mountains. Those on S.W. and N. are covered with eternal snow. The mildness of the winter in this valley may readily be imputed to the immense number of Hot Springs which rise near the head of the river. I visited but one of those which rise to the south of the river in a level plain of prairie, and occupies about two acres; this is not so hot as many others but I suppose to be boiling as the outer verge was nearly scalding hot. There is also an Oil Spring in this valley, which discharges 60 or 70 gallons of pure oil per day. The oil has very much the appearance, taste and smell of British Oil. From this valley we proceeded by S.W. direction over a tolerable route to the heads of Sweet Water, a small stream which takes an eastern course and falls into the north fork of the Great Platt, '70 or 80 miles below. This stream rises and runs on the highest ground in all this country. The winters are extremely, and even the summers are disagreeably cold.

We past here about the middle of July last, the ice froze near half an inch in a kettle. Notwithstanding the intense cold this country is well covered with grass herbage and numberless Alpine plants. After crossing the above mentioned stream, we took a more westerly direction over high rolling Prairies to a small branch of a considerable river, known to us by the name of Seet Kadu, and to Spaniard, by Green River, and is supposed to discharge itself into the Bay of California. This river has a bold running current, 80 or 90 yards wide, & bears a S.E.

direction. It falls from the Rocky Mountains in many small rivulets, on which were considerable beaver. This valley, like all others I have seen in this country, is surrounded by mountains, those to S.W. and N. are covered with eternal snow, near the tops. Columbia Mountain, lying N. is the highest I ever saw, and perhaps the highest in North America. It stands rather detached and majestic, beginning abruptly towards the E. and terminating toward N.W. Its tops are the repository of eternal winter. In clear weather its appearance is truly sublime and reflects the brilliancy of the diamond in its various colours. This mountain gives rise to many streams, the principal are the Yellow Stone and Wind River. [Note, The "mountain" Potts is refering to is the Continental Divide. At this point there should be an "and" after Wind River so that the next sentence is a continuation. A newspaper typesetter may be to blame, Author].

The southern branches of the Missouri are [this "are" should be "and"] Seets Kadu and Lewis river, and others of smaller note. After passing from this valley, in a S.W. direction we had very good travelling over an inconsiderable ridge, we fell on a considerable river, called Bear River, which rises to the S. in the Utaw Mountains, bears N. 80 or 90 miles, when it turns short to the Great Salt Lake. On this river and its tributary streams, and adjacent country, we have taken beaver with great success. Since the autumn of 1824, you have no doubt heard, and will hear by the public prints, of the furs brought in by Gen. Ashley, which were the product of our toils. The first valley as you approach from the head of the river, is a small sweet lake, [Bear Lake] about 120 miles in circumference, with beautiful clear water, and when the wind blows has a splendid appearance. There is also to be found in this valley a considerable sour spring [Soda Springs] near the most northerly swing of the river. The valley is scantily supplied with timber, as is the case with most of the low grounds of this country. The second, or Willow Valley, [Cache Valley] is better supplied on this point--this valley has been our chief place of rendezvous and wintering ground. Numerous streams fall in through this valley, which, like the others, is surrounded by stupendous mountains, which are unrivalled for beauty and serenity of scenery. You here have a view of all the varieties, plenty of ripe fruit, an abundance of grass just springing up, and buds beginning to shoot, while the higher parts of the mountains are covered with snow, all within 12 or 15 miles of this valley. The river passes through a small range of mountains, and enters the valley that borders on the Great Salt Lake. The G. S. Lake lies in a circular form from N. E. to N. W. the larger circle being to S. it is about 400 miles in circumference, and has no discharge or outlet, it is generally shallow near the beach, and has several islands, which rise like pyramyds from its surface. The western part of the lake is so saturvated with salt, as not to dissolve any more when thrown into it. The country on S. W. and N. W. is very barren, bearing but little more than wild sage and short grass. The S. E. and E. are fertile, especially near the outlet of Utaw Lake and Weber's river. The former is about 30 yards wide at its mouth, the latter from 50 to 60, and very deep. This river rises to the E. in the Utaw Mountains, and in its course passes through three mountains, to where it enters the lake. We expect to start in a short time to explore the country lying S. W. of the Great Lake, where we shall probably winter. This country has never yet been visited by any white person--from thence to what place I cannot say, but expect the next letter will be dated at the mouth of Columbia. My long absence has created a desire to hear from you, as well as the rest of my people, also my associates. I have been on the very eve of returning this summer, but owing to this unexplored country, which I have a great curiosity to see, I have concluded to remain one or two years. We celebrated the 4th of July, by firing three rounds of small arms, and partook of a most excellent dinner, after which a number of political toasts were drunk.

D. T. P.

LETTER OF DANIEL T. POTTS TO ROBERT T. POTTS, 1827

Sweet Lake, July 8, 1827

Respectid Brother

A few days sinci our trader arived by whom I received two letters one from Dr. Lukens the other from yourself under date of January 1827 which gives me great congratulation to hear that you are both happy wilst I am unhappy also to hear from my friends Shortly after writing to you last year I took my departuri for The Black-foot Country much against my will as I could not make a party for any other rout. We took a Northerly direction about fifty miles, where we cross Snake river or the South fork of Columbia at the forks of Henrys & Lewis's forks at this place we was Dayly harrased by the Black-feet from thence up Henry's or North fork which bears North of East thirty miles and crossed a large ruged Mountain which separates the two forks from thence East up the other fork to its source which heads on the top of the great chain of Rocky Mountains which separates the water of the Atlantic from that of the Pacific. At or near this place heads the Luchkadee or Calliforn Stinking fork Yellow-stone South fork of Masuri and Henrys fork all those head at an angular point that of the Yellow-stone has a large fresh water Lake near its head on the verry top of the Mountain which is about one hundrid by fourty miles in diameter and as clear as Crystal on the South borders of this Lake is a number of hot and boiling springs some of water and others of most beautiful fine clay and resembles that of a mush pot and throws its particles to the immense height of from twenty to thirty feet in height The Clay is white and of a Pink and water appear fathomless as it appears to be entirely hollow under neath. There is also a number of places where the pure suphor is sent forth in abundance one of our men Visited one of those wilst taking his recreation there at an instan the earth began a tremendious trembling and he with dificulty made his escape when an explosion took place resembling that of Thunder. During our stay in that quarter I heard it every day. From this place by a circutous rout to the Nourth west we returned two others and myself pushed on in the advance for the purpose of accumalatin a few more Bever and in the act of passing through a narrow confine in the Mountain we where met plumb in face by a large party of Black-feet Indians who not knowing our number fled into the mountain in confusion and we to a small grove of willows here we made every prepparation for battle after which finding our enemy as much allarmed as ourselves we mounted our Hourses which where heavyly loade we took the back retreat. The Indian raised a tremendious Yell and showered down from the Mountain top who had almost cut off our retreat we here put whip to our Horses and they pursued us in close quarters until we reached the plains when we left them behind on this trip one man was closely fired on by a party Black-feet several others where closely pursued. On this trip I have lost one Horse by accident and the last spring two by the Utaws who killed them for the purpose eatting one of which was a favourite Buffaloe Horse this loss cannot be computed at less than four hundred and fifty Dollars by this you may conclude keeps my nose cllose to the grind stone A few Days previous to my arival at this place a party of about 120 Black feet approachid the Camp and killed a Snake and his squaw the alarm was immediately given and the Snakes Utaws and Whites sallied forth for Battle the enemy fled to the Mountain to a small concavity thickly groon with small timber surrounded by open ground In this engagement the squaws where busily engaged in throwing up batterys an draging off the dead there was only six whites engaged in this battle who immediately advanced within Pistol shot and you may be assured that almost every shot counted one The loss of the Snakes was three killed and the same wounded that of the Whites one wounded and two narrowly made their escape that of the Utaws was none though who gained great applause for their bravery the loss of the enemy is not known six where found dead on the ground besides a great number where carried off on Horses. Tomorrow I depart for the west we are all in good health and hope that this letter will find you in the same situation I wish you to remember my best respects to all enquiring friends particularly your wife

Remain yours most affectionately Vo

Danl. T Potts

I inform you I wrote Dr. Lukens under the same date an wish you to write me immediately on the receipt of this after the former direction giving me the price of Bever

LETTER OF DANIEL T. POTTS TO DR. LUKENS, 1827

The Gazette and Daily Advertiser

September 27, 1827

SHIP NEWS FROM THE ROCKY MOUNTAINS

A letter dated "Sweet Water Lake, July 8th, 1827," received by a gentleman [likely Dr. Lukins] of this city, says–"Mr. Smith, one of our traders, arrived a few days since, in forty days from the Gulf of California. He has explored the country south of this. He informs us that he was on board of two merchant vessels from Boston–the ship *Courier*, Capt. Cunningham, and a schooner the name of whose master is not recollected. Capt. C. was taking in a cargo of hides and tallow. Mr. Smith had been given up for lost. His sufferings were extreme, owing to the vast sandy deserts lying between this place and the gulf."

The same letter gives a *price current* of various articles in the region of the Rocky Mountains. This together with other extracts we shall take advantage of an early opportunity to lay before our reader. On the first page of to-day's paper they will find a letter from the same writer, giving a faithful picture of a Western Hunter's life, in a Western Hunter's unadorned language.

Oct. 19, 1827

The following letter was communicated during the "month of politics," but knowing that no other journalist could anticipate us, we delayed the publication to a convenient season. It comes from a native of Pennsylvania, who, actuated by a spirit of romantic adventure, has left a good mill in Montgomery county, to wander in the wilds of the west.

Sweet Water Lake, July 8th 1827.

Shortly after our arrival last fall in winter quarters, we made preparation to explore the country lying south west of the Great Salt Lake. Having but little or no winter weather, six of us took our departure about the middle of February, and proceeded by forced marches into the country by way of the Utaw Lake–which lies about 80 miles south of the Sweet Water Lake, is thirty miles long and ten broad. It is plentifully supplied with fish, which form the principal subsistence of the Utaw tribe of Indians. We passed through a large swamp of bullrushes, when suddenly the lake presented itself to our view.

On its banks were a number of buildings constructed of bullrushes, and resembling muskrat houses. These we soon discovered to be wigwams, in which the Indians remained during the stay of the ice. As there is not a tree within three miles, their principal fuel is bullrushes.

This is a most beautiful country. It is intersected by a number of transparent streams. The grass is at this time from six to twelve inches in height, and in full bloom. The snow that falls, seldom remains more than a week. It assists the grass in its growth, and appears adapted to the climate.

The Utaw lake lies on the west side of a large snowy mountain, which divides it from the Leichadu. From thence we proceeded due south about thirty miles to a small river heading in said mountain, and running from S. E. to S. W. To this I have given the name of Rabbit river, on account of the great number of large black tail rabbits or hares found in its vicinity. We descended this river about fifty miles to where it discharges into a salt lake, the size of which I was not able to ascertain, owing to the marshes which surround it, and which are impassable for man and beast. This lake is bounded on the south and west by low Cedar Mountains, which separate it from the plains of the Great Salt Lake. On the south and east also, it is bounded by great plains. The Indians informed us that the country lying southwest, was impassable for the horses owing to the earth being full of holes. As well as we could understand from their description, it is an ancient volcanic region. This river is inhabited by a numerous tribe of miserable Indians. Their clothing consists of a breechcloth of goat or deer skin, and a robe of rabbit skins, cut in strips, sewed together after the manner of rag carpets, with the bark of milkweed twisted into twine for the chain. These wretched creatures go out barefoot in the coldest days of winter. Their diet consists of roots, grass seeds, and grass, so you may judge they are not gross in their habit. They call themselves Pie-Utaws, and I suppose are derived from the same stock.

From this place we took an east course, struck the river near its head, and ascended it to its source. From thence we went east across the snowy mountain above mentioned, to a small river which discharges into the Leichadu. Here the natives paid us a visit and stole one of our horses. Two nights afterwards they stole another, and shot their arrows into four horses two which belonged to myself. We then started on our return, The Indians followed us, and were in the act of approaching our horses in open daylight, whilst feeding, when the horses took fright and ran to the camp. It was this that first alarmed us. We sallied forth and fired on the Indians, but they made their escape across the river.

We then paid a visit to the Utaws, who are almost as numerous as the Buffaloe on the prarie, and an exception to all human kind, for their honesty . . . .

There is a poor prospect of making much here, owing to the evil disposition of the Indians and the exorbitant price of goods. For example,

Powder $2.50 per lb.
Lead 1.50
Coffee 2.00
Sugar 2.00
Tobacco 2.00
Vermilion 6.00
Beads 5.00
Pepper 6.00
Blankets [three point] 15.00
Cotton Stripe, per yard 2.50
Calico do.[likely means: ditto]
Scarlet Cloth [coarse] do 10.00

Blue Cloth [coarse] do 8.00
Ribband, per yd 0.75
Brass nails, per dozen 0.50
Horses cost from 150 dollars to 300, and some as high
as 500.

Tomorrow I start for the west, and shall not return under
a year, when I expect to start for St. Louis.

LETTER OF DANIEL T. POTTS TO ROBERT POTTS

St. Louis, October 13th 1828

Respected Brother

with congratulation and a heart overflowed with joy to
think that I can write to you from a place incompassed within
the bounds of civilition I arrived at this place about a week
since after a long and fatigueing journey of about seventy days
after which my mind has become more tranquil. Directly after
my arrival at this place I hastened to see genl Ashly to receive
some tidings from you but to my sad disappointment, there was
none this was rather a strange circumstance as I had wrote to
you last July was a year also to Dr Lukens at the same time At
that time I received yours & his letters of the 23rd and 24th of
January 1827 both much interesting and very entertaining in my
leisure moments since my arrival for the want of language I am
scarcely able to converse with any men of talents which
occasiond verry disagreeable feelings. now to affairs more
interesting my adventures and escapes for the last year in the
mountains farr exceeds all the remainder part of my stay in the
mountains as I had risked everything to make or die in the
attempt in this fortune froune though preservation smiled
through the Indians on one part and the hard winter on the other

has been my sad ruin and [I] have lost not less than one thousand dollars the first snow fell on the third of September when it snowed for three days without intermission the snow remained on the ground upwards of knee dep and I think must have felt fully waist deep this had not the least effect on any kind of vegetation as it appears addepted to the climate the winter remained gentle until the first of December when the power vengence was poured out on us the N. E winds and more particularly South accompanied with a continued snow until the first of march when it somwhat abated the snow remained upwards of four feet deep on the level the sweet lake was bridged over on the 8 of may for twenty days in succession the great spirrit the sun refused to visit us the like has been known by the oldest livers which I suppose is not less than one hundred or upwards the horses which the winter did not destroy the early visits of the Black feet swept away with from twelve to fifteen scalps of our hunters A party of about one hundred Black feet mounted attacted thrty odd of our hunters with their familys this engagement lasted for upwards of three hours when a couple of our men mounted two of their swiftest horses dashed through their ranks of the horrid tribe where the balls flew like hail and arrived with express at our camp in less than one hour a distance of more than sixteen miles in this we had one man killed & two wounded one child lost. that of the enemy six or eight killed and wounded I shall now discontinue any further particulars as it is growing late in a few days I shall leave this place in steam boat for New Orleans where I shall remain during the winter and spring if successfull any thing like to my expectations I shall return but you may rest assured if I am by no means successfull you may dispense of ever seeing me there. though contentment I profess not West of the Alleghany I find this place somewhat sickly though for my part never enjoyed better health my weight is one hundred and eighty nine pounds five pounds more than ever before I have a small capital which I flatter myself with is pretty good business I shall furthermore dispense of giving you so minute particulars and beg leave to be excused for the past though I feel somewhat delicate in writing least it should not be exceptable if not remember my best respects to all my friends particularly your wife who from the little acquaintance I respects on the highest terms

Remain your most affectionat Brother

Danl T Potts

Direct your letters to New Orleans wher I shall remain until New Years whereas it is necessary for you to write in haste previous to leaving that place I shall inform you where I go and my business

Since writing this letter I have received your and Weirs letters which alters the case amazingly those letters wher mislaid. Tomorrow I embark

BIOGRAPHY OF DANIEL T. POTTS

From The Potts Family, Published in Cannonsburg, Pennsylvania, 1901

Daniel T. Potts, [Zebulon, Nathan, David], son of Zebulon and Martha [Trotter] Potts, was born 7 mo. 18, 1794. Born and raised on a farm, he was a lad of excellent habits and sound principles. When he reached manhood, anxious to see life and the country, he went west. In 1822, he joined the Henry and Ashley expedition, bound for the Rocky Mountains and the Columbia River and served as a scout. Gen. Ashley wrote to his brother Robert of his integrity and courage. His letters written to friends at home were graphic and full of interest. After leaving this service he went to Texas, and from there wrote to his friends that he was buying and shipping cattle to the New Orleans market. His brother Robert placed several thousand dollars to his credit with merchants in New Orleans and wrote to him to that effect. The money was never drawn and he was never heard of again. About this time a vessel loaded with cattle encountered a storm and went down, and all on board were lost. Daniel Potts is supposed to have perished on this vessel. He is not known to have been married.

BIBLIOGRAPHY

Books

Alter, Cecil. *Jim Bridger*. Norman, Oklahoma: University of Oklahoma Press, 1962.

Beal, Merrill D. and Merle W. Wells. *History of Idaho*. New York: Lewis Historical Publishing Co., 1959.

Blaire, Walter and Frank Meine. *Half Horse, Half Alligator*. Chicago: University of Chicago Press, 1956.

Bolton, Herbert. *Pageant In the Wilderness*. Salt Lake: Utah Historical Society, 1950.

Bonner, T. D., ed. *The Life and Adventures of James P. Beckwourth*. New York: Alfred A. Knopf, 1931.

Brackenridge, Henry M. *Views of Louisiana, Together With a Journal of a Voyage up the Missouri River in 1811*. Pittsburgh: Cramer, Spear and Eichbaum, 1814.

Camp, Charles C. *James Clyman, Frontiersman*. Portland: Champoeg Press, 1960.

Chittenden, Hyram M. *The American Fur Trade*. New York: Rufus Rockwell Wilson, Inc., 1963.

Chittenden, Hyram M. *The Yellowstone National Park*. Cincinnati: Stewart and Kidd, Co., 1915.

Cook, Philip St. George. *Scenes and Adventures in the Army*. Philadelphia: Lindsey & Blakiston, 1857.

Dale, Harrison, C. *The Ashley-Smith Explorations and the Discovery of the Central Route to the Pacific, 1822-1829*. Cleveland: Arthur H. Clark Co., 1918.

Ferris, Warren A. *Life in the Rocky Mountains*. Edited by Paul C. Phillips. Denver: The Old West Publishing Co., 1940.

Frost, Donald M. Notes on General Ashley, *The Overland Trail and South Pass*. Barre, Massachusetts: Barre Gazette, 1960.

Gowans, Fred R. *Rocky Mountain Rendezvous*. Brigham Young University, 1976.

Hafen, LeRoy R. and W. J. Ghent. *Broken Hand*. Denver: The Old West Publishing Co., 1931.

Hakola, John W., ed. *Frontier Omnibus*. Missoula: State University Press, 1963.

Harris, Burton. *John Colter*. New York: Scribner, 1952.

Irving, Washington. *Astoria*. New York: R. F. Fenno, 1900.

James, Thomas. *Three Years Among The Indians and Mexicans*. Philadelphia: J. B. Lippincott Co., 1962.

Lawrence, Paul. *John Colter, Journey of Discovery*. Jackson Wyoming, Unita Pioneer Press, 1978.

Lindsley, Marian D.*Major Henry In Idaho* [n.p. c 1985].

Louie, Robert. *The Crow Indians*. New York: Farrar and Rhinehart, 1835.

Morgan, Dale L. *The Great Salt Lake*. Indianapolis: Bobbs-Merrill Co., Inc., 1947.

Morgan, Dale L. and Carl I. Wheat. *Jedediah Smith and His Maps of the American West*. San Francisco: San Francisco Historical Society, 1954.

Morgan, Dale L. *The West of William H. Ashley*. Denver: Old West Publishing Co., 1963.

Oglesby, Richard E. *Manuel Lisa, and the Opening of the Missouri Fur Trade*. Norman: University of Oklahoma Press, 1963.

Parkman, Francis. *The Oregon Trail*. Garden City, New York: Doubleday and Co., Inc., 1946.

Paullin, Charles C. *Atlas of the Historical Geography of the United States*. Washington: Carnegie Institute, 1932.

Rollins, Phillip A. *The Discovery of the Oregon Trail, Robert Stuart's Narratives*. New York: Edward Eberstadt and Sons, 1935.

Ross, Alexander. *The Fur Hunters of the Far West*. Edited by Kenneth Spaulding. Norman: University of Oklahoma Press, 1956.

Russell, Carl P. *Guns on the Early Frontiers*. Berkeley: University of California Press, 1957.

Russell, Osborne. *Journal of a Trapper*. Edited by Aubrey L. Haines. Portland: Champoeg Press, 1955.

Ruxton, George F. *Life in the Far West*. Edited by LeRoy R. Hafen. Norman: University of Oklahoma Press, 1951.

Sullivan, Maurice S. *The Travels of Jedediah Smith*. Santa Anna: Fine Arts Press, 1934.

Sunder, John E. *Bill Sublette, Mountain Man*. Norman: University of Oklahoma Press, 1959.

Talbot, Vivian L. *David E. Jackson, Field Captain Of the Rocky Mountain Fur Trade*, [Jackson, Wyoming, Jackson Hole Historical Society and Museum, 1996].

Thwaites, Reuben G. *The Original Journals of the Lewis and Clark Expedition, 1804-1806*. New York: Antiquarian Press Ltd., 1959.

Vinton, Stallo. *John Colter, The Discoverer of Yellowstone Park*. New York: Edward Eberstadt, 1926.

Webster's New International Dictionary of the English Language, Unabridged. Springfield, Massachusetts: G. & C. Merriam Co., 1949.

Periodicals

Barry, J. N. "Autobiography," *Wyoming Annals*, Vol. X [July, 1838], p. 117.

Camp, Charles L., ed. "The Chronicles of George C. Yount," *California Historical Quarterly*, Vol. II [April, 1923], pp. 24-33.

Elliott, T. C., ed. "Peter Skene Ogden Journal, 1827, 1828," *Oregon Historical Society Quarterly*, vol. XI [December, 1910], pp. 355-399.

Linford, Dee. "Wyoming Stream Names," *Wyoming Annals*, Vol. XV [July, 1943], p. 269.

Mattes, Merrill J. "Behind the Legend of Colter's Hell," *Mississippi Valley Historical Review*, Vol. XXXVI [September, 1949], pp. 251-282.

Miller, David E. "Peter Skene Ogden Snake Country Journals," *Utah Historical Quarterly*, Vol. XX [April, 1952], pp. 159-186.

Miller, David E. "William Kittson's Journal," *Utah Historical Quarterly*, Vol. XXII [April, 1954], pp. 25-142.

Newspapers

Ashton Herald [Ashton, Idaho], 1906-1956, Golden Anniversary Edition.

Gazette and Daily Advertiser [Philadelphia], Oct. 19, 1827.

Missouri Republican [St. Louis], July 16, 1823.

Salt Lake Tribune, July 4, 1894.

San Francisco Bulletin, Oct. 29, 1858.

Government Publications

Breckenridge, Roy and Hinkley, Bern, "Thermal Springs Of Wyoming," *Geological Survey of Wyoming*, [Laramie, 1978].

Carter, Clarence E., ed. *Territorial Papers of the United States*. Washington: Govt. Print. Off., 1934-. Vol. XIII. Territory of Louisiana-Missouri, 1803-1806 [1948], 196-99, 243.

Hayden, F. V. *Sixth Annual Report of the Geological Survey of the Territories Embracing Portions of Montana, Idaho, Wyoming and Utah, 1872.* Washington: Govt. Print. Off., 1873.

Writers Program, W. P. A.., Wyoming, A Guide to its History, Highways, and People. New York: 1941.

Unpublished Sources

Interview by Jerry Bagley with Hazen Hawkes, August, 1963, Drummond, Idaho.

Interviews by Jerry Bagley with W. C. Lawrence, 1962-1963, Jackson, Wyoming.

Letters of J. Nielson Barry to W. C. Lawrence, Jackson, Wyoming: March 14, 1949; March 21, 1949; March 22, 1949; January 23, 1953; February 3, 1953.

Letters of Daniel T. Potts - See Appendix

To T. [Thomas] Cochlen, dated "Rocky Mountains," July
    7th, 1824.

To Robert Potts, dated "Rocky Mountains," July 16, 1826.

To Robert T. Potts, High Street, Philadelphia, Pennsylvania,
    dated "Sweet Lake," July 8th, 1827.

To Dr. Lukens, Philadelphia, dated "Sweet Water Lake," July
8th, 1827.

To Robert Potts, dated St. Louis, October 13th, 1828.

INDEX